Also by Mohamed Heikal

THE CAIRO DOCUMENTS
THE ROAD TO RAMADAN
THE SPHINX AND THE COMMISSAR
IRAN: THE UNTOLD STORY

AUTUMN OF FURY
The Assassination of Sadat

MOHAMED HEIKAL

Random House New York

 Published in the United States by Random House, Inc., New York. Originally published in Great Britain by Andre Deutsch Ltd.
Library of Congress Cataloging in Publication Data
Haykal, Muhammad Hasanayn.
Autumn of fury.
1. Egypt—Politics and government—1970- . 2. Sadat, Anwar, 1918- —Assassination.
3. Assassination—Egypt. I. Title.
DT107.85.H39 1983 962'.054 82-42806
ISBN 0-394-53136-1
Manufactured in the United States of America
24689753
First American Edition

To Hedayat

CONTENTS

INTRODUCTION

THIS HAS NOT been an easy book to write. In the first place it aims at telling a story which has been concealed from most people in the West, and which I fear is bound to come as a considerable shock to many of them. But it is a story which must be told if similar misconceptions, with all their disastrous consequences, are to be avoided in the future.

Secondly, there is for me a personal problem. The burden of this book is that the outside world completely failed to understand what President Sadat was doing and the effect his policies were bound to have. To that extent it represents an adverse judgement on Sadat. But it is in no sense the expression of a personal grudge against him, although, because he ended up by putting me, like so many others, in prison, there are certain to be those who will assume that it is.

I was, in fact, very fond of Sadat as a man. For the first four years of his presidency I was, as he acknowledged in 1974 in an interview with a Lebanese magazine, *Al-Asbu' al-Arabi*, closer to him than anyone else. I played a leading part, as Minister of Information and member of the National Security Council, as well as one of the inner circle round the late President, in the deliberations from which Sadat emerged as the agreed successor to Nasser. While fully conscious of his shortcomings I hoped that the responsibilities of office would strengthen the positive elements in his character and enable him to overcome the weak ones. The example of Truman was always present in my mind. I managed Sadat's campaign to confirm him in the presidency, and remained in almost daily contact with him until we fell out over the policies he pursued in the wake of the 1973 war.

Nor is it true, as is sometimes said, that he dismissed me from my editorship of *Al-Ahram*, and that thereafter there was a total breach between us. Differences of opinion there certainly were, and on matters of such fundamental importance that it was impossible for me to continue to be responsible for the conduct of Egypt's leading newspaper. But the decision to quit was mine. Nor did we suddenly switch from being friends to being enemies. Sadat subsequently offered me on various occasions positions of importance – as Counsellor to the President, as his National Security Adviser, as Deputy Prime Minister. I did not accept, because I did not believe I could have performed any useful function, but the offers were without doubt sincerely made.

There was a time when our long-term aims were the same, when we both wanted peace and a just overall settlement in the Middle East, and when we both wanted to see Egypt free and prosperous and the Arab world united. But as things turned out there was no chance of reconciling our views as to how best these aims could be realized. I did not regard myself as being in opposition to Sadat, but as trying to preserve an independent voice. When later Sadat began to attack me regularly by name in public, and even when eventually he put me in prison, there was still on my side no feeling of personal animosity. Indeed, when a president makes you a special target for his denunciations it adds more to you than it takes away, so in a sense I must be grateful to Sadat for enhancing my stature both nationally and internationally.

It must therefore be emphasized that this book is not an attack on Sadat, nor is it in any sense a biography of him, even though it goes into detail about some parts of his career, examines his personality and tries to analyse his motives. Nor have I written a book about economic and social conditions in Egypt today, or about the enduring characteristics of Egypt, though these aspects too are touched on. Nor, yet again, is this a book about Islamic fundamentalism, or the Coptic Church, or about terror as a political weapon. All these themes will be found in the book, but only inasmuch as they lead to one particular point in time and space – that moment on the morning of Tuesday 6 October 1981, when the shots were fired which brought to an end the life and achievements of President Anwar Sadat of Egypt.

At the time, a good many people in the West saw the assassination of Sadat as just another of those apparently senseless acts of violence which have destroyed, or threatened to destroy, so many prominent public figures in this age of violence. They put it in the same category as the murders of Jack and Robert Kennedy, or the attempted murders of President Reagan and Pope John Paul II. Nothing could be further from the truth. Such assassins or would-be assassins in the West have usually been loners or belonged to some stray peripheral group. In the more structured societies of the West the mainstream is fairly constant. The different classes are there – a higher bourgeoisie, perhaps an aristocracy of wealth or privilege, a petit bourgeoisie and a working class. These classes are not rigid. They may change dramatically (compare the working class in Europe today, for example, with the working class in Karl Marx's day) and there is movement between them. But together they form a recognizable whole – a majority in the nation, which may or may not deserve the title 'silent' but which is very definitely a majority.

The nation-states of the West have evolved over centuries. Their evolution has been accompanied by wars, civil wars, revolutions, and every sort of political upheaval. They are still evolving, and still often convulsed. The countries of the Third World are at an earlier stage of development. Their societies are in some ways more rigid (tribal and traditional) but also more formless, and therefore more explosive.

It does not, of course, follow that Third World countries will have to pass through all the stages that produced the nation-states in the West – conditions in the late twentieth century, thanks to developments in technology and communications, have quickened the pace and broken down barriers of all sorts. But observers need to be very careful if they are to discover where the cohesive forces, the majorities, are to be found in the Third World. The murderers of the Kennedys were isolated from the society to which they nominally belonged. The forces which conspired against Sadat were just as much a part of the mainstream in Egyptian society as were the forces which overthrew the Shah from the mainstream in Iran.

My purpose in writing this book will be served if people in the West start asking themselves questions – and if it helps them to find answers to their questions. They must ask why it was that a man so much admired in the West was so isolated in his own world; why the man whom Henry Kissinger had dismissed as a 'bombastic clown' before the 1973 war should in the space of a few years become in the opinion of the same judge 'the greatest since Bismarck'[1]; why a man

[1] A strange, if flattering, comparison, since Bismarck created a united Germany round the strongest German state, whereas Sadat, at the head of the strongest Arab state, fragmented the Arab world.

who was mourned as a heroic and far-seeing statesman in the West found hardly any mourners among his fellow-countrymen; why a man who had for so long filled the television screens and captured the headlines should, so soon after his death, be almost completely forgotten. The West must finally ask why it is that foreign leaders whom it has taken so fervently to its bosom because they seemed to speak its language – Chiang, Suharto, the Shah, Marcos, Sadat, and many others – have so significantly failed to win the affection of their own people.

I know that what I have written will cause offence to some people in Egypt. Sadat's policies did benefit a small, privileged circle, and their fortunes must inevitably fluctuate with his reputation. But Egypt, like the West, needs to take a long hard look at what happened. La commedia é finita. The play is over. The stage is in darkness.[1] The day of the superstar has passed, and ordinary mortals must learn to recognize and to live with each other.

I began to think about writing this book almost from the first moment I was arrested, on 3 September 1981. When I saw all the others who had been rounded up at the same time – many of the best-known public figures in Egypt – I realized that this was the last desperate throw of a gambler. I felt convinced that this was the penultimate scene in the drama, which must end soon one way or another, and that as a newspaperman I would one day have to write about it.

In prison I talked at length with others about what had been happening (there was, in any case, little else to do), first with those in my own cell, and later, as we were allowed more contacts, with many others. I talked with ex-Ministers (there were enough former Cabinet Ministers in Tora prison to form a highly qualified government), with economists and union leaders, with sheikhs and fundamentalists and with Coptic priests. I am grateful to all of them for their friendship and for the stimulus of their conversation. I am no less indebted to those with whom I have had discussions since being released.

I have in particular to thank Dr Hassan Hanafi, Professor of Islamic

---

[1] The Egyptian elder statesman, Dr Mahmoud Fawzi, Prime Minister for a time under Sadat, once said to me, while Sadat was still alive: 'We are in the unique position of being part of the audience in a theatre which has no play. There is scenery; there are sound effects, lights, a curtain – but no script.'

Philosophy at Cairo University, as well as Dr Murad Wahba and Dr Milad Hanna, two scholars who helped me to understand the Coptic inheritance. I owe a great debt to Adel Hussein for his monumental studies on the Egyptian economy, and to Dr Saad Ibrahim, Professor of Sociology at the American University of Cairo, for his writings on the social structures of Egypt, and to others too numerous to mention. But I must emphasize that any errors of fact or judgement are mine, not theirs. Finally, I would again wish to thank my friend and colleague, Edward Hodgkin, for all the assistance he has given me in writing this book.

Cairo, October 1982

Part I

THE MAKING OF A SUPERSTAR

I have ventured
Like little wanton boys that swim on bladders,
This many summers in a sea of glory,
But far beyond my depth.

Shakespeare *King Henry the Eighth*

I

IN SEARCH OF SADAT

EVERY AGE needs its heroes. They may be prophets or priests, kings or warriors, discoverers or explorers, philosophers or poets, but some extraordinary people for the ordinary men and women to look up to and in their own fashion to imitate there must always be.

When we look at the present century, and more particularly at the political heroes of the last forty or fifty years, we can see a certain pattern emerging. First there were the giants of the war – Roosevelt, Churchill, Stalin, de Gaulle and even Hitler, since without his malevolent genius the others would not have had their capacities brought on to greatness. Then, in the wake of the war, came the revolutionaries whose personalities and ideas had an influence far beyond the confines of the countries in which they assumed power – Mao Tse-tung, Ho Chi-Minh, Nehru, Tito, Nasser.

While these first two generations were dominating the international scene, a new scientific revolution, no less far-reaching in its implications than the industrial revolution of two hundred years ago or the harnessing of nuclear power, was hatching a third generation of heroes. This was the revolution in communications, which ushered in the world of television, of satellites and computers, the revolution which brought the faces as well as the voices of famous and infamous men and women into almost every home, and which created perhaps the most remarkable phenomenon of our time – the superstar.

Politicians and others in public life were quick to appreciate the potentials of this new force seemingly at their disposal, but only a handful proved themselves its real master. Who have been the superstars of our time? Probably everybody's lists would include the names of Pope John Paul II, Jacqueline Kennedy, Henry Kissinger, and Lech Walesa. They would also include the name of President Anwar Sadat.

A President of the United States, a Secretary-General of the Communist Party of the USSR, a Chairman of the Chinese party, can, by his position as a leader of a superpower, command automatic attention whatever he says or does. If they have a flair for superstardom, so much the better for them; but if they lack it, no great matter – they are still super even if not stars. But other political leaders have to compete for the lights, and if the lights are turned off them they almost cease to exist. They are like actors without a play to appear in, or novelists deprived of pen and paper. But as long as the lights are focused in the right direction, they not only lend tremendous backing to a superstar's policies, they can even act as a substitute for policy. It is those who are left in the shadows who find that what they have to say is being ignored and their arguments neglected. Thus, as long as the lights were on him, Kissinger could afford to be cavalier in his treatment of Congress, and even of the White House, and Pope John Paul II has been able to make almost inaudible his many critics in the Curia, because it is him alone that the world wants to see and hear.

The trouble about the modern superstar is that, like a bicyclist, he has to keep pedalling all the time if he is not to fall off. Indeed, he has to pedal faster and faster, because it is an uphill race he is engaged in. Yet in the long run fame itself can never be a substitute for ability, nor any substitute for a strong power-base or for a clearly contrived and executed political strategy. The lights can conceal the weaknesses in a person's make-up and can dazzle the eyes of his opponents, but the day has to come when the pace slackens, and when attention is diverted, perhaps by the rise of a new superstar in the firmament.

But by that time superstardom will have proved as addictive as any drug, and as with drugs the dose has to get stronger and stronger. Thus the first time Kissinger indulged in shuttle diplomacy, and had the eyes of the world focused upon him as he stitched together a cease-fire after the October War, it needed only four journeys between Aswan and Tel Aviv to get an agreement signed between Egypt and Israel. But when the shuttle was resumed between Israel and Syria it took Kissinger forty days to emerge triumphant. True, the Syrians were more obstinate than the Egyptians, but the fact of the matter is that in his new superstar role the Secretary of State simply could not afford to fail, and by then the other parties to the negotiations had come to realize this.

Nobody can achieve or maintain the position of a superstar by doing the usual. It is the unusual, the unexpected – the horrible even (and it is this which has turned some hijackers and terrorists like Carlos into superstars of a sort) – which is required of the superstar. The October War brought Sadat greater fame than he had ever enjoyed before. The successful crossing of the Suez Canal astonished the world, but then came setbacks. Israeli commanders like Sharon began to share the honours of war with him, and Kissinger ran away with the honours of peace. For audiences who had watched men walking on the moon something more was required than a mere battle, and this was what Sadat achieved when he made his historic journey to Jerusalem in November 1977. By making this journey Sadat crossed the sound barrier between the normal and the abnormal, between the thinkable and the unthinkable. Jerusalem made Sadat a superstar.

When Sadat landed at Ben Gurion airport on 20 November 1977 people were not so much concerned with asking themselves whether his mission would succeed or not as with the simple fact that the journey had been made at all. Of course many in the West hoped, with an almost desperate hope, that it was going to solve all their problems – the problem of the Jews and Zionism, the problem of energy costs, the problem of a possible superpower confrontation in the Middle East. But there was little attempt to work out how these eminently desirable ends were to be achieved.

It is not always appreciated that a superstar creates his own constituency. Lesser men have to deal with the traditional limitations imposed on them by the facts of history and geography, but a superstar leaps over the frontiers of time and space, grasping the hands and caressing the ears of millions of people unknown to him. His measure of success or failure is not the number of votes cast for him in an election or his majority in Parliament, but the number of times his face is shown on the cover of *Time* magazine and *Newsweek*, and the number of times he is asked to appear with Walter Cronkite, Barbara Walters or David Frost.

By going to Jerusalem Sadat achieved a world-wide constituency, but lost the constituency which was naturally his as President of Egypt – the Arab world. This was tragically and graphically illustrated at his funeral, when he was taken to his grave by a most imposing galaxy of foreign statesmen, including three former Presidents of the United States and the Prime Minister of Israel, but with only a handful of his own fellow-countrymen as mourners.

Sadat was one of the Third World leaders who realized the implications of the communications revolution. In a country like Egypt television has changed the lives of the ordinary people in a manner it is almost impossible to exaggerate. Before the television era they may have known the face of the ruler from photographs in the newspapers, and heard his voice from time to time on the radio, but television brought his every gesture into their homes. He became a real person, sharing their sitting room and even their bedroom with them. Sadat's trouble was that, though he was in so many ways a child of the television age, he could not resist the temptation to overdo it. He was the first Egyptian Pharaoh to come before his people armed with a camera; he was also the first Egyptian Pharaoh to be killed by his own people. He was a hero of the electronic revolution, but also its victim. When his face was no longer to be seen on the television screen it was as if the eleven years of his rule had vanished with a switch of the control knob.

2

ROOTS

IT WOULD BE HARD to imagine a less auspicious setting for a future superstar than that into which Sadat was born on 25 December 1918. As his fame grew, Sadat became increasingly conscious of the contrast between his origins and his later power and glory, and it was a contrast which obsessed him. From 1974 onwards it was his custom on his birthday to go back to the village where he was born, Mit Abu el-Kom, and there, wearing the *galabiyeh* and *abayeh* of the fellahin, he would reminisce in front of the television cameras about his early life for two or three hours. The trouble was that no two reminiscences were the same; they all differed in detail, and differed too from the accounts in the autobiographies which were published during his lifetime, either in book form or in the form of articles and interviews for the many newspapers and magazines which he either controlled or sponsored. Indeed, Sadat set up a special committee charged with the task of producing an edited version of his life and opinions, though its labours were never completed.

It was a harsh start in life that fate had decreed for him – harsher even than any of the versions which he was later to give the world. The truth, if Sadat had told it, could only have increased respect for him and for the way in which he had overcome the obstacles in his path. But he preferred to doctor the true story, to embroider or suppress; and since the true story helps to explain so much in the character of the man, it is essential to try to reconstruct it.

Sadat was the son of a certain Mohamed Mohamed El-Sadaty.[1] Sadat's grandmother was Sitt Om-Mohamed El-Sadatieh, and before her only son was born she had four daughters. But, as is the custom, even before any male child had been born to her she was known as

---

[1] Sadaty means 'followers of the masters', referring to one of the many Sufi sects flourishing in Egypt. This does not mean that Sadat's father was himself a Sufi, but that his family had originally been connected with them. After the Revolution of 1952 Sadat was to drop the final syllable of his name, but in the Military College he is still to be found listed as Anwar El-Sadaty.

'mother of the hoped for son', 'Om-Mohamed', mother of Mohamed, and when this son did at last come into the world, it can be imagined how he was welcomed and how inevitably he was spoiled in comparison to his four sisters.

Sitt Om-Mohamed was the strongest influence in Sadat's childhood. 'How I loved that woman!' he says in the autobiography which he wrote for Western readers towards the end of his life.[1] 'She had a very strong personality and enjoyed a rare wisdom.' She was a very poor woman, going round the houses of the better-off families in the village selling things like butter, but she worked hard, determined that her only son should have an education. This she secured him, first at the primary school in the larger nearby village, Shebin el-Kom, of which Mit Abu el-Kom was a sort of satellite.

In Shebin el-Kom there was a detachment of the British army medical corps (the British having been in occupation of Egypt since 1882) engaged in research on local tropical diseases such as bilharzia and hookworm. After gaining his certificate of education Mohamed Mohamed el-Sadaty went to work with this medical group, acting as liaison and interpreter with the local villagers. Now that he was educated he became an effendi, and his mother thereby became known as 'mother of the effendi'. She was eager to arrange the next step in his career, and so, while he was still only thirteen years old, she married him to a local girl. This first wife, Sadat's step-mother, has completely vanished from the pages of history. Even the closest members of his family have forgotten her name, and she produced no children to perpetuate it.

After a few years the British medical group to which Mohamed Mohamed el-Sadaty was attached was ordered to the Sudan, and he was happy to go with it because, though few Egyptians readily accepted exile from their own land, it meant an increase in salary. But before he went Om-Mohamed had arranged a second marriage for him.

The bride she had chosen was called Sitt el-Barrein, 'girl of the two banks'. She was the daughter of a man called Kheirallah, brought originally as a slave from Africa. After the British occupation, when pressure to abolish slavery intensified, his master (whose identity is unknown) freed Kheirallah. His daughter, Sitt el-Barrein, was, like

---

[1] *In Search of Identity*, p. 3.

her father, completely Negro, and the fact that Sadat inherited her complexion and some of her features was to have a profound effect on him.

So, shortly before the 1914 war started, Mohamed Mohamed el-Sadaty set off for the Sudan with a wife, who, he could reasonably suppose, would fit in well with his new surroundings. But he did not intend that any children of the marriage should be born in the Sudan. As soon as Sitt el-Barrein's pregnancies became noticeable she was put on the so-called Post boat which went up the Nile, its deck always crowded with passengers, their baggage and animals, to Shellal and the First Cataract, and from there, probably on foot, to Aswan where she would take the train to Cairo and so to the Delta and Mit Abu el-Kom. There the child would be born in the house of Om-Mohamed, and there mother and child would stay until the child had been weaned. When this age had been reached Sitt el-Barrein would return to the Sudan, leaving the child behind with its grandmother.

This process was repeated four times, for three boys and one girl – Talaat, Anwar, Esmat and Nefissa – names reflecting their father's admiration for the leaders of the Young Turks after the Revolution of 1908.

Sadat claims that his father left the Sudan in 1925 when the Egyptian army was ordered out of the Sudan following the murder of the Sirdar, Sir Lee Stack, in the previous year.[1] But the British medical unit to which Mohamed Mohamed el-Sadaty was attached was brought back to Egypt in 1922, two years before the Sirdar's murder, and stationed in Abbasiyeh barracks near Cairo. Mohamed Mohamed el-Sadaty proceeded to look for somewhere for himself and his family to live, and found it in the first-floor flat of a two-storey house in Kubri el-Kubba, a Cairo suburb, No. 1 Sharia Mohamed Badr.

The wife who had fitted so well into her surroundings in the Sudan was not so suitable for Cairo, so Sitt Om-Mohamed, watchful as ever over the interests of her cherished only son, began the search for a replacement. This she found in a girl from Mansura, called Fatoum. Mohamed Mohamed el-Sadaty duly married her, and brought her to his house.

It is important to take a close look at No. 1 Sharia Mohamed Badr because it is here that Sadat passed the formative years of his life, and

---

[1] *In Search of Identity*, Collins, London 1978, p. 53.

the extreme complexity of his character cannot be explained without some knowledge of the conditions in which he grew up.

Mohamed Mohamed el-Sadaty moved into his new flat in 1924 and a year or so later summoned his children by his second wife to join him there. Until then Sadat had been living with his grandmother in Mit Abu el-Kom, and in retrospect these were for him the golden years: 'Everything made me happy in Mit Abu el-Kom, my quiet village in the depths of the Nile Delta,' he wrote,[1] and there is no reason to suppose that here he was not speaking the truth from his heart.

Now consider what the boy found in Cairo. His father's flat was of the usual pattern in Egyptian cities. The front door led into a central hall with four rooms opening off it. One room was occupied by the master of the house and his new wife, Fatoum; one by his grandmother, Om-Mohamed, now removed from her home in Mit Abu el-Kom, and one by Sitt el-Barrein and her four children. The fourth room was available for visitors.

Or was so available for a time. One day some visitors from Mit Abu el-Kom called to see Om-Mohamed. They brought with them a daughter, Amina, aged eighteen. She was fair-skinned, and Mohamed Mohamed el-Sadaty fell in love with her. He proposed marriage, and was accepted. The unfortunate Fatoum, who had borne her husband no children, was expelled into the visitors' room, and Amina installed in her place.

It will be readily understood that Sitt el-Barrein, now superseded by two rivals, occupied the lowliest position in this menage. Amina quickly established an ascendancy over her husband, who handed over to her most of the £E30 a month which he earned. She presented him in rapid succession with nine children, two boys and seven girls.[2] By the time Amina's family was complete the Mohamed Badr Street flat contained the master of the house, his mother, his three wives and thirteen children. Nor was this the end of the story, for when Talaat married, and when Anwar married for the first time, they brought their brides back to the flat, and when Amina's eldest daughter, Sakina, became married (to a musician) she brought him to live there too.

All this time young Anwar had not just to regret the loss of the

[1] *In Search of Identity*, p. 2.

[2] The names of Amina's children, Sadat's half-brothers and sisters, were Sakina, Effat, Zeinab, Zein, 'Aisha, Atef, Soheir, Hoda and Azza.

freedom and excitement of life in the village, but to watch his mother reduced to a position of servitude no less harsh than that from which her father, Kheirallah, was supposed to have been rescued. Sitt el-Barrein, the black wife, became the household drudge. When she made a mistake she was beaten by Mohamed Mohamed el-Sadaty in front of her children.

What sort of a life was this for Sadat? Homesick for his village, the neglected second son in an inferior family, watching every day the humiliation of a mother despised for her colour and punished for shortcomings for which she was not to blame, he spent much of his time in a corner of their overcrowded room, retreating into a private world of fantasy. The boy became submissive – he had to be – but beneath the submissiveness there was lurking a hidden streak of violence, which was to make him in later life a ready participant in assassination conspiracies. It is significant that in all the long rambling reminiscences to which, when President, he treated his audiences on his birthday broadcasts he never once referred to this period of his life. The picture which he wanted the world to have of him – and the picture which he wanted to preserve for himself – was of the village boy who became an officer and a revolutionary. The miseries of Mohamed Badr Street had no part in this picture. They were better forgotten.

3

FLIGHT TO FANTASY

SADAT called the authorized story of his life, published both in Egypt and in the West in 1978, *In Search of Identity*. Whether the choice of title was his own or his publishers' does not matter, but it was certainly appropriate. His life in the Mohamed Badr Street flat left him with a feeling that he belonged nowhere. He feared his father but could not love him; he could not respect his unfortunate mother, and had come to resent the badge of colour which he inherited from her. He longed for sympathy and understanding, and this eagerness to please and to be accepted, which remained with him throughout his life, is one of the most attractive aspects of his character. It meant that he was ready to give his allegiance to a stronger personality when he came into contact with one, and that he knew how to accept rebuffs and humiliations. But it also meant that somewhere inside him was the need to seek revenge for his sufferings. Meanwhile the only road of escape was into the world of dreams and fantasies.

Sadat followed his elder brother Talaat in the normal state education for boys of his class, but while in secondary school something happened which resulted in his being obliged to leave and to go instead to one of the inferior *ahli* schools. These, privately run, usually by a former state teacher, tended to provide a less adequate education than the official schools. Sadat refers obliquely in his autobiography to what was evidently a somewhat traumatic experience: 'That result was a turning point in my life. I realized that my failure was a sign God was not satisfied with me, perhaps because of my negligence, perhaps because of my overconfidence . . . So, in that mood and with that vague feeling – a combined sense of guilt and a resolve to repent – I submitted my papers to another school.'[1]

Sadat the escapist became Sadat the dreamer; Sadat the dreamer

---

[1] *In Search of Identity*, p. 11.

became Sadat the actor. Most of his life Sadat was acting a part – or sometimes several parts at the same time. He never, as will be seen, made any secret of the fascination which acting had exercised over him, but the first public manifestation of this enthusiasm he preferred not to be remembered.

In the mid-1903s, in the early days of the Egyptian cinema, a lady film producer called Amina Mohamed put an advertisement in a magazine asking for young boys who could act. They were requested to submit their particulars and a photograph, preparatory to an interview. Sadat answered the advertisement. 'I am,' he wrote, 'a young man, with a slender figure, well-built thighs, and good features. Yes – I am not white, but not exactly black either. My blackness is tending to reddish. (Signed) Anwar el-Sadaty.'

Oddly enough the copy in the national archives of the magazine which contained this advertisement has at some time been torn out. But Sadat must have known that people were on the track of the story because, when he was editor of *Gomhouriyeh* after the revolution, he wrote an article containing his version of what happened:[1]

> All my life I have felt attracted to acting. Even in the 1930s, before going to military college, I was always trying to meet anyone who would give me a part in a play. I saw an advertisement by Amina Mohamed, asking for new faces for a film with a Chinese setting she was going to produce called *Tita Wong*, so I went along to the offices of the film company in Sharia Ibrahim Pasha, and stood in a row with some other candidates. Amina came in and looked at us – we were about twenty young men – but unfortunately she only picked out two, and I was not one of them. She told the rest of us to send her two more photographs, one in profile and one full-face, but I later found that this was simply a way of getting rid of us.

Sadat described in the same article how there had been a time later when he called himself Haji Mohamed, although he had never been on the Haj, and grew a little beard to sustain the role. 'It is true,' he wrote, 'that I called myself Haji Mohamed, as part of an act, but nobody asked me any questions so I went on with it. I only feel myself really at home in the company of actors.'

★ ★ ★

---

[1] *Gomhouriyeh* No.705, 28 November, 1955.

There was to be no career for Sadat in acting, but a career of some sort had to be found for him, and it was here that Mohamed Mohamed el-Sadaty's connections with the British army came to be useful. The officer who had been in charge of his medical unit, Dr Fitzpatrick, had since his return from the Sudan been working in cooperation with the Egyptian army medical department at Abbasiyeh Hospital. He undertook to have a word with the Under-Secretary for War, and afterwards father and son intercepted the Under-Secretary at the door of the Ministry to introduce him to the young man about whom Dr Fitzpatrick had spoken. The proposal was that Anwar should go to the Military College, and this was not as unlikely a proposition as it would have been a few years before. The Anglo-Egyptian Treaty, signed on 26 August 1936, envisaged a considerable expansion in the Egyptian armed forces. The previous property qualification for officers was abolished, and the way opened for young men like Anwar Sadat and Gamal Abdel Nasser to obtain commissions. After being accepted for a shortened course of only nine months, Sadat emerged from the Royal Military Academy a second-lieutenant in the infantry in February 1938.

The actor side of his nature immediately began to take over now that he had a definite role to play. The most admired officer caste in those pre-war days was the German, and Second-Lieutenant Sadat decided that he would take them as his model. So he had his hair cropped close, bought himself a monocle at a shop in Sharia Suleiman Pasha, and went about with a swagger-cane under his arm. His more conventionally minded father decided that the equipment he now stood in need of more than a monocle or swagger-cane was a wife. Accordingly he arranged for his son what must have seemed to him the most suitable match possible – to the daughter of the *omdah* (headman) of Mit Abu el-Kom. She was called Ekbel Mady, and by her Sadat had three daughters – Rokaya, Rawiya and Camelia. This was a union which must have been particularly gratifying to Sitt Om-Mohamed.

Sadat was soon posted to Manqabad, a town in Upper Egypt, and it was here that he first met Nasser. In his autobiography Sadat represents himself as arriving at Manqabad already a secret revolutionary, much more mature than his brother officers 'who mostly lacked any political education', and maintains that he 'worked hard during long conversations to open my colleagues' eyes to the realities of the situation in general and the position of the British in particular.' There is no supporting evidence for this claim. On the contrary, he was remembered at Manqabad as being in no way particularly outstanding, though his ability to sing and act and to mimic his superior officers gained him a certain popularity. There is no question that it was Nasser who, at Manqabad, was accepted by all as being the leader in political discussions. As Sadat himself wrote:

> Around this man a group of young men collected. Nobody could then tell that this was to be the nucleus of something much bigger. Nasser used to talk to us, educating us. We all had the greatest admiration for him. We would watch his silences, wondering what he was thinking. Then Gamal would start talking to us, explaining to us that the British were the source of all our troubles. Gamal made us all feel prematurely old, because he made us feel that we had the whole burden of our country's future on our shoulders.[1]

Looking back later Sadat saw that first meeting in a rather different light:

> Although Nasser and I had come to know each other at the tender age of nineteen, I cannot say that our relationship ever exceeded mutual trust and respect; it was hardly what you'd call a friendship at all. It wasn't easy for Nasser to have anybody for his friend, in the full sense of the term, because of his tendency to be wary, suspicious, extremely bitter and highly strung.[2]

In 1940 Nasser was posted to the Sudan and Sadat was chosen to join the Corps of Signals at Maadi, a few miles south of Cairo. By now the long-expected war in Europe had broken out, and though Egypt was not a combatant the presence on Egyptian soil of a large British army ensured that the country would be directly involved and, as was soon made clear, that it would become one of the war's principal battlefields.

There were at this time three main political forces in Egypt whose permutations and combinations shaped its destinies. These were the Royal Palace, whose incumbent since May 1936 had been the young

---

[1] *Unknown Pages*, p. 26.

[2] *In Search of Identity*, p. 101.

King Farouk, the Wafd,[1] and the British, whose representative in Cairo since 1934 had been, first as High Commissioner and after the 1936 Anglo-Egyptian Treaty as Ambassador, Sir Miles Lampson (Lord Killearn). King Farouk's sympathies were with the Axis, and Germany's early victories in Norway and France only strengthened his conviction that Britain was certain to be defeated. His Prime Minister, Ali Maher, largely shared this view, though he was more interested in developing Egypt's leadership among her eastern neighbours (an embryonic vision of Arab unity as it was to emerge after the war).

The two elements inside Egypt which the Palace habitually looked to for support were the army and Al-Azhar, the oldest and most influential religious university in the Islamic world. The Wafd, which, in spite of rigged elections, still enjoyed more popular backing than any other political party, had recently clashed with both Palace and al-Azhar, with Mustafa Nahas Pasha, the leader of the Wafd, insisting that King Farouk could not exercise full sovereignty until he reached the age of twenty-one (which would have been in 1941) whereas the King claimed the right on reaching his eighteenth birthday. Sheikh Mustafa el-Maraghi, Rector of al-Azhar, issued a *fetwa* (ruling) favouring the King, and Nahas was obliged to back down.

One of those who were attracted by Ali Maher's ideas of an eastward-looking policy for Egypt was Hassan el-Banna, founder and first Guide of the Moslem Brotherhood. King Farouk and his Prime Minister saw the growing influence of the Brotherhood as a possible weapon to be used against the Wafd, and Hassan el-Banna was allowed to go round some of the army barracks to expound his views. The Signals Corps camp at Maadi was one of those he visited and Sadat was among his audience. He found himself deeply impressed by what he heard: 'My admiration was unbounded.' He introduced himself to the speaker, and thought seriously of joining his organization. But though Sadat was soon to be actively committed politically, it was not to be through the Moslem Brotherhood.

Another man whom Sadat met at Maadi was to have a more significant influence on his career. This was an air force officer called Hassan Ezzat who was on a signals course there. Ezzat belonged to a

---

[1] The main nationalist party, formed in 1918 by Saad Zaghlul, and since his death in 1927 headed by Mustafa Nahas.

clandestine group in the air force which included Abdel Latif Baghdadi, and had contacts with General Aziz el-Masri, Inspector-General of the army. The intention of the group was to get in touch with the Germans and to make use of their advancing armies to drive out the British and, it was confidently hoped, thereby secure the true independence of Egypt. They needed a trained signals officer for their work, and Sadat appeared to be a promising choice.

The story of el-Masri's abortive conspiracy has often been told. From the point of view of Sadat's story the important thing is that, thanks to Hassan Ezzat, he now found himself belonging to a genuine secret organization. For Sadat, as for many people, the act of belonging to such an organization was to provide an inner sense of security, through becoming a part of something stronger and more vital than himself. Unfortunately for Sadat it was the same sense of belonging which was to give strength to his assassins forty years later.

Sadat's involvement with two German spies, Hans Eppler and his colleague known only as Sandy, is described in *In Search of Identity*, but it was told in rather greater detail in a somewhat different version in the book called *Unknown Pages*, which he wrote soon after the revolution and which was withdrawn from circulation when be became President.

'It all started with a knock on my door by my friend Hassan Ezzat,' he recalls. 'The spies, one of whom was German born but brought up in Egypt and speaking perfect colloquial Arabic, had slipped into Egypt through the oases in a captured British jeep and wearing British uniforms. They had with them a transmitter and £25,000 in forged notes. The transmitter proved in need of repair, and Ezzat, their contact man in Cairo, thought I was the man to repair it. I was more than willing.' Sadat goes on to give a graphic description of his rendezvous with the Germans:

> I had an appointment to see the transmitter. The first thing that surprised me was that they were living on the Nile houseboat belonging to the famous dancer, Hikmet Fahmy. The surprise must have shown on my face, because Eppler laughingly asked 'Where do you expect us to stay? In a British army camp?' He said Hikmet Fahmy was perfectly reliable. They had exchanged their British uniforms for civilian clothes, and were living there without arousing any suspicion. They were trying to assess feeling in the country and, if possible, to get information about the movement of British troops.

> The Germans were spending their evenings at the Kitkat nightclub, coming back drunk to the houseboat which they also used as their transmitting base. They told me with much satisfaction that the Bank of Egypt had changed a lot of money for them. They had found a Jewish intermediary who was prepared to undertake the exchange for them on the basis of a thirty per cent commission. I was not surprised at a Jew performing this service for the Nazis because I knew that a Jew would do anything if the price was right. But I was worried on behalf of Eppler and Sandy over this contact with the Jews.[1]

Sadat describes Eppler as being sexually more animal than man, constantly playing Rimsky-Korsakov's *Sheherazade* on the gramophone. 'One night I looked at him when he was drunk. [Sadat had by this time come to spend some nights on the houseboat.] "How happy that man Shahriar must have been," he said, "getting a fresh virgin every night and killing her the next morning. That is my ideal life! Why shouldn't I become a second Shahriar?" ' But apparently Eppler's attempts to emulate Shahriar aroused Hikmet Fahmy's jealousy, especially when one night he obtained from somewhere two Jewish girls to play the part of virgins.[2]

There were now two transmitters in the houseboat – the German one Eppler had brought with him, which proved useless, and a powerful American one obtained through the Swiss Legation in Cairo. Sadat was asked to do some repairs on this, so he took it back to the Mohamed Badr Street flat in a taxi. It was still in the flat when the British security police, who had already picked up Eppler and Sandy, came to arrest Sadat. They did not find it, because it had been hidden in the room occupied by the women of the family, which the British were too tactful or too embarrassed to search. What he later persuaded himself was the worst aspect of his arrest was that, as he wrote in *Unknown Pages*, 'Thus I was prevented from sending my treaty to Rommel.' In retrospect he could dream up a scenario in which he, a captain in the Egyptian army, was to negotiate a treaty with the German government, via a field-marshal, which would bring Egypt its freedom.

Sadat was taken first to the Aliens gaol in Cairo and then to Makousah prison in Minieh, 160 miles further south. This transfer

---

1 *Unknown Pages*, p. 59ff.

2 *Unknown Pages*, p. 77.

was late in 1942, by which time the events of 4 February 1942, when British tanks surrounded Abdin Palace and forced King Farouk to choose between abdication and appointing Nahas Pasha as Prime Minister, had taken place. Farouk's humiliation became the nation's, and in particular the army's, the King being supreme commander of the armed forces. The Palace brooded on revenge, and the King's chief adviser, Ahmed Hassanein Pasha, identified three targets – the Wafd must be broken; Killearn must be transferred; and Nahas and Amin Osman,[1] regarded as the principal architects of the February 4th ultimatum, must be appropriately dealt with.

The first objective was realized when, early in 1943, Makram Ebeid, a Copt and number two in the Wafd, published his *Black Book,* a detailed accusation of corruption inside the Wafd, particularly in Nahas's own family. The second, in spite of intensive lobbying in London by the Egyptian ambassador, Abdel Fetah Amr Pasha, Farouk's friend and champion squash player, was not achieved until 1946, when Britain's new Labour government was in any case bent on opening a new page in Anglo-Egyptian affairs. Achievement of the third objective was to involve Sadat.

Whether Hassanein countenanced assassination as suitable punishment for Nahas and Amin Osman is not known, but someone in authority must have given the go-ahead. The task was assigned to a certain Yussef Rashad, who had been a surgeon in the Egyptian navy and come to the attention of King Farouk when he attended him after the King had been injured in a motor accident. Farouk liked him, made him one of the royal doctors and his beautiful wife one of the Queen's ladies-in-waiting. It so happened that Sadat had previously got to know Yussef Rashad when they were both stationed in Mersa Matruh. Rashad had now risen to the rank of colonel and was in charge of a group of young officers calling themselves the Iron Guard, dedicated to defending the honour and rights of the King at all costs.

At this time, with the war ending and Egypt, together with most of the other Arab countries, flexing its muscles for the next round in the struggle for independence which was obviously coming, many clandestine organizations with broadly nationalist aims sprang up. One of these was led by a young man from a rich family called Hussein

---

[1] Former Under-Secretary of Finance, later Minister of Finance, close associate of Nahas and the Wafd's liaison with the British.

Tewfiq and included Mohamed Ibrahim Kamal, who was much later to be Foreign Minister under Sadat until he resigned in opposition to Camp David. This particular organization specialized in assassinating British soldiers in and around Cairo, usually when drunk and on their own.

Yussef Rashad had recruited Hassan Ezzat into the Iron Guard – though arrested at the same time as Sadat he had been released, as no evidence had been produced against him. Hassan Ezzat suggested Sadat's name as that of another useful candidate. Accordingly an emissary from the Palace visited him in Makousah prison, and after he had been enrolled in the Iron Guard it was arranged for him to be moved to Zeitoun camp, near Cairo. This was, in fact, a large private house which had been converted into a prison, and it was here that friends of the Palace were confined. (The fact that the Director of Prisons was a Palace man, and that all prisoners worked on the royal estates, made this sort of special treatment easy.)

Conditions in Zeitoun were so lax that Sadat and a friend were able to leave the prison, take a taxi into the centre of Cairo, spend the night at a pension kept by a Frenchwoman, and the next day go to Abdin Palace and write their names in the book there, Sadat adding the remark that they were prisoners in Zeitoun and wanted to complain about the treatment they were receiving. Sadat returned to Zeitoun camp, but after a month escaped again, and this time permanently.

While he was on the run a representative of the Palace arranged a meeting between him and Hussein Tewfiq at the Casino Opera nightclub in Cairo. At this meeting Tewfiq was told by Sadat that he was pursuing the wrong tactics. What was the use of attacking individual British soldiers, of which there was an almost endless supply? Much more to the point would be to attack Britain's Egyptian friends, and so intimidate them that they would cease their collaboration. Sadat identified the two most guilty men to Tewfiq, now being enlisted as hit-man for the Palace, as Nahas and Amin Osman.

Although sometimes it was to be a source of some embarrassment to him, Sadat never made any secret of the part he played in the successful attempt on the life of Amin Osman or in the unsuccessful attempt on the life of Nahas in September 1945. On this occasion, though Hussein Tewfiq (under Sadat's instruction and supervision, as he says) managed to throw a grenade at Nahas's car, the Wafd leader was saved by his driver's being obliged to accelerate suddenly to avoid a tram.

There were later to be two other attempts against Nahas, and Sadat's involvement in them is recorded in the files relating to Iron Guard activities found in the royal archives after the revolution. On the first occasion, in April 1948, Sadat was specially smuggled out of prison so that he could take part. He and another officer, Abdel Raouf Nureddin, were in a car belonging to the Palace fire brigade driven by Captain Hassan Fahmi Abdel Meguid, use of the car for this purpose having been authorized by Captain Abdullah Sadiq of the fire brigade. Shots were fired at Nahas from the car, but missed. The next attempt took place a month later, when a car loaded with explosives was left outside Nahas's house in Garden City. According to the Palace archives, the participants in this venture were Captain Mustafa Kamal Sidqi, Abdel Raouf Nureddin and Anwar Sadat.

All this was more than two years after Amin Osman had been shot, on 6 January 1946. Hussein Tewfiq was caught red-handed in the attack, and the police had little difficulty in tricking him into a confession which implicated Sadat. Once again he found himself in the Aliens gaol, but it was not until January 1948 that he and Tewfiq were brought to trial.

The trial proved more or less farcical. It lasted from January to July 1948 and was spread over eighty-four sessions. Two former Prime Ministers, the Speaker of the Senate and several ex-ministers appeared for the defence. The state prosecutor acted more as defence counsel, and was to be rewarded when Sadat became President with the newly invented post of 'Socialist Prosecutor'. The principal judge in the court, which eventually acquitted eleven of the accused including Sadat, was later to receive at Sadat's hands Egypt's highest decoration, the Nile Collar. Hussein Tewfiq was sentenced to fifteen years' imprisonment, but the Palace secured his escape and spirited him away to Syria, where he became something of a public hero.

During all the time he was under investigation, and while the trial was going on, Sadat had enjoyed most unusual privileges. As has been seen, the influence of the Palace was able to secure his temporary freedom for the purpose of taking part in an attempt on the life of a former Prime Minister, and he was continually in receipt of funds from Yussef Rashad through the agency of one of the prison guards, Major Marei. The Palace also tried to help the defendants by arranging for the documents in the case to be stolen while they were being transferred from the prosecutor's office to the court, and though this endeavour failed, it is clear from the testimony of Mohamed Ibrahim Kamel that Sadat had been told about it in advance.

After Sadat was released he published extracts from his prison diary, first in the pages of the weekly magazine *El-Mussawar* in 1948, and later in book form. *Thirty Months in Prison*, as his book was called, was subsequently suppressed, but after Sadat became President the Saudis republished it. It sheds some interesting light on Sadat's character, and so is worth quoting from.

> *Friday, 18 January 1946* Yesterday after midnight I was taken to the Aliens gaol. Once again the Aliens gaol! This is where I had found myself with Eppler and the others some years ago!
> *Sunday, 20 January* Nothing much happened. I sent a letter to the Public Prosecutor protesting against my bad treatment.
> *Monday, 21 January* My letter seems to have had some effect, because the *Mamur* [Governor] himself brought me some soap, fresh pyjamas, blankets, and a dressing gown, and arranged for me to have a hot bath.
> *31 January* I am beginning to be annoyed. I feel nervous and tired. I sent another telegram to the Public Prosecutor.
> *4 February* It seems to me that Leila the Indian [in the women's wing of the prison] is in love with Prisoner No. 14 [Mohamed Ibrahim Kamel, later Foreign Minister] because she has gone to the *Mamur* to ask for his exercise period to be extended. Everybody is talking about this.
> *8 February* As I came out from my cell I met a soldier coming in with a lot of kebabs. I protested, asking who these were intended for. Apparently they were for the first of the accused [Hussein Tewfiq]. I went to the *Mamur* and talked roughly to him. I was allowed to order some kebabs from Shimi [a kebab shop].
> *17 February Al Muqattam* reports that Killearn is to be transferred from Cairo. How I hate that creature! He tarnished the dignity of Egypt. I decided to celebrate the occasion, and sent out for twelve pieces of cake. These I distributed to Leila the Indian and others, keeping three for myself. Unfortunately there must have been something wrong with the cakes, because I woke at two in the morning with diarrhoea. My hatred for Killearn increased.

As time went on Sadat began to organize his fellow prisoners.

3 July We had a meeting at which the following resolutions were passed:
1. All appetising food received by any prisoner should be distributed among all of us.
2. Those prisoners from good families who receive food from their homes should share it with the others, because prison food is unsatisfying, and food is the only source of pleasure in prison.
3. The prison authorities should give permission for the playing of chess and card games and for smoking.
4. Anyone who observes an attractive woman in the women's wing of the prison should inform the others and not monopolize the view.
5. We should seek entertainment by the production of a newspaper.
10 July How delightful is movement after stillness! Today we are all busy because we are producing our newspaper.
August God save our souls from the press and from pressmen! The problems of the newspaper are dominating the prison because everyone is jockeying for position.
September God confound all propaganda and propagandists!

In February 1948, when war in Palestine following Britain's decision to evacuate the country, was imminent, Sadat was engaged in a new enterprise very much after his own heart. This was the production of a play by and for the prisoners, which he had written and in which he was to take the lead.

The scene of the play was the court of the Caliph Haroun al-Rashid (played by Anwar Sadat). Other parts were taken by Hussein Tewfiq (Mansur, the executioner), Said Khamis (leader of the singers) and Murad (the 'Hawajah', or leader of a delegation from the Emperor of Roum (Byzantium)). The first act opened with the Caliph giving a signal to the master of ceremonies for the music to start. He is carried away by the sound – 'Let us enjoy it! Sing again!' Then the master of ceremonies comes to report that a delegation of foreigners craves permission to present their gifts. 'I grant permission, and the delegation enters, bearing a gift of cigarettes, and begging me to authorize the signing of a treaty of friendship and brotherhood with the Emperor of Roum. The executioner is indignant and accuses me of collaborating with foreigners who do not keep their word. "Oh Caliph," he exclaims, "do not, I beg you, cooperate with foreigners who never keep faith or respect frontiers." I try to argue with him, but he rushes at me and asks my permission to behead the foreign delegation. I forbid him.'

But apparently the play was not a success, because Sadat sadly reports: 'The audience began shouting at me "stop all this nonsense". So I stopped.' His final attempt to entertain his fellow-prisoners took the form of a daily 'broadcast' from his cell which included a programme for children in which Papa Anwar gave a talk and then imitated birds and animals and puppets, and sang a new song, written and composed by 'the beggar Anwar Sadat'.[1]

When Sadat left prison he was without a job. He had naturally been dismissed from the army at the time of his first arrest, much to the disgust of his father. But the Palace looked after people who had been useful to it. Hassan Ezzat had been supplied with sufficient finance to set up business as a contractor, and he took Sadat in as a partner. Ezzat was still in touch with Yussef Rashad and the Iron Guard, but the Palace was anxious to keep things quiet for the time being.

However, Sadat's relations with the Palace were a matter of common knowledge, and after his acquittal led to a rather curious incident. One day in 1948, while he was working in the contracting business, he was approached by Hassan el-Banna who asked if Sadat could arrange a meeting between him and King Farouk. This incident is described by Sadat in his suppressed autobiography.[2] El-Banna said he knew that the Moslem Brotherhood was mistrusted by foreigners, and that this mistrust prejudiced the King against them.

'I assure you, Anwar,' the description of their interview goes on, 'I want to put an end to these misunderstandings. I am sure foreigners will feel safe with us if the King feels safe with us. If I meet the King I am sure I can win his confidence. One meeting between us would be sufficient. I am not asking the King to cooperate with us; I only want to assure him that he has nothing to fear from the Moslem Brotherhood. You know Yussef Rashad. Can you explain my wishes to the King – that I will never be a danger to him?' Sadat said he would do his

---

[1] *Thirty Months in Prison*, pp. 45-49.

[2] *Unknown Pages*, p. 100.

[3] An investigation after the 1952 revolution proved that the assassination had been carried out on orders from the Prime Minister, Ibrahim Abdel Hadi, by General Mohamed Wasfi, director of the special force responsible for protecting government ministers. Abdel Hadi was tried on this charge by a revolutionary court, of which Sadat was a member, and sentenced to death, later commuted to life imprisonment.

best. A year later, on orders from the Palace, Hassan el-Banna was assassinated.[3]

One day Ezzat and Sadat went from Cairo to Suez to make some deliveries. They called in on some of Ezzat's relations, and there met a beautiful and vivacious girl, sixteen years of age, Jihan Safwat Raouf. She had seen Sadat's photograph day after day as his trial proceeded and had formed a romantic crush on him. Now she came face to face with her hero. The meeting was no less momentous for Sadat, who fell instantly and desperately in love with the girl. Her father, Safwat Raouf, was an official in the Ministry of Health who had married a Maltese girl called Gladys,[1] and Jihan appealed to Sadat not only because she was beautiful and adoring but because she was white. Colour had been, and was always to be, almost an obsession with him.

Sadat proposed to Jihan and was accepted. But before the marriage could be solemnized certain preliminaries had to take place. His first wife, Ekbal, had to be divorced, and he had to have a regular livelihood. The first was comparatively easily arranged; the second took a bit more time.

Sadat says that he received eighty gold sovereigns from Ezzat as his share of the contracting business (and should have received one hundred and eighty), and that at the time the gold sovereign was worth £E6.[2] This may be so. At any rate, many years later a statement of account was found in the house of Yussef Rashad showing that the sum of £E1000 had been paid out to Sadat on the occasion of his marriage to enable him to buy a car and to help him to start this new chapter of his life.

After a holiday in Helwan Sadat obtained a temporary job in the publishing house Dar el-Hillal, but what he and Jihan and her family wanted for him was not a job in journalism but a return to the army. So Sadat approached Yussef Rashad, pointing out that as he had been acquitted in the Amin Osman trial there should be no obstacle to his reinstatement. Rashad advised him to throw himself in the way of King Farouk when he went to the Friday prayers in the Hussein mosque in Cairo. This he did, kissing the King's hand, and asking forgiveness for anything he had done wrong. Farouk gave a nod of

---

1 When she became a President's wife Jihan pursued the idea that her mother's family originated in Sheffield, but exhaustive searches failed to find any trace of them there.

2 *In Search of Identity* p. 97.

acknowledgement. The next day Yussef Rashad told him to go and see Mohamed Haidar Pasha, Commander-in-Chief of the armed forces. This he did. Haidar Pasha greeted him severely: 'You're a criminal! You have a very black record.' Sadat tried to protest. Haidar Pasha interrupted him: 'Don't say anything.' Then he pressed a button and an orderly came in. 'This boy should be returned to the army today,' the Commander-in-Chief told him.

So on 15 January, 1950 Sadat was once again a captain in the Egyptian army. He had already married Jihan, and they had taken a flat in the Manial quarter of Cairo. But the army authorities thought this controversial individual would be better out of Cairo, so he was posted to Rafah, in northern Sinai.

I had covered the Palestine war for my paper, *Akher Sa'a*, and had subsequently revisited the Gaza Strip from time to time. On one of the visits, while at the headquarters of the 1st Infantry Division in Rafah, I ran into Sadat, whom I had met briefly at the house of Yussef Rashad in Cairo a year earlier. He invited me to lunch at the house in El-Arish he was occupying alone, Jihan having remained behind in Cairo. He gave me the impression of being keen on returning to the career in journalism he had briefly experienced a year or two earlier. He showed me some short stories he had been writing, and a novel, the manuscript of which I still have. It is called *The Prince of the Island* and is about a young ruler surrounded by old men who give him bad advice and young men who give him good advice. It has never been published.

It was in 1951 that Nasser again got in touch with Sadat. He of course knew of Sadat's record – of his trial and of his relations with the Palace, and thought he might be a useful source of information about what was going on in the Palace. Sadat was not at first told anything about the Free Officers movement, only given the impression that there was some undefined nationalist organization which might wish to make use of his services.

4

IN THE SHADOW OF NASSER

LATE IN 1951 Sadat was officially invited to become a member of the Free Officers movement. Almost all the others in the leadership of the movement except Nasser were strongly opposed to his inclusion. They knew of his record – of his comic opera dealings with the Germans, and his membership of the Iron Guard and the part he had played in the assassination of Amin Osman, and his kissing King Farouk's hand in the Hussein mosque. But Nasser's point of view was that all junior officers with some political experience were potentially useful to the movement, and that Sadat's Palace links ought not to be wasted. He could bring them information about what was going on in the Palace and perhaps supply the Palace with misleading information about the Free Officers. Most of Nasser's associates feared that Sadat was more likely to operate as a double agent.

Not that in Rafah there was much that Sadat could do. During the whole of 1951 he only attended one meeting of the Free Officers. This was after he had had a meeting with Yussef Rashad (with whom he was still in contact) at which he had been told about some impending army postings and promotions. Nasser thought these might be important, and invited him to Cairo to report to the Executive Committee of the movement. In 1952 Sadat attended two more meetings of the Executive Committee. Looking back a quarter of a century later these contacts had for him come to take on a different aspect:

> He [Nasser] always rushed to see me, whenever I arrived in Cairo on leave, to complain about the difficulties some members [of the Free Officers movement] created for him. It is no exaggeration to state, recalling the events of that distant period, that out of a seven-day army leave five would be spent with Nasser, during which the situation within our organization

and the problems that lay ahead would be thoroughly studied. Nasser always respected my experience.'[1]

The chief representatives of the Free Officers movement in the 1st Infantry Division in Sinai, with its headquarters in Rafah, to which Sadat was attached, were Gamal Salem and Salah Salem. In the original plan for the coup a signals officer was needed who could cut telephone communications in Cairo, and Nasser wrote down Sadat's name for the job, but with a query against it in red pencil. Sadat had been told that the coup was to take place some time in August, but the date had to be brought forward, and one of the officers, Hassan Ibrahim, was sent to Rafah to inform the Salem brothers of the revised deadline and to tell Sadat to present himself in Cairo on 22 July.

That day he duly took the train to Cairo, went home, collected Jihan and took her to a movie. In the summer open-air cinemas of those days it was common for there to be three feature films in one programme. Sadat and Jihan sat through them all.[2] While in the cinema Sadat had a loud quarrel with another member of the audience who had in some way offended him. Later the uncharitable were to say that this quarrel was designed to provide an alibi, should something go wrong with the coup, but there is no reason to suppose this was the case.

Sadat and Jihan did not return to their flat until about 12.45 on the morning of 23 July. There he found a hand-written message from Nasser, telling him that the operation was to take place that night – where was he? Sadat put on his uniform and went round to army headquarters, but by then the operation had been successful and the headquarters had been taken over. Sadat was refused entrance until Abdel Hakim Amer heard his voice raised in expostulation and let him in.

I remember seeing Sadat when he arrived at army headquarters at about 3.00 a.m. By then there was no need to cut the telephones, but Sadat went down to the cellar where the communications system was located to check that telephone links with the Suez Canal and the Gaza Strip were functioning properly. The proclamation announcing the

---

[1] *In Search of Identity*, p. 101.

[2] When he saw President Reagan in Washington in 1981 Sadat told him Reagan had a part in one of the films he saw that night. Reagan said: 'So I had a role in the Egyptian revolution without knowing it!' But the film has not been identified.

success of the revolution was now ready, and the broadcasting studios were reported occupied, so it was time for the world to be told. Nasser handed the proclamation to Sadat, saying: 'Anwar, you've got a good voice and know how to act. Go to the broadcasting studios and read this.'

Sadat went off, and all those at army headquarters waited eagerly to hear his voice over the air. It was a long time coming, but eventually at seven o'clock the announcement was made. When he came back a little later Nasser asked him the reason for the delay. 'There was a Sheikh reading the Koran in the studio,' said Sadat, 'and I didn't like to interrupt him.'

The other part played by Sadat on this first day of the revolution came after the Prime Minister, Nagib Hilaly Pasha, had resigned, and it was decided to ask Ali Maher to take his place. Somebody was needed to go to Ali Maher's house to sound him out, and as Sadat said he knew where he lived, he was sent.

Two days later Sadat was sent to Alexandria, where as usual King Farouk had gone to spend the summer months, with the text of the ultimatum calling on him to abdicate. From the first hours of the revolution Zakariyeh Mohieddin had been in charge of the military side in Alexandria and Gamal Salem of the political side. The British Consul-General came to see them to express the fears of the foreign community, but in the course of an extremely cordial interview received assurances that there was no cause for alarm. Somehow in *In Search of Identity* this incident is transmogrified into a scene in which Sadat confronts the British Chargé d'Affaires and Military Attaché who make demands which rouse Sadat to 'teach them a lesson'. The scene ends in the total discomfiture of the British and another personal victory for Sadat: ('the Chargé d'Affaires beat a hasty and apologetic retreat' – but in fact all the time he was in Cairo). In the version of history which has developed since 1970 it thus became Sadat who organized the Free Officers, proclaimed the revolution, put the British in their place and forced Farouk into exile. Sadat the actor took over from Sadat the soldier and Sadat the politician.

After July 1952 for a while Sadat more or less vanishes from the scene. The other members of the Revolutionary Command Council were still suspicious of him and frequently made him the butt of far from friendly jokes, but he enjoyed Nasser's protection. As often before and afterwards the submissive side of Sadat's nature was now most in evidence. He was always happiest when he could attach himself to a personality stronger than his own, and though Nasser himself was too busy to spare any time for this particular colleague, Abdel Hakim Amer – he who had recognized the voice of the locked-out Sadat in the early hours of 23 July – was more accessible. Amer had quickly emerged as number two in the revolutionary hierarchy (excluding Neguib who was never more that a figurehead, though the outside world took a long time to realize this), and Sadat cultivated Amer as his patron.

In 1953 it was decided that members of the RCC should be allotted Ministries, Nasser himself taking the Ministry of the Interior and Wing-Commander Baghdadi that of War. No Ministry came Sadat's way, but because of his brief journalistic experience he was made editor of *Gomhouriyeh*, the daily newspaper which had been started to express the views of the Revolutionary Command Council. Sadat wrote a good many articles in *Gomhouriyeh* which he later collected and published in *Revolt on the Nile* and *Unknown Pages*, but not all were equally worthy of preservation. One day at the beginning of 1955, when preparations for the mutual defence agreement sponsored by Britain and backed by America, soon to emerge as the Baghdad Pact, were under way, the American Ambassador came to see Nasser and pointed indignantly to an article in *Gomhouriyeh* which said: 'we must hit [Secretary of State] Dulles on his piggish neck.' Not only had this article appeared in the official newspaper, complained the Ambassador, but it was signed by the editor, Anwar Sadat, a member of the RCC. Nasser summoned Sadat: 'What's all this about Dulles and his piggish neck?' Sadat looked at the paper: 'I'm sorry, Mr President, but I haven't read it.' It had apparently become his practice to lend his signature to leading articles in *Gomhouriyeh* but to leave the writing of them to others. Not long afterwards he was relieved of the editorship.

A new post was found for Sadat when he was appointed Secretary-General of the recently formed Islamic Congress which had its headquarters in Cairo. It was a position which he thoroughly enjoyed. Many ideas were being suggested for films and other forms of publicity explaining Islam and this gave Sadat the excuse to mix once again with actors and producers. It also gave him the opportunity to travel and make new acquaintances. One such who was to prove of great value to him was Kamal Adhem, later to become head of Saudi intelligence, whom he first met in the house of the well-known singer Farid el-Atrash. Adhem's sister was married to Prince Feisal, the most important man in the kingdom after his brother King Saud whom he was to succeed in 1964. In 1955 Sadat was a witness at Kamal Adhem's own marriage. As Secretary-General of the Congress Sadat was the recipient of a great many gifts, which encouraged a natural tendency for him to compensate for long deprivation with excessive luxury. But he could be generous too, and one of the Cadillacs presented to him he passed on to Amer. When a power struggle erupted in the Revolutionary Command Council – not over who should be number one; there was never any question about that – Sadat always shrewdly backed Amer against his rivals, Baghdadi, Zakarieh Mohieddin or Salah Salem.

In 1958, after the union between Egypt and Syria and the formation of the United Arab Republic, Sadat was made Speaker of the Joint Parliament – 'he can orate as well as the Syrian Baathists,' was Nasser's comment. But at the end of that year he suffered a personal blow.

For some time Sadat and Jihan had been living in a modest house on the Pyramids Road, and Jihan's mother, Gladys, had come to live with them. Sadat tried the experiment of bringing his own mother from Mit Abu el-Kom to join the menage, but it was not a success. Gladys naturally expected and received much better treatment than Sitt el-Barrein, so after a few weeks his mother asked to be allowed to go away. Sadat found her a small flat near where his brother Talaat was living in Kubba, and on 12 December, on his way back from an unsuccessful attempt to see Nasser in Heliopolis, he called in to see how his mother was. He found her listening to a play on the radio. She offered to get him a cup of coffee, and as she came into the sitting room from the kitchen she called out: 'Anwar, take the tray.' She collapsed and died in his arms.

Sadat wanted to bury his mother in Mit Abu el-Kom, but he had no family tomb in the village graveyard. So he asked the father of his first wife, the Omdah, if she could be laid in their family tomb until a new one could be prepared. This was agreed. The Sadat family tomb was duly built, and Sitt el-Barrein laid in it. Later Sadat was to buy a seventeen-acre plot in the village and to build himself a house there. It was from this time that his association with Mit Abu el-Kom, which played such a big part in the image presented to the world after he became President, was renewed.

Though no longer directly associated with the Islamic Congress Sadat kept up many of the connections he had formed while he was Secretary-General, and in 1962 one of these was activated which was to have far-reaching consequences both for him and for Egypt. In the summer of that year a merchant from Taiz in Yemen, Abdel Ghani el-Mutahhar, got in touch with Sadat and told him that an army group, led by Colonel Ali Abdel Mughni, were planning a coup which would replace the Imamate by a progressive republic along the lines of Egypt. He wanted to know whether they could expect Egypt to help them.

Sadat brought the news to Nasser. He argued strongly in favour of giving the republican Yemenis all the help they could; it would, he said, help to compensate for the setback Egypt had suffered when the Syrians broke up the UAR the previous year. He was also influenced by a certain Abdel Rahman el-Bidany, a Yemeni refugee living in Cairo. The death of the old Imam Ahmed in September precipitated the coup, but unfortunately Mughni was killed in the first encounter with the royalists. There were long discussions in the RCC about what should be done, Sadat always urging intervention. All that would be needed, he said, was for the air force to make some overflights to scare the tribesmen – 'just a few planes tossing bombs out of the windows' was the expression he used, and one with which Nasser was later to tease him when Egypt became bogged down in Yemen, with almost everyone, including the CIA, the Saudis and even the Israelis involved on the other side. 'We sent a battalion to Yemen and reinforced it with two divisions,' said Nasser. But Sadat continued to be the political link with Yemen, his patron Amer in charge of the military side of the operation.

It was round about this time that Sadat developed a somewhat surprising new sideline, as manager of the business affairs of Sheikh Mubarak el-Sabah, the former Minister of Interior of Kuwait, who had quarrelled with the rest of the ruling family and come to live in Cairo. This came out a good deal later when Sheikh Mubarak sued a Palestinian called Mohamed Barakat, who had been acting as his agent, accusing him of embezzling some of the funds entrusted to him.

Barakat pleaded that he had only paid out as he had been instructed, and quoted payments made to Sadat among others. The case was withdrawn after Sadat became President. But Nasser had earlier got wind of what was happening when Sadat asked if Sheikh Mubarak could be given diplomatic status, which would have enabled him to import into Egypt anything he wanted free of duty. Nasser refused, and blamed Sadat for getting himself involved in this sort of thing.

Another occasion for Nasser's annoyance came in 1966, when Sadat had an invitation from Congress to visit the States (he was by then Speaker of the Egyptian Parliament). Sadat complained to Sheikh Mubarak that the official allowance he was to be given for the visit was insufficient. So Sheikh Mubarak wrote him a cheque for $35,000. When Nasser heard of this he was extremely angry and made Sadat return the cheque – but not before Intelligence had had it photographed and copies deposited in its archives.

As the Yemen war dragged on it had a generally corrupting effect on Egyptian life. It also corrupted Abdel Hakim Amer in various ways, which was to become apparent in his behaviour in June 1967. Sadat saw that Amer's influence was waning, so he once again cultivated a direct relationship with Nasser.

After the 1967 war and the suicide of Abdel Hakim Amer, only Hussein Shafei and Zakariyeh Mohieddin were left besides Sadat from the original group which had made up the Revolutionary Command Council. It was a grim period for Egypt and for Nasser in particular. He was working night and day to the limit of his endurance to rebuild the army and to recover what he could, politically and economically, from the ruins of defeat. In these difficult times Sadat became closer to Nasser than he had ever been before. His home was somewhere where Nasser could go and briefly relax in the company of an old and unexacting friend. It was natural therefore that, when Nasser suffered his first stroke in 1969, Sadat should have been named as head of the committee set up to act while the President was incapacitated.

However, Nasser soon recovered, and in December was due to attend the Arab summit conference in Rabat. I was going with him in the same plane, and as we took our seats he said to me with a laugh: 'Do you know what I did today? Sadat was coming to see me off at the airport, so I told him to make certain he brought a Koran along with him – I think he took the hint. I've sworn him in as Vice-President while I'm out of Egypt.' I was greatly surprised, and asked him why he had done this. 'Read these,' said Nasser, handing over a bunch of telegrams from the advance party which had been sent to Rabat to check on security. Among these was a report that General Mohamed Oufkir, Moroccan Minister of the Interior, was collaborating with the CIA in a plot to assassinate Nasser. If anything did happen to him, said Nasser, Sadat would be all right for the interim period. People in the Socialist Union and the army would look after the real business, and Sadat's job would be largely ceremonial. 'Besides,' said Nasser, 'all the others have been Vice-President at one time or another; it's Anwar's turn.' He added that in any case it was only for a week, and he didn't set much store by this assassination report – he had seen too many of them.

The nine months between the Rabat summit and Nasser's death on 28 September 1970 were a period of intense diplomatic activity. William Rogers, the American Secretary of State, launched a new peace initiative on 25 June 1970, and to the astonishment of the Russians and of many Arabs, Nasser decided to accept it. To the astonishment too of Sadat, who had seen a copy of the initiative and, while Nasser was abroad in Tripoli, had confidently told a meeting of the Socialist Union that the plan would be rejected. He was unaware of the strategy Nasser had in mind, which was to exploit the war of attrition then in progress across the Suez Canal by raising the conflict from a local level, in which Israel enjoyed unchallengeable superiority, to the superpower level, where the balance of diplomatic and military power was much more even.

It was while Nasser was in the Soviet Union in the summer of 1970 that Sadat got into trouble which might well have cost him his position as Vice-President and so altered the course of history. He and Jihan felt that their existing house on the Pyramids Road was not worthy of the Vice-President of Egypt and cast anxious eyes on a grander one next door. This belonged to a retired general, Ibrahim Mogi. They offered to rent it from him, but he refused, whereupon Sadat arranged to have it sequestered. On his return Nasser received a full report of what had happened, which annoyed him greatly, and Sadat was admonished. He retired to Mit Abu el-Kom saying that his master's anger had given him a heart attack.

In the end Sadat was rewarded rather than punished for the house affair. Nasser ordered that a house on the Nile, near the Soviet Embassy, which had belonged to a Jewish millionaire called Castro and had been turned into a government guest house, should be made the official residence of the Vice-President. After Nasser's death Jihan asked for this house to be redecorated. This was supposed to be a comparatively modest undertaking, but the bill eventually came to £E650,000. Following the example of Jackie Kennedy when she redecorated the White House, Jihan transferred objects she admired from the royal palaces to this house, which she and the family continued to use.

Nasser died from a heart attack at five o'clock in the afternoon of 28 September 1970. Immediately after the doctors had confirmed his death, those of us who had been at his bedside, and Sadat who had arrived at the house about an hour and a half later, had a meeting in the sitting room on the ground floor to discuss what should be done next. It was a moment of great tension. As well as grief, it was possible to see in the faces of those round the table the seeds of future conflicts and divisions.

Sadat asked my opinion as to what should be done. I told him I thought the most important thing was to give the nation a sense of continuity. We should not innovate, but follow the rules laid down in the Constitution. This states that on the death of a President the Vice-President should take over for a period of sixty days until a plebiscite to choose a successor can be held. I said I also thought it was essential to move step by step. Settle the matter of the presidency first; if we started at the same time discussing who should be Prime Minister or fill other positions, we should get caught up in endless deals and compromises.

Sadat was still at this time officially the sole Vice-President. With the pressure of other business – after the Rabat summit came Nasser's visit to Moscow, his illness, the Rogers initiative, further Israeli raids, the showdown between King Hussein and the Palestinians and much else – it had simply not occurred to Nasser or anyone else to bother about making any change. Besides, his new honorific position gave Sadat such obvious pleasure. Certainly, all of us taking part in this meeting were conscious of his limitations, but I felt strongly that the need for continuity overrode all other considerations. Also I hoped that the exercise of responsibility would help to mature the good qualities in the man, and quoted the example of Harry Truman.

There was general agreement on these principles. The next question was how to put them into practice. I recommended that there should be a joint meeting of the Cabinet and the Higher Executive Committee of the Socialist Union to declare to the nation and the world that the Vice-President was taking over. I suggested to Sadat that he himself should make the broadcast announcement of Nasser's death and of the procedure which was to be adopted. Thus Egyptians would hear the voice of their new President. I reminded the meeting how the American people had found reassurance after President Kennedy's assassination by seeing on television the swearing in of Vice-President Johnson on the plane taking him back to Washington.

Sadat welcomed the suggestion, and we went together in my car to my office to prepare the broadcast. He asked me to go to the broadcasting studio with him, but I said it was better that he should go alone. However, as he had forgotten to bring his spectacles with him he borrowed mine to read the announcement.

The broadcast was made, and Sadat had to face up to the realities of his new position. The group which afterwards became known as 'the centres of power' were content with Sadat as President because they thought he was a weak man whom they could manage. I told some of them that I knew what they were thinking but they ought to remember the example of Nahas Pasha, another political leader whom others had tried to manage only to find that they were out in the cold while he remained on top. Sadat asked me to run his presidential campaign for him, and since, as had always been my intention, I had resigned my ministerial post (Minister of Information) a few days after Nasser's death, I agreed to do this. We campaigned on the platform that Sadat had been Nasser's own choice for the post. After he had been duly elected Sadat appeared before Parliament and pledged himself to carry on along the path Nasser had charted. 'My programme is Nasser's,' he said. But when he had finished speaking he made the mistake of bowing to a bust of Nasser which stood in the chamber. There was a murmur of disapproval; such a gesture smacked of idolatry.

5

ON TOP OF EGYPT

ON 15 OCTOBER 1970, Sadat was confirmed as the new President of the Egyptian Republic in a plebiscite which gave him 90.04 per cent of the votes. He was now master of Egypt. Or was he? But before turning to the challenge to his authority which Sadat was soon to be called upon to meet it is necessary to consider the person who, in this and in all the difficult times to come, was closest to him – his wife Jihan.

There is a story which Jihan used sometimes to tell of how, when they were engaged, she and Sadat were having dinner together in a restaurant called Casino des Pigeons in Giza. An old gipsy came up to their table and offered to tell Jihan's fortune. After studying her palm the gipsy turned to Jihan and said: 'You are going to be Queen of Egypt!' Jihan says that she and Anwar both laughed, but if the story is true there can be little doubt that she more than half believed what had been told her. She was always extremely ambitious and prepared to work hard to achieve her ambitions. She was beautiful, with a beauty which reflected her mother's foreign origin, but she had a shrewdness of intellect which she inherited from her Egyptian father.

Jihan was to prove an enormous help to her husband, whom she always encouraged and whose streak of submissiveness was more than compensated for by her own domineering energy. Sadat was by nature lazy, at any rate as far as paper work was concerned; it is significant that after he became President no official photographs were ever released showing him sitting at a desk. A routine had been established under Nasser by which four reports were prepared for the President every morning when he began work – a summary of telegrams from Egyptian Ambassadors abroad; a report from the Ministry of Interior about conditions inside the country; a report from the *Mukhabarat* (Intelligence) about counter-espionage, security on the frontiers, the state of the army, etc; and a financial and economic report listing such items as the level of foreign reserves, stocks of food and so on. Nasser also liked to have before him Arabic newspapers, not only all the Egyptian ones but also all those from Beirut at a time when the Lebanese press was the most free and varied in the Arab world, as well as newspapers from Britain and America.

Soon after he had taken over Sadat protested: 'Don't ever bring all this paper to me; I'm being smothered by a mountain of paper.' It is probably true that Nasser spent too much of his time reading reports and newspapers, but certainly Sadat spent too little. However, Jihan did her best to make up for his omissions. She became an omnivorous reader of reports, showing a special predilection for transcripts of tapped telephone conversations and intelligence reports and for any matters which concerned the state of public opinion, though less interested in foreign affairs and economics. Her willingness to undertake this work was all the more valuable because Sadat became an increasingly restless traveller, spending less and less time in the presidential office. Indeed, it is probable that he and Jihan did not spend more than half the year together.

So Jihan became Sadat's eyes and ears, and quickly gathered round her an entourage of her own – wives of businessmen, politicians, service officers, as well as ladies from the old aristocracy who had been leaders of society before the revolution. She paid particular attention to the officers of the Presidential Guard and their wives, and at one time arranged a marriage between one of the officers and her eldest daughter, though in the end it never came off.

Jihan had the sense to realize her limitations. Her formal education had stopped when she was sixteen and she had married soon after. Now she was the wife of a head of state and knew that she would have to meet and make conversation with distinguished foreign visitors. She did not want to be an embarrassment to her husband or to her country, so she consulted some of her friends about what should be done. They suggested that, as foreigners were bound to ask her questions about Egypt, she had better start by learning more about her country's history. She agreed that this was a good idea, and it was arranged for her to have a course of instruction from one of the country's leading Egyptologists, Professor Abdel Munim Abu Bekr. They met for a while several times a week, and he took her round the principal archaeological sites in the neighbourhood of Cairo as well as, of course, the Egyptian Museum. The intention was that after she had finished the course on ancient Egyptian art and culture she would move on to the Islamic period and then to modern times, but these projects were never realized. After the events of 15 May 1971 Sadat bestowed on Jihan the official title of 'First Lady of Egypt' (*'sayidat misr el-aula'*). This was obviously modelled on the title accorded to the wives of American Presidents, but it does not sound so well in Arabic as in English.

The date of what Sadat called 'The Corrective Revolution' was 15 May 1971 and it was a date he would celebrate in later years with considerable éclat. The crisis which ended with the disappearance from office and into prison of what were known as 'the centres of power' had begun on 21 April at a meeting of the Higher Executive Committee of the Socialist Union. The subject for discussion at this meeting was theoretically the proposal for a union between Egypt, Syria and Libya, but the real issue was much deeper, because if the union was accomplished it would mean new institutions and new elections, which would give Sadat the opportunity to remove his opponents. This they of course realized, and it was a bitter attack on the proposed union by his leading critic, Ali Sabri, which brought the quarrel out into the open.

After this meeting it looked as though Sadat stood no chance. Only three hands out of about four hundred members present had been raised in his support. The politicians appeared to have everything in their power. The only organized political grouping in the country was ranged almost solidly against the President, and General Mohamed Fawzi, the Commander-in-Chief, was known to lean towards the camp of Sadat's opponents. Yet three weeks later the tables had been completely turned and Sadat was triumphant. How had this been achieved?

The story of Sadat's dismissal of Ali Sabri on 2 May and the events which followed are well known. It was on the night of 9/10 May that Sadat was brought tangible evidence to show that his telephone had been tapped, and three days later Sharawy Gomaa, the Minister of the Interior, was dismissed. This was followed by the resignations of the other leading members of the group, including the head of the Presidential Office, the Director of Intelligence, the Minister of Information and others. They calculated that by their action the government would be paralyzed and Sadat compelled to yield.

But what has never been clear is whether or not there was an actual conspiracy to seize power. Did the opposition simply want to assert themselves against someone whom they had always regarded as a figurehead who had no business taking an active part in the framing of policy, or were they prepared to go further? Obviously no proof of a conspiracy was ever forthcoming; if there had been, nobody can doubt that the conspirators would not have escaped, as they did, with only prison sentences.

In fact a conspiracy did exist and Sadat was saved from it by one thing and one thing alone – the superb discipline of the Egyptian army and particularly of some of its senior officers.

On 21 April, the day of the confrontation between Sadat and his critics at the meeting of the Central Committee of the Socialist Union, General Fawzi wrote out in his own hand an order to General Mohamed Sadiq, Chief of Staff of the Egyptian Army. This reads:

United Arab Republic
Ministry of War
21.4.71

General Sadiq

Tomorrow you coordinate, organize and plan with:

1. Military Intelligence
2. 6th Mechanized Division
3. 22nd Mechanized Infantry Brigade
4. Military Police

with the object of securing Cairo against all eventualities. Ensure control of cypher network, assembly places, telex system, etc. (orders to be taken only from Fawzi, Sharawy, Sami.)

Duties

Secure: 1. broadcasting
2. entrances to Cairo
3. electronic – close down all embassy radios

(Signed) Mohamed Fawzi[1]

[1] When this order was eventually made public in 1982, General Fawzi defended himself by saying that it had nothing to do with a *coup d'état* but was connected with preparations for the coming battle with Israel. His defence is not entirely convincing.

These orders remained waiting to be acted upon, but known only to the officer who had issued them and to the officer who had received them. Meanwhile the crisis was moving to a head.

The only hint I received of what was in the wind was when, at a meeting with General Sadiq, he whispered to me: 'Tell that man to take care.' When I saw Sadat shortly afterwards I advised him to get in personal touch with General El-Leithy Nassif, commander of the Presidential Guard. Strictly speaking the Guard came under the control of the Minister for Presidential Affairs, who was Sami Sharaf, one of Sadat's principal opponents, so a direct approach was necessary. This he did.

William Rogers, the American Secretary of State, arrived in Egypt on 4 May bringing with him new proposals to which Sadat made counter-proposals. Sadat summoned General Fawzi to keep him informed of the position, and was understandably astonished when the general told him that the army found both Rogers's proposals and the President's counter-proposals 'unacceptable'. It was not explained how 'the army' had been consulted or what made it the army's business to pronounce on these matters.

On 13 May, the day when Sharawy Gomaa was dismissed and the others resigned, General Fawzi summoned the service chiefs of staff to the Ministry of War and told them that Sadat was selling out Egypt to the Americans. He turned to Sadiq: 'Are you ready?' he asked him. General Sadiq had all this time been sitting on the orders he had received, not yet understanding the occasion for which they were to be implemented. Now he understood. He bluntly accused Fawzi of dragging the army into politics. 'If you want to resign, you can,' he told him, 'but the army is not going to move. It's all over.' Sadiq turned to the other senior officers present. 'Are the armed forces of Egypt prepared to get themselves mixed up in politics at a time when we are preparing for the battle?' he asked. They remained silent.

Sadat himself was under the impression that Sadiq had joined the 'centres of power'. He invited me to his house that night and I assured him that this was not so. I urged him, on the contrary, to make

---

It is not usual for the military command to start a war by cutting off its own capital, nor were the three men named those who would in such conditions be in control. In any case, at this time the country was totally unprepared for a war, as General Fawzi himself knew better than anyone.

General Sadiq Minister of War. He telephoned to General Sadiq, who came round straight away. Sadat appointed him Minister of War and promoted him to full general.

So the coup failed. But although Sadat emerged the hero of the hour, who had almost single-handedly routed the formidable phalanx of his enemies, he had not had to do anything at all. He had been rescued by luck, and by the discipline of the army. When it came to the trial of the 'centres of power' the death sentences passed on the leaders were commuted to life imprisonment because there was no evidence of an actual conspiracy. Had General Sadiq produced the orders sent to him by General Fawzi the evidence would of course have been there for all to see. The death sentences would certainly have been carried out. But General Sadiq thought that the shedding of blood in such circumstances could only have a devastating effect on morale in the army and on public opinion in general. He preferred to suppress the incriminating document, and hid it at the back of a mirror in his house. There it remained until after Sadat's death.

Sadat was now President in fact as well as in name. But just because he had achieved so much, more was expected of him. When he was preparing the address he intended to make to the nation, telling them about what had happened, I found he planned to concentrate on the way in which his opponents had tried to prevent him from negotiating with Rogers. I told him I thought this was misjudging the mood of the country – what the people wanted to hear was that there was going to be a return to greater democratic liberties. 'They know they have had a narrow escape,' I told him. 'They want to be reassured.' When Sadat did make democracy the main theme of his address, a great sigh of relief went up in the country. Incidentally, he showed on this occasion that his ideas about democratic procedures were still rather hazy. 'I have decided to come to talk to you, the People's Assembly,' he told the deputies. 'By the way, your name is no longer the National Assembly, but the People's Assembly.' The deputies took this change of title, on which they had not been consulted, with due humility.

Then there was the problem of the army. The armed forces were now geared to one sole aim – a war to liquidate the consequences of enemy aggression. But, though he never said so openly, Sadat had always thought that Nasser had made a great mistake in not admitting after the 1967 war that he had been defeated; nor had he ever been happy about the Soviet alliance. Now he began to think back to some of the ideas which had been in vogue at the end of World War Two – that what Egypt really needed was its own Marshall Plan, the sort of programme of economic recovery which only America could finance and organize.

But paradoxically the first major foreign policy act of Sadat's was to sign a treaty of friendship and alliance with the Soviet Union (27 May 1971). This greatly puzzled the Americans. What did it mean? Why had Sadat first got rid of those members of the government who were regarded as pro-Soviet, and then gone and signed a treaty with the Soviets, which was something Nasser had never done?

To find an answer, the Americans naturally consulted the Saudis. King Feisal and his brother-in-law, Kamal Adhem, Director of Saudi Intelligence, happened to be in Washington when the treaty was signed. The Americans knew that Adhem not only worked in the closest possible cooperation with the CIA, but also had a close personal association with Sadat, dating back to the days of the Islamic Congress and consolidated during the Yemen war. So close indeed had this association been that, as was later revealed in the *Washington Post*, Adhem had during the 1960s 'provided Sadat with a steady income'.[1]

After Sadat became President, Adhem had been one of the first people to visit him. He had described the efforts the Saudis were making to get the Americans more closely involved in Middle East affairs, but said that they always came up against the problem of the Russian presence in Egypt. Sadat had explained his dependence on Russian aid as long as the Americans went on providing Israel with everything it needed, but volunteered the information that, if the first phase of an Israel withdrawal was completed, he would get rid of the Russians. This significant undertaking was transmitted to Washington, but its effects were largely undermined thanks to a deliberate leak by Senator Jackson.

On his way back from Washington to Riyadh Feisal stopped off in Egypt, and towards the end of the King's visit I was surprised to be rung up in my office by Sheikh Taher Radwan, the Saudi Arabian representative at the Arab League, saying that Feisal wanted to see me

[1] *Washington Post*, 24 February 1977.

at Kubba Palace on Friday. I was surprised because I had been outspoken in my criticisms of Feisal in the columns of *Al Ahram* over the Yemen war and other matters and knew that Feisal was not a person who easily forgave. This was Wednesday. I told Sheikh Radwan that unfortunately I must excuse myself because I was going to Alexandria to be with my family, whom I had not seen for three weeks. 'When are you going?' he asked. I told him I was going that same day. 'Very well,' said Sheikh Radwan, 'the King is in Alexandria now, and comes to Cairo tomorrow. He will see you in the Palestine Hotel in Alexandria this evening.'

There was nothing more to be said, so I went to the Palestine Hotel and was received by Feisal. He told me how surprised the Americans had been over the treaty with the Soviet Union. I was close to Sadat and knew his thinking, what did it mean? I explained what I believed to be the President's point of view – the need to keep a balance between the various forces inside and outside the country – though I had to confess my personal dislike for treaties as such. The King then expounded to me some of his theories about Communism and Zionism being the same thing, and told me how greatly this theory had interested Richard Helms, the head of the CIA, when he had explained it to him.

We talked for about two hours, Feisal showing himself extremely affable. When I came out I found Kamal Adhem waiting in the anteroom. 'I wanted to leave you and the King together,' he said, 'so that you could talk freely. I hope it went well.' I said it had: 'His Majesty was most gracious. Bygones are bygones, and we are starting a new page. But I confess that I can't go along with his theories about Communism.' (Among his other ideas, Feisal was convinced that Brezhnev was a Jew, because he thought his first name, Leonid, was derived from Leon, which he was persuaded was a Jewish name.)

Kamal Adhem said they wanted to arrange for there to be closer coordination between the King and Sadat, and I agreed that this was desirable. Kamal Adhem explained that there had been technical developments in communications of a revolutionary nature, and that the Russians had not made them available to us. 'You are the only person the President really trusts,' he went on, 'and he asked us to talk to you. We want to arrange for the installation of a hot line between my house and your house.' 'My house?' I exclaimed in astonishment, 'or do you mean in *Al Ahram*?' 'No, no,' said Kamal Adhem. 'This is a top secret matter. It couldn't be in *Al Ahram.*' Knowing as I did that Saudi intelligence was a step-child of the CIA, I could only apologize and say that it was quite impossible for me to consider any arrangement of this nature.

Later I told Sadat what had happened and said I felt offended as well as astonished by the proposal. 'Forget about it, Mohamed,' he said, 'forget about it.' Some weeks later General Sadiq mentioned to me that some of the army's detector apparatuses had spotted powerful new signals being put out from somewhere in Giza (where Sadat lived). Did I know anything about them? I said I did not, but in fact I realized that Sadat must have chosen a member of his staff to act the part I had turned down. The hot-line terminal had been installed in his house, and was later moved to Abdin Palace.

This was another example of Sadat's love of cloak-and-dagger operations and of how easily he let himself be influenced by a stronger character than his own. No doubt the arguments Sadat used to himself were that it was only realism to acknowledge that the Americans were the masters of the world, and that if there was going to be any change for the better in the political or military situation it would have to come from them and from the Saudis.

But whatever Sadat's real thoughts and intentions may have been, this was a time when he managed to conceal them from more or less everyone. In spite of the constant scrutiny to which he was subjected – by the Americans via the Saudis and by the Russians from their vantage point in Cairo – he managed to keep both superpowers guessing. So it was that only two months before he ordered the Russian experts out of Egypt he prepared for Marshal Gretchko, the Soviet Commander-in-Chief, on his arrival in Cairo, a particularly effusive welcome. The Marshal had been invited to the President's house at seven o'clock for a drink before going on to a dinner party arranged for him at the Officers' Club by General Sadiq. But Gretchko was unable to leave until almost eleven, Sadat insisting that he stay to listen to songs his eldest daughter had learnt while she was at a students' camp in the Soviet Union. I myself was rebuked by him for a series of articles I wrote at this time in *Al Ahram* in which I had argued that the Soviet Union was benefitting from the condition of 'no war, no peace'. 'Stop writing this stuff, Mohamed,' he told me. 'The Soviet

Union is my only friend.' My answer was that if anybody had only one friend in the world he was certain to find himself in trouble.

It is now known that Sadat had already secretly resolved that the Russians must go; his only problem was how to do it. When Prince Sultan, the Saudi Defence Minister, and Kamal Adhem came to Cairo at the end of June they renewed the pressure on Sadat to get rid of the experts. If he did decide on dismissing them, they said, would he be sure to let them know in advance, so that they could tell the Americans. But this was precisely what Sadat was determined not to do. He knew that the expulsion of the experts would be an extremely dramatic act which would create an international sensation, and he had no intention of sharing the limelight with anybody else. He thought that once the expulsion had been announced the Americans would be so delighted they would give him anything he asked for. In this of course he miscalculated. As Kissinger said afterwards: 'Why didn't he tell us what he was going to do? We would have paid well for it.' But once the deed had been done there was no need for the Americans to pay anything.

General Sadiq was as surprised as everybody else by Sadat's action, being only told about it on 7 July, the day before it happened. Although he had the reputation of being anti-Soviet the general was far from delighted by the news. 'Don't do it this way,' he begged the President. 'The Russians are our only source of arms.' As it turned out he need not have worried. After the break Moscow speeded up the supply of arms to Egypt to an extraordinary extent. It was as if the Russians were telling Sadat that if he did not proceed to the battle he had been so long talking about he could not blame them for his failure.

Sadat needed an excuse. The year 1971 had been proclaimed 'the year of decision', when the fighting war would be resumed. But nothing happened, though, not altogether convincingly, the delay could be blamed on the superpowers' distraction through the war between India and Pakistan. Nothing happened again in 1972, this time the excuse being Russia's failure to deliver the necessary arms. But what about 1973? There had already been ominous signs of disaffection in the army at the end of 1972, when on 12 October an army officer led some of this troops to the Hussein mosque in central Cairo, publicly demanding 'immediate war' with Israel. The official version was that the officer was off his head, but General Sadiq was made a scapegoat. He was accused of having lied to the President about the state of the Egyptian army's preparedness and was replaced by General Ahmed Ismail.

It was not just in the armed forces that discontent erupted. The whole nation was becoming restless, continually exhorted to prepare for a climax which never materialized. Students demonstrated; hundreds were arrested and the universities closed.

Some members of the Writers Association and other intellectuals wrote an open letter in which they pleaded the case of the students, pointing out that these young men could look forward to being drafted into the army for an unknown number of years to prepare for a battle which seemed to be growing more and more elusive. They said that preparation for the battle was proving an enormous drain on Egypt's resources, human and financial, and that therefore it might be worthwhile – though this was only hinted at – to explore the possibility for a peaceful rather than a military solution. Dr Abdel Kader Hatem, who was both Deputy Prime Minister and Minister for Information and Culture, asked two of the signatories of the letter, Tewfiq el-Hakim and Negib Mahfuz, both authors with international reputations, to come and see him and to discuss the content of the letter. This they did.

Needless to say, the letter could not be published in Egypt, but copies of it were smuggled out of the country and appeared in some Beirut newspapers. Sadat was furious when he heard about it, and attacked the writers in Parliament. He even summoned a special meeting of nearly two hundred people connected with the press, including seven representatives from each publishing house, in which he accused Tewfiq el-Hakim personally of defeatism and of writing 'with black hatred in his heart'. He said it was tragic that a man whom Egypt had raised so high should have sunk so low.

Sadat also accused me of being behind the writers' open letter and their discussion with Dr Hatem, though when all this took place I had been in China and knew nothing about it. However, when I came back to Cairo I had a visit from Tewfiq el-Hakim, who said he wanted the President to know the truth of what had happened and asked me to take a letter to him explaining it all. This I did, and this is the text of the letter which has never previously been published.

Cairo, 7 March 1973

Mr President,

It is my duty not to conceal from you anything which passed at the meeting between us and Dr Hatem in which it appears that an expression was wrongly attributed to me and the writers who took part in the meeting. The truth of the matter is as follows:

1. Dr Hatem asked to see myself, Negib Mahfuz and Sarwat Abaza. At our meeting he was the first to speak, outlining the situation and expressing the view that the tragic circumstances in which Egypt now found herself were due to our failure to acknowledge defeat after the June War. He told us to treat what he was saying as strictly confidential, and up to this moment I have so treated it. If it had not been for your speech in which you accused us of defeatism none of us would have allowed ourselves to make any reference to it.

2. Dr Hatem also said that the current talk about a peaceful solution was more dangerous to the President than talk about an impending battle because it would expose him to the attack of all those who opposed a peaceful solution. These include Libya, the PLO, the army, and the adventurous Left. Our answer was that we felt it our duty, as writers and patriots, to help the President in the interests of Egypt. It would be wrong for us to leave him unsupported when he is facing obstacles which may prevent him from securing the best interests of the nation. (This was the point at which the phrase was used about 'helping the President towards any solution he thinks desirable' which was quoted out of context in the President's speech.)

3. When we asked Dr Hatem what would be the nature of the battle which Egypt sees as necessary, his answer was that it would in fact amount to no more than a skirmish aimed at drawing the attention of the world to the explosive situation in the area, and so stimulate international pressure for a peaceful solution. He said that the settlement which Egypt was willing to accept would not necessarily be an immediate and complete withdrawal within the framework of an overall solution.

This is the point which I wish to make clear. My two colleagues have reminded me of what passed at our interview with Dr Hatem, because the accounts which have appeared in the newspapers are extremely inaccurate.

I assure you, Mr President, of our confidence in your ardent nationalism, with which we have long been acquainted, and of our consciousness of your great love for Egypt and of the struggles which you have made on her behalf all through your life.

Please accept my greetings and deepest respect,

Tewfiq el-Hakim

I confess that I was disturbed by this letter and its implications, though when I saw the embarrassment it obviously caused the President I did what I could to restore harmony between him and the writers. Not that my good offices were really necessary. It was strange that some time later Sadat should have awarded Tewfiq el-Hakim Egypt's highest civilian honour, the Nile Collar.[1]

I saw a lot of Sadat at this time and could understand the conflict which was going on in his mind. He was in a real dilemma. The mood of the country was one of frustration and anger. In the army the sense of being let down was much worse; the ever-receding vision of the battle for which they had so long been trained had had a disastrous effect on the morale of all ranks. Sadat realized that all the tensions which had been building up were bound to explode, and that unless he could control the explosion it might prove his undoing. But how to act? His preference was for a limited battle which would quickly involve the superpowers. But could he be sure of the Americans?

In February 1973 he sent his National Security Adviser, Hafez Ismail, to Washington for a well-publicized meeting with President Nixon, and for secret talks with his opposite number, Henry Kissinger, at the private residence of Donald Kendall, the chairman of Pepsi-Cola, who was a close friend of President Nixon.[2] Nothing really concrete emerged from these talks, but as the months went by Sadat began to get an increasing number of messages about American intentions through his most consistent channel of information – Kamal Adhem and the CIA. These were to the effect that Kissinger (as he had explained in an interview with Arnaud de Borchgrave) would not want the administration to get more directly involved in the Middle East's problems as long as these were more or less dormant. But if the area began to show signs of hotting up, that would be a different matter. When I was in London many years later,[3] Kamal Adhem confirmed this to me, saying he had spoken to the CIA man in charge of Middle East affairs, and that now, with the Israelis showing signs of increasing obstinacy, it might be that the Americans were willing to do a little heating up themselves. As late as 23 September,

[1] By that time Tewfiq el-Hakim had published a book called *The Return of Awareness* in which he attacked Nasser.

[2] Richard Nixon himself had been lawyer for Pepsi-Cola.

[3] March 1982.

when David Rockefeller met Sadat at Bourg el-Arab, he passed on the same message – a little heating up would be in order.

But what Sadat had all along found so difficult to determine was what temperature to heat things up to. He could accuse others, like Tewfiq el-Hakim, of defeatism, but in fact nobody had dragged their feet more than he had. This indecision was to have serious consequences for the battle, even after the signal to go ahead had been given, for whereas the operation which the Syrians were told was to be activated was that known as Granite 2, which involved an advance to the Sinai passes, the orders given to General Ahmed Ismail, the Minister of War, were to implement Granite 1, which only envisaged a five-point crossing of the Canal. This not only caused serious misunderstandings with the Syrians, but meant that when the initial attack proved far more successful than Sadat had expected there was no prepared plan to exploit it. Planning for the second stage of the battle was really only begun on 12 October, six days after the initial attack, by which time of course it was much too late.

Nobody expected the Egyptian army to behave as it did. Its performance came as a complete surprise not only to the Israelis and Americans but also to Sadat himself. He was astonished in particular by the meticulous nature of the preliminary planning and by the proliferation of anti-tank and anti-aircraft missiles which played so large a part in the victory. Not long before the battle began he said to me: 'Whatever happens now, I have done my duty. If we are defeated in the Canal crossing, well, that's our fate. But the nation won't be able to blame me. We have to defend the honour of Egypt, whatever the cost, even if crossing the Suez Canal costs us twenty thousand casualties.'

As it turned out, of course, Egypt was not asked to pay anything like this price. The courage and determination of the Egyptian troops, who swarmed across the Canal as if they were simply taking part in another full-scale rehearsal (they had already had twenty-three) was beyond all praise. In twenty-four hours after hostilities began at 2.05 p.m. on Saturday, 6 October 1973 five divisions were on the east bank of the Canal in Sinai. For a second time Sadat had been rescued by the discipline and courage of the Egyptian armed forces.

Once Sadat had overcome his hesitations he showed to the full the overwhelming sense of relief and pride felt by all Egyptians now that the humiliations of 1967 were being wiped out. But what he was thinking of was a limited battle. He was not really interested in exploiting the initial victories of Egyptian arms or in continuing the close political and military alliance which had transformed the strategic balance in the Middle East. For the first time all Arabs were united in action. The two superpowers were impotent; Western Europe distraught; Israel under great pressure; the oil weapon really biting. But what Sadat wanted to do as quickly as possible was to get in touch with the Americans and arrange matters with them.

Part II

THE SECOND RUIN OF EGYPT

Geography is the constant factor in the making of history.

Handwritten letter from President de Gaulle to President Nasser. 26 August 1967

I

THE WORLD IS A STAGE

Before considering how Sadat was to make use of the new position which he occupied in the world it is, I think, necessary to look briefly at the problems of legitimacy confronting all leaders of Third World countries, at the historical pressures to which the Arab world as a whole is subject, and at the special circumstances of Egypt.

A majority of Third World countries are in a transition period between the traditional legitimacies, usually tribal or religious, and the constitutional legitimacy enjoyed (in theory at any rate) by the more advanced nation states of the West. Countries in this transitional period depend as a rule on a form of legitimacy based on two elements – a bureaucracy, including the army, which alone holds out the hope of some degree of continuity, and so of stability, and the personality of one man, alive or dead, that one man being usually the individual who secured his country's independence from colonial rule.

The problem however is that this one man, however respected or even idolized, cannot rest on his laurels. Nor can he transmit his authority intact to his successor. A new President or Prime Minister in the West will no doubt be expected to implement at least some of the programme he offered before his election, but his legitimacy, and so his tenure of power, comes from the institutions of the state. In the Third World the leader's legitimacy, and so his survival, depends on his achievements.

Almost every Third World leader likes to talk about 'development' as a touchstone of what he has achieved, usually without appreciating that development is not just a matter of building factories but rather an integrated process in which all aspects of the life of the country – cultural and political as well as economic – go forward together along parallel lines. There can be no true development unless the institutions exist in which it can be contained and flourish, and no effective institutions unless they reflect the realities of the society they are supposed to represent.

Because internal development presents so many problems it is easier for a Third World leader to try to confirm his legitimacy by a foray into foreign fields. Indeed, he is often forced to do this, since no ruler nowadays can remain isolated behind his natural boundaries (and many states, because of the frontiers drawn in colonial times, lack natural boundaries). The air waves are open to his rivals and enemies; television recognizes no national frontiers. No longer is national independence symbolized by a flag, an anthem, and a seat at the United Nations. Every ruler must ensure his control over the main instruments of continuity – the bureaucracy, the police and the army. But these cannot control the minds of his people. To do that he must tighten his grip on press, radio and television. A powerful transmitter becomes a more important symbol of independence than a flag; a television studio of more use to the ruler than a seat at the UN.

Generalizations have to be treated with care, and although in one sense the Arab countries can be regarded as properly belonging to that amorphous political concept, 'The Third World', in another sense they must be regarded as a special case. The Arab countries do not suffer from too little history but from too much. They are burdened by their past. It could almost be said that the Middle East epitomized history. These were the lands which produced the earliest civilization, writing and the arts, prophets and religions, which were the battleground for every conqueror from Sargon to Alexander, from Caesar to Allenby, and which are equally the ideological battleground for the superpowers of today. When it comes to ideas and knowledge the Middle East has been more a giver than a receiver. The European Renaissance, through the cultural florescence of Spain and Sicily, through the Crusades and Byzantium, had a strong Islamic infusion.

But though giving out so much in the past the Middle East has more recent memories of encirclement. In the eighteenth and nineteenth centuries the Ottoman Empire, which was supposed to be the Islamic fortress within which an Arab civilization could flourish, proved an increasingly feeble protector. When it finally collapsed the Arabs were left exposed and undecided. They were linked together by language, religion, law, culture, by trade, by intermarriage and by common interests, but a political framework for this linkage was lacking, and in spite of all that has been achieved, practically and theoretically, in the name of Arab nationalism and Arab unity, it is still lacking. The Arab world today presents a mosaic of political entities which, for all the richness of their past, by and large follow the general pattern of the Third World. There are countries like Saudi Arabia and Morocco whose rulers owe their legitimacy to their religious sanction; there are others where society is still purely tribal, and still more where legitimacy is represented solely by the army, that most enduring element in the bureaucracy.

Among the Arab countries Egypt must occupy a special place, and unless the reasons for this are appreciated both by her friends and her enemies, there are bound to be misunderstandings, or worse.

Egypt is the subject of many popular misconceptions. Everyone knows Herodotus's apothegm that Egypt is the gift of the Nile, but the Egyptian historian Dr Shafiq Ghorbal came nearer the mark when he said that Egypt was the gift of the Egyptians. Then there is the often repeated idea that Egyptian history is an unchanging record of misery; as Edward Dicey said,[1] 'The fertile Nile-watered lands [of Egypt] have been ruled over for unknown ages by one endless series of taskmasters.'

In fact, a society which does not show itself capable of change must be a fossilized society, but in the last two thousand years Egypt has changed its language three times and its religion three times, and nothing is more important in the life of any people than language and religion. That is not fossilization. The mistake made by so many who have written about Egypt from Herodotus onwards is to mix up the constants in Egyptian life and the variables. The true story of Egypt is the interplay between the necessity for continuity and the necessity for change.

The constants in Egyptian life are, first and foremost, the Nile and the deserts. The Nile creates life; the deserts prevent expansion. An Egyptian either lives in the Nile valley or he perishes. Because everything depends on the control of the river there must be a single central authority, backed by a bureaucracy descending in stages from the pharoah to the village elder. The political Egypt is always the same as the geographical Egypt. And because the waters rise at the hottest

---

[1] *England and Egypt*, Chapman & Hall, London 1981, p. 304.

time of the year from some invisible source there is always the need for religious belief to acknowledge this annual miracle.

The variables in Egyptian life have all been brought in from outside. Foreign invaders and rulers have left bits of themselves behind in the language and customs of the people of the Valley, but in the end all the invaders have either been absorbed or expelled.

Egypt, with its unitary structure and its annual miracle, created the concept of the God-King, and consciously or unconsciously each new arrival on the scene has acknowledged this. Egypt turned Alexander and Julius Caesar into pharaohs. Napoleon declared himself a Moslem, and Arabic broadcasts from Berlin talked of 'Haji Mohamed Hitler'. Farouk, though by blood a mixture of Turkish and Circassian, tried to prove his descent from the Prophet, and at the time of Suez, when Moscow threatened Britain and France with nuclear war, enthusiastic crowds in Cairo chanted 'Bulganin – Seifeddin' (sword of God). True to this tradition Sadat chose for himself the title 'the pious President'.

The ruler of Egypt, the God-king, was at the apex of the pyramid. Immediately below him were the royal family and the high priests, below them the senior bureaucrats and lesser priests, below them again the artisans and the lowest ranks of the priesthood, and finally at the base of the pyramid the great mass of cultivators. The ruler interceded between God and man, planned the distribution of the water which was God's gift to man, while his bureaucrats collected the taxes and organized the labour, voluntary or forced, who tilled the soil or filled the ranks of the army. In modern times Mohamed Ali showed himself well aware of the significance of the Egyptian pyramid of power and the essential trinity of ruler, land, and cultivator, by making himself the ultimate owner of all the land of Egypt. But by the time of the last of his descendants to rule Egypt, King Farouk, the social structure had become so distorted that one half per cent of the population owned a third of the land and drew half of the total income derived from it.

The Nile is one constant; the fact that Egypt forms a land bridge between two continents and the link between two principal waterways is another. This means that Egypt must always occupy a key strategic position. Egypt is bound either to dominate the area herself or, if not strong enough for that, to become part of some alien empire. If Egypt cannot exploit her own strategic position someone else will exploit it for their benefit. The real significance of the 1952 revolution is that for the first time in two thousand five hundred years the Egyptians themselves changed their rulers and that for the first time the new ruler was one of themselves.

The Egypt which Sadat inherited was largely the creation of Gamal Abdel Nasser. It may be true, as Lenin said, that there is no such thing as a revolutionary, only people who know how to seize and exploit a revolutionary hour. Nasser was certainly one such. As he often used to say: 'I am the expression of a movement.'

Though so recent in time, it is already hard to recapture the ferment in the Arab world in general, and Egypt in particular, at the end of the Second World War. Two old empires were in the last stages of their decline; two new empires were flexing their muscles to take over. Heady new ideas were proliferating in an area shaken out of its former mould through the clash of foreign armies, inflation and the first stages of the communications revolution. Before the war Roosevelt's New Deal had aroused much admiration and high hopes. During the war the Beveridge Plan had had an almost equal impact among intellectuals. More extreme political bodies, such as the Communists and the Moslem Brotherhood, were gaining new adherents. Arab nationalism and the dream of Arab unity, accepted as a desirable necessity in spite of its Islamic flavour by Egypt's Copts and Lebanon's Maronites, were enshrined in 1944 in the Charter of the Arab League. In these conditions Egypt's traditional politics, which amounted to little more than complicated manoeuvering between the Palace, the British and the Wafd, appeared increasingly irrelevant.

Change there had to be, and it was no use expecting change to be brought about by some political party, old or new. The class structure in Egypt was still too unformed to provide the social base without which a genuine political party can never flourish. So when change came, it inevitably came through the only element in society which combined a sense of continuity with a capacity for action – the army. Not that this was a *coup d'état* in the by now familiar pattern, where the army ousts an incompetent civilian government and takes over control itself. It was, rather, a revolution organized by a group of young men in the armed forces who, reflecting the overwhelming sense of discontent in all sections of the population, undertook to lay the foundations for a complete social transformation which they, like so many others, knew to be essential.

The important thing about Nasser, and the reason for his success, is that like Mohamed Ali he instinctively understood the geographical and historical constants which are bound to govern Egypt's destinies. He realized that Egypt's security depended on two things – the Nile, which meant that the ruler of Egypt must have an African policy; and the land bridge to Asia, which meant that he must have an eastern policy. It is worth pointing out that one of the formative influences on Nasser's espousal of the idea of Arab unity (which was the form his eastern policy was to take) was his study as a young officer of the campaigns of Allenby in the First World War. He had lectured on these campaigns in the Military Academy before the war and knew that Allenby appreciated Egypt's two lines of defence – the first from Gaza to Beersheba, and the second, should the first fail, along the Sinai passes. Nasser also realized from his reading of history that, long before Allenby, the great rulers of Egypt, from Thutmosis III to Saladin and Mohamed Ali, had regarded the true frontier of Egypt as being much further east, in Syria. (But the real impetus for his commitment to the cause of Arab unity came from practical experience, not from theory. It was when serving in Palestine in 1948 that he saw and understood the involvement of all Arabs in the fate of an Arab country.)

In *The Philosophy of the Revolution* Nasser explained his concept of Egypt's interlocking interests by the analogy of the 'Three Circles' – Islamic, Arab and African – of which she was the centre. But it was not his ideas which gave him his legitimacy; it was his achievements – land reform, nationalization of the Suez Canal and of all other major enterprises including banking and insurance, industrialization, the redistribution of wealth and the involvement of workers and farmers in all elected bodies, building the High Dam, the emancipation of women, free education at all levels, and of course his assumption of political leadership in the Arab world as a whole.[1]

---

[1] The transformation Egypt underwent between 1952 and 1970 cannot be properly measured in figures, but all the same some statistics (and these are all based on World Bank reports) are worth giving as a reminder. During this period the area under cultivation increased by 15 per cent, for the first time more than keeping pace with the rise in population. (Nasser was the first ruler of Egypt actually to increase the size of the Nile Valley.) During the same period the number of those of both sexes in schools

Nasser saw that the Arab world possessed one great asset and faced one great danger. The asset was its central geographical position in the world, to which was now added the unlooked for wealth from oil. Together these gave the Arabs great potential strength which, if properly used, would enable them to work out their own salvation. The danger was the continued threat of outside interference. This had not been removed by the disappearance of the British and French empires. Indeed, through the new Western agency imposed in the heart of the Arab world, Israel, it had become more real than ever.

It is wrong to suppose that Nasser wanted war with Israel. Though he thought that a direct confrontation was probably inevitable it was not what he wished to see. He preferred that Israel should be encircled and isolated. He used to make a comparison with the way the Egyptian fellahin treat warts – they take a hair from a horse's tail, tie it tightly round the wart so that the blood cannot reach it, and wait until it drops off. 'We must defend our frontiers against Israeli aggression,' he would say, 'but it's impossible for us to start an offensive war.' Because of his reading of history, one of Nasser's main objections to Israel was that it stood as a barrier between Egypt and the Arab lands in Asia. This is why, when he was asked at the Bandung Conference in 1953 whether he was prepared to accept the existence of Israel, he said he was, provided it was an Israel confined within the boundaries Count Bernadotte had recommended before he was murdered – in other words, provided the Negev remained in Arab hands and so remained a link between Egypt and Syria.

Nevertheless, Israel was to prove the cause of Nasser's greatest failure in foreign affairs, just as true democratic participation by the people in government was to prove his greatest failure in domestic affairs. Israel and democracy remained his stumbling-blocks.

This was the land, and these were the problems, which Sadat was to inherit. I recall an occasion in the summer of 1969, shortly before his first stroke, when Nasser, Sadat and I were talking together in the

---

and institutions of higher education increased by 300 per cent, and instead of there being only one doctor for every five thousand of the population there was, by 1970, one doctor for every two thousand, and the average life expectancy had risen from forty-three to fifty-two.

garden of the Mamourah rest house overlooking the Mediterranean. Nasser was already worrying about his health, and it may be that this prompted Sadat to say, 'You know, *mu'allim* (teacher), you have made it very hard for anyone to succeed you. What have you left him to do? You got rid of the King and the British. You built the High Dam and forged Arab unity, you have transformed the face of Egypt. Poor chap – whoever he is, I pity him.' Nasser's answer was: 'Don't suppose for a minute that when I'm gone the Americans will leave us alone. Somewhere at this moment they must be grooming a Suharto in the ranks of the army.' 'A Suharto in Egypt!' exclaimed Sadat. 'My God! If anyone could point him out to me I'd wring his neck!'

Though untried, and by many underestimated, Sadat started well. He had the great advantage of being accepted as Nasser's designated successor. To this he added, after his political triumph in May 1971, a measure of political freedom which won him much popularity. And then, in October 1973, came the crossing of the Suez Canal. It might have been thought that thereby Sadat had built an almost unassailable position for himself. But this was to prove not so.

Part of the trouble was Sadat's own character. He had never had the education – or, indeed, the time – to give serious consideration to the problems which were going to confront him. He had no real understanding of Egyptian history. After a miserable childhood he had spent his adolescence and early manhood in underground adventures, and, once learned, conspiratorial habits are hard to shake off. He enjoyed the trappings of supreme power without appreciating the responsibilities which go with it. Nor did he understand the true nature of Egypt's relations with the rest of the Arab world. He saw that Egypt was a natural leader among the Arabs, but assumed that wherever she led the others would follow. The subtleties of leadership, the inevitable give-and-take demanded of it, completely eluded him.

Evidence of these shortcomings was made immediately apparent in the aftermath of the October War. Sadat failed to recognize the magnitude of the victory that was now within his grasp. He held all the trumps. The oil weapon was his to command; public opinion among the Arabs and in much of the rest of the world was solidly behind him; the Soviet Union was still prepared to support him. But he turned his back on all this. Instead, he opted for the victory parades and the cameras, and, ignoring his Arab allies and friends, resolved that he would rebuild the area alone with his new friend, Henry Kissinger.[1]

[1] 'Why, then, didn't Sadat use the situation to press for a total Israeli retreat? Because, Kissinger answered, Sadat had fallen victim to human weakness. It was the psychology of a politician who wanted to see himself – and quickly – riding triumphantly in an open car through the city of Suez with thousands of Egyptians cheering him.' *The Secret Conversations of Henry Kissinger* by Matti Golan, Quadrangle Press, New York 1976, p. 152.

2

RESTRUCTURING THE AREA

ALTHOUGH SADAT often gave the impression of being a creature of impulse, this was not really so. In small matters he could be, but his big decisions were always the result of careful calculation, and none more so than the major upset in Egyptian foreign policy which he engineered, whereby the country ceased to be one of the foremost exponents of non-alignment and became instead a close ally of one of the superpowers, the United States.

It has been seen how, soon after he became President, Sadat began to receive hints via the Saudis that the Americans would be able to assist him towards a settlement which could secure to Egypt the return of her lost territories, but only on condition that the Russians were got rid of first. Unofficial contacts with the Americans developed (there were still no formal diplomatic relations, since these had been broken off at the time of the 1967 war), channels being opened between General Ahmed Ismail, Sadat's Director of Intelligence, and Eugene Trone, the CIA representative in Cairo, and in Washington with Kissinger and the National Security Council. These supplemented the official channel which operated through the American Interests Section of the Spanish Embassy in Cairo, headed by Donald Bergus. It took Sadat quite a long time to make up his mind to follow the advice he was receiving, but once he had done so he acted in his own way, without telling anyone or sharing the credit with anyone. It was his natural secretiveness which helped to give the impression of impetuosity.

After he had expelled the Russian advisers in the summer of 1972 he waited for his reward, but this never came. He realized that a different approach was necessary, and the messages he began to receive from Washington that some hotting up of the situation would not be unacceptable reinforced pressure from the army and mounting public dissatisfaction to draw him to the battle. But the conduct of the war, and its consequences, came as a big surprise to him and the Americans alike. Never had the Americans dreamed that the Egyptians could plan and fight as they did. They thought they had the measure of Sadat as a politician, but the capabilities of the men he led came as a revelation to them.

The first message the Americans sent to Sadat, as usual via the intelligence channel, came on 10 October, four days after the opening of the battle. It came from Kissinger, and was to the effect that he thought the situation had now reached a point which offered a good chance for a satisfactory settlement, based on a ceasefire and some sort of international conference. When Sadat received this message he was still elated by the initial successes of the Egyptian armed forces and was making belated preparations for a second phase of the attack. So he sent only an equivocal reply. Kissinger decided to try again. Edward Heath, the British Prime Minister, was contacted, with the result that on the night of 12 October the British Ambassador in Cairo, Sir Philip Adams, called on the President in Tahra Palace, bringing him a message from Heath asking Egypt to agree to a standstill ceasefire on the positions then occupied by the opposing armies. Sadat's answer was that if there was to be a ceasefire the Israelis would have to give some positive evidence that they were preparing to evacuate Egyptian territory occupied in 1967.

Receipt of this reply, and the opening of Egypt's renewed attack on 14 October, persuaded Washington to authorize the airlift of weapons to Israel. It may be that Kissinger thought Sadat was being evasive, or that it was time for him to be cut down to size. Whatever the thinking behind it, the airlift enabled the Israelis to commit their strategic reserves to the battle, and so changed the course of the war.

Kosygin came to Cairo on 16 October. The Russians had been in continual close touch with the Americans and were in favour of a ceasefire. Kosygin was able to give Sadat evidence of the scale of the Israeli counter-attack and of the recrossing of the Suez Canal by Israeli forces. Sadat was persuaded. He was ready to agree a ceasefire and negotiations along the lines of the Security Council Resolution 242. On 21 October, as a result of Kissinger's hurried journey to Moscow the day before, a new Security Council Resolution, Number 338, co-sponsored by the two superpowers, was agreed. It called for a ceasefire, full implementation of Resolution 242, and the start of negotiations for a 'just and durable peace' in the Middle East. On 25

October came the American nuclear alert. The Americans were now masters of the situation.

Sadat sent his Foreign Minister, Ismail Fahmy, to Washington at the end of October to prepare for Kissinger's projected visit – a 'largely psychological' assignment, as Kissinger was later to describe it,[1] for this was to be his first journey to the Arab world, and he had no idea what to expect. As he once told me, when he was appointed Nixon's National Security Adviser he had wanted if possible to keep out of the Middle East, and its problems, because he knew that, being a Jew, he would inevitably be accused of being biased in favour of Israel. Instead, events were to ensure that, as Secretary of State, he was to be more deeply involved in the Middle East than any of his predecessors.

Kissinger had naturally embarked on his Middle East journey armed with a great number of position papers, but the document which he particularly valued was a semi-humorous semi-philosophical essay prepared for him by a Harvard professor with the title 'The Bazaar and the Tent'. This was supposed to brief the Secretary of State on how to deal with the Arabs, with whom he would now be negotiating for the first time. The message of this paper was that among nomad Arabs there was always one person in authority – the sheikh – and that in the bazaar you must be prepared for bargaining. In other words, find out who is in charge, and then haggle.

Before Kissinger's arrival in Cairo on 6 November Sadat had discussed with me the form the negotiations should take. I suggested either a fairly large team of negotiators, including, besides himself, his Vice-President for Foreign Affairs, Dr Mahmoud Fawzi, his National Security Adviser, Hafez Ismail, and the Foreign Minister, Ismail Fahmy, or a small delegation with just one of these. In either case I thought it would be a mistake for the President to do more than preside at the opening session before turning over detailed discussions to the Minister or Ministers concerned. Kissinger would know that, as President, Sadat had full and final authority, which would put him at a disadvantage compared with his opposite number in the negotiations, Golda Meir, who would always be able to gain bargaining space by

---

[1] Henry Kissinger, *Years of Upheaval*, Michael Joseph, London 1982, p. 617.

saying she had to consult her Cabinet, or the Knesset, or her Party. Sadat rejected my arguments, saying that Kissinger always had *tête-à-tête* meetings with other political leaders like Brezhnev and Mao, and saw no reason why it should be different this time. I said that these *tête-à-tête* meetings of Kissinger's only came as the climax to thorough preliminary work by officials on both sides. But again my arguments had no effect.

So it was that, at the critical meeting in Tahra Palace on 7 November which opened at 11.00 a.m., after the photographers had done their stuff, everyone was told to withdraw, leaving Sadat and Kissinger alone. When I saw Sadat the next day he gave me some account of what had happened at the meeting. Kissinger had begun by congratulating Sadat on the performance of the Egyptian armed forces, which Sadat naturally found very gratifying. In return, he asked Kissinger why he had taken so long to come to Cairo: 'I've been asking for you for a long time. Where have you been? I've been wanting you to take over.' Then, as Kissinger began to open his briefcase and take out some papers: 'What are you doing? Do you think I'm going to argue about the ceasefire lines of 22 October or about disengagement? No, Dr Kissinger. You are a man of strategy; I am a man of strategy. I want to talk to you at the strategic level.' When he was recounting this to me, Sadat added: 'Then I began to talk to Kissinger about matters he'd never dreamed I was going to raise.' But he didn't tell me what these were.

But from what has subsequently been revealed the general lines of the discussion at this momentous meeting have become more or less clear. Sadat seems to have begun by saying that he was finished with the Soviet Union. He told an astonished Kissinger that he regarded the Soviet Union as 'the real enemy'. Next he said (and this is something he told me the following day) that Egypt had fought her last war with Israel. From these premises Sadat drew the conclusion that peace in the Middle East should in future be organized and supervised by the United States. He added that he would even be ready in due course for direct negotiations with Israel, but that would have to wait until the people in Egypt had begun to appreciate the benefits flowing from the ending of hostilities and the beginning of the peace process.[1] He also

---

1 This was later to be confirmed by Itzhak Rabin in an interview given to the *Jerusalem Post* on 16 April 1982, in which he said: 'Back in 1974 there was a tacit

talked a bit about what he called 'the failure of the socialist experience' in Egypt, and said he wanted to develop the country along different lines. He had already discussed this with David Rockefeller. He made one specific request – that the United States would in future make itself responsible for his personal safety, since he knew that there were many who would be plotting against him – Russians, Arabs and even some inside his own country.

Towards the end of the meeting, Sadat asked Kissinger what he had discussed with Golda Meir. Kissinger took out from his briefcase the paper on which Golda Meir's six points were written – points which Kissinger had told her when she was in Washington he was sure Sadat would reject. Sadat glanced at the paper, and said: 'All right; I accept.' Later that day Sadat was to tell the waiting journalists that he and Kissinger had agreed 'on my six points', and without batting an eyelid handed out copies of Golda Meir's proposals as his own.

Meanwhile, direct contacts between delegations from the Egyptian and Israeli armies at Kilo 101 on the Cairo-Suez road, which had begun on 28 October, were continuing. 'Unfortunately,' Kissinger wrote later,[1] 'neither negotiator spoke fully for his government.' This was hardly the fault of General Gamasy, who headed the Egyptian delegation, for Sadat was engaged in a complicated piece of deception to which the general had not been made party. Sadat had come to the conclusion that in the conflict between the Israeli Prime Minister, Golda Meir, and her Defence Minister, Moshe Dayan, the Americans were backing Dayan, and he thought he could exploit this split between the Israeli politicians and soldiers to his own benefit – just as he was later to try to exploit the disagreement between Begin and Weizmann. General Aharon Yariv, Israeli's representative at Kilo 101, he took to be a Dayan man, so while he was sending messages via Ismail Fahmy to the Americans (which of course he knew they would pass on to Golda Meir) that Egypt insisted on Sinai being handed back

understanding between the United States, Egypt and Israel as to a common strategic concept based on three points: 1. That the United States would lead the peace process amidst the neutralization [?] of the Soviet Union and Europe; 2. That Egypt and Israel would be regarded as twin cornerstones of a US-led peace policy; and 3. That the peace process would be a gradual one. There was Kissinger's step-by-step approach and President Carter's policy which produced the Camp David agreement.'

[1] Kissinger, *op. cit.*, p. 751.

up to the line El Arish-Ras Mohamed, to Dayan, via Gamasy and Yariv, he was sending the message that Egypt would be content with no more than the line of the passes. Naturally these conflicting signals puzzled Kissinger.

The three-hour meeting Kissinger had with Sadat on 7 November left Kissinger dumbfounded. He has sometimes been accused of seeing the Middle East entirely in terms of superpower rivalry, but in fact when he first came to it the Jewish problem was uppermost in his mind. It was Sadat, with his proposal for strategic coordination between Egypt and America, who raised the discussion from the local to the superpower level. Suddenly the very reasons which had made Kissinger reluctant to come to grips with the Middle East made it and its problems all the more attractive to him. Was it possible that he, a German Jewish refugee from the holocaust, might prove to be the agent fate had chosen by which the legacy of the holocaust would be resolved?

Kissinger's immediate reaction was, admittedly, one of scepticism. Certainly, the Americans had had plenty of contacts with Sadat over the past year, and they had seen how he had dealt with the Russians in 1972, but they were not ready for such radical and wide-ranging proposals. Kissinger did not know how far he could believe or act on what he had been told, and so was reluctant to pass on the gist of it officially to the Israelis, though he did discuss it with his friend Itzhak Rabin, the Israeli Ambassador in Washington. What Sadat was suggesting would involve profound changes. Was he strong enough to see them through? After prolonged discussion it was agreed that perhaps he was.

As Sadat had requested, the Americans now made themselves responsible for his personal security. Not only was his special bodyguard sent to the States for training, but a new unit was formed specially equipped to deal with international terrorism. A CIA employee called John Fiz, who could read and speak Arabic, was installed in the presidential office and had the task of dealing with all matters regarding security.[1] Then came the close alliance between the intelli-

[1] John Fiz is now a businessman in Switzerland, having been in partnership with Kamal Adhem. Like most senior CIA officials in the Middle East, he has found it more profitable to switch over to business in, or connected with, the Middle East.

gence services and Saudi Arabia, Iran, Morocco, and Egypt (the special intelligence connected with the office of the President), which led on to the formation of the Safari Club of which I have given a fuller account elsewhere.[1] This remarkable body, the brain child of Comte de Marenches, head of the French Securité d'Etat et Contre-Espionage (SDECE), was born in 1972 and included the French and Moroccan as well as three other intelligence services. Its aim was to counter communist activities in Africa, and more specifically to protect the heavy investments in Africa of French companies and of banks such as Chase-Manhattan. Its first successful achievement was when Egyptian and Moroccan troops came to the rescue of Mobutu's threatened régime in the Congo. The Safari Club's existence was particularly welcomed by Kissinger, who was being prevented by Congress from direct intervention in Africa but was thus enabled to intervene indirectly, and without any expense.

Kissinger was no less pleased with Sadat's new policy over arms supplies. Sadat called this 'diversification', but in fact it meant replacing Russia as the main source of Egyptian armaments by the West, and particularly by America, since it is not sound policy for any country to draw its main armaments from a variety of suppliers. The Soviet Union had in fact treated Egypt well after the October War, all the victories in which of course had been won by Soviet arms. The Central Committee of the Party gave Egypt 250 TU-62 tanks, and Egypt was able to purchase three squadrons of Mig-23s. Their reward was to be effectively excluded from the Geneva conference in December 1973 where they were supposed to be participating on equal terms with the Americans. By April 1974 Sadat was open in his reproaches against the Soviet Union as an arms supplier, maintaining that they had an obligation to 'compensate' Egypt for the arms which had been lost in the fighting, but without explaining why this should be expected of them. They were, after all, not in any way responsible for Egypt's losses.

Between the so-called Czech arms deal in 1955 and 1975 Egypt bought arms from the Soviet Union to the value of 2,200 million roubles (a rouble being approximately equal to a dollar), of which 500

[1] *The Return of the Ayatollah*, André Deutsch, London 1981, pp. 113–6.

million roubles were paid back, leaving 1,700 million roubles still owing at the end of the period.[1] Between 1975 and 1981 Egypt bought from the West arms to the value of $6,600 million. The twenty years during which the Soviet Union was Egypt's sole source of arms covered Suez, the war in Yemen, the 1967 war, the attrition war, and the October War. In the following six years, when three times as much was spent on arms as in the previous twenty, there was no fighting except for a half-hearted attack on Egypt's Arab neighbour, Libya, and the one thing which was abundantly clear was that no Egyptian arms were going to be used against Israel. The Americans would see to that. A certain posturing might be permitted, as between those two other ancient rivals who had also become militarily dependent on America, Greece and Turkey, but nothing more. By switching to America as Egypt's source for arms Sadat ensured that there would never be any alternative to negotiating with Israel. Successive American Presidents have reiterated their undertaking to ensure the protection of Israel ever since the foundation of the state. That this involves guaranteeing Israeli superiority in armaments over all the Arab states combined was spelled out explicitly in the letter sent by President Reagan to Mr Begin after the evacuation of Yamit in Sinai. Consequently, not only was Egypt now committed to indefinite negotiations with Israel, but to do so from so weak a position that she would always be obliged to settle on any terms Israel was willing to concede.

This much had already become apparent in the secret commitments Egypt made to Israel after the first disengagement agreement. In the first place an undertaking was given that almost all Egyptian armour would be withdrawn from Sinai. I recall the scene in the Cataract Hotel at Aswan in December 1973 when these discussions were taking place. It had been accepted that Egypt would keep no more than thirty tanks in Sinai, and then Sadat, as a gesture of goodwill, said these thirty could be withdrawn too. General Gamasy, the Director of Operations, could not believe his ears. 'What a heavy price we paid to get our tanks into Sinai,' he said. Thirty tanks was a ridiculously low figure, but to reduce that to none . . . ! He went over to the window, and I saw that he was in tears. Kissinger, who had come from a meeting with Sadat bringing news of this new concession, noticed Gamasy's emotion and was irritated by it. 'Is anything the

---

[1] Figures given at a closed session of Paliament in 1975.

matter, General?' he asked. 'No sir,' said Gamasy. 'Orders are orders.'

In the same way Sadat agreed to withdraw all Egyptian artillery from Sinai except for thirty-six small guns. A pledge was given that there would be no fedayin raids from Egypt into Israeli-occupied territories, and that there would never be a blockade of the Straits of Bab el-Mandeb at the southern exit from the Red Sea. All Israeli prisoners were to be unconditionally returned, and cargoes for the Israeli port of Eilat were to be allowed through the Suez Canal. The rebuilding of the devastated cities in the Suez Canal area was to be begun immediately – the Israelis set particular store by this as the new towns would be hostages against a renewal of the conflict. Finally, Egypt agreed not to initiate or take part in any propaganda hostile to Israel.

What in these weeks Sadat was in effect doing was placing Egypt fairly and squarely in a new military alliance of which America and Iran were the other principal partners. Ever since the end of World War II two rival defence systems had competed for the allegiance of Egypt and other Middle Eastern countries. The first was one sponsored by the West, of which the abortive Middle East Defence Organization of 1951, the Baghdad Pact, and the Eisenhower Doctrine were examples. The other was an Arab system, whereby the countries of the area aimed at banding together in their own defence, not committing themselves in advance to either of the superpowers. This was what, for over twenty years, had been the aspiration of most Arabs, in spite of many setbacks and disappointments. Now Egypt, the leading Arab country, had abandoned it. A main difference between the two systems is, of course, that in the Arab system Israel is necessarily excluded; in the Middle East system, Israel is, if not formally a partner, inevitably the principal beneficiary.

Thus it came about that the whole area was restructured. One inevitable consequence of Egypt's surrendering her traditional role as the main modernizing and unifying Arab country was that the Arab world split up into small political and geographical entities, busy with their own affairs and often squabbling among themselves – the Fertile Crescent, North Africa, the Arabian Peninsula and the Nile Valley. And this was being done at a moment when, as events were shortly to confirm, the world centre of gravity was shifting to the Gulf area – a fact which, it might have been supposed, ought to have bound Egypt closer to her Arab sisters rather than cut her off from them.

Naturally Sadat's reversal of alliances received an enthusiastic welcome in the Western – and particularly in the American – media. When Kissinger was in Cairo in January 1974 he arranged that President Nixon should pay a state visit to Egypt. He also persuaded Sadat to use his influence to get the oil embargo lifted – it was embarrassing, said Kissinger, for him to try to negotiate a settlement under the shadow of an embargo. This Sadat succeeded in doing, though King Feisal was cunning enough to agree only if he got a written statement that lifting the embargo was important from the point of view of the 'confrontation states', meaning mainly Egypt and Syria.

As this was the time of Watergate Nixon's visit was intended more to impress public opinion in America than to bolster Sadat's position. The cheering crowds (carefully organized) were to show how universally respected was Nixon the peacemaker. Another visitor to Cairo, returning a state visit to Tehran by Sadat, was the Shah, coming there for the first time since as Crown Prince he came to marry King Farouk's sister, Fawzia, in 1938.[1] Sadat arranged to take him to see the High Dam, and sent his wife, Jihan, on ahead to supervise the preparations. She noticed that there was a picture of Nasser on the route which the Shah and the President would have to travel, and ordered it to be removed, fearing that it might give offence to the Shah. It could be replaced after the Shah had gone, she said. But it never was.

[1] At this meeting Sadat told his royal guest that this, by his reckoning, was the third time they had met. The Shah was puzzled. 'I can only recall one previous meeting,' he said, 'which was at the Rabat Islamic Summit Conference in 1968.' 'But I had seen you once before that,' said Sadat. 'I was a member of the guard of honour which greeted you when you came to marry Princess Fawzia.'

This is another example of Sadat's inability to resist making a good story better. The platoon which provided the guard of honour when the Crown Prince landed at Suez in 1938 was drawn from the Royal Guards, of which Sadat was never a member.

3

DÉJÀ VU

ACCORDING TO STRICT CHRONOLOGY Sadat came to the presidency as successor to Nasser, but this was not exactly the pattern of things as he himself began to see it. He once said to me, 'Gamal and I are the two last great pharaohs of Egypt,' but he gave President Jimmy Carter a rather different version of the same theory; it was a mistake, he said, to look on him simply as a successor to Nasser – his real predecessor was Rameses II. His manner certainly began to be increasingly autocratic, even pharaonic, though now, as an ally of America, he was careful to talk in terms of democracy. 'You know, Mohamed,' he told me, 'Gamal and I always wanted the same things. The difference is that he tried to get them through a dictatorship; I try to get them by democratic methods.'

Sadat consciously cultivated the pharaonic image, preferring to be photographed in a stern Ramesesian profile, holding his field-marshal's baton as if it was a sceptre. But if there was one previous ruler of Egypt whom more than any other he resembled it was not any of the pharaohs but the Khedive Ismail.[1] Both men had the good fortune – or perhaps it would be truer to say the misfortune – to come to power at a moment when an economic boom was beginning. In Ismail's case this was the cotton boom which resulted from the American civil war and the interruption to cotton supplies for Europe from the South; in Sadat's case it was a boom caused by an influx of Arab oil money. Each succeeded a ruler who had understood the strategic position of Egypt and had managed to use this understanding to make Egypt a significant counter in international affairs. No doubt both Mohamed Ali and Nasser suffered severe military setbacks in the process, but there is equally no question their vision transformed Egypt and Egypt's position in the world. Both were succeeded by lavish spenders.

---

[1] Ismail, grandson of Mohamed Ali, founder of the dynasty, and grandfather of its last representative, King Farouk, ruled from 1863 to 1879.

Ismail's reckless expenditure resulted in the accumulation of debts on so vast a scale that his foreign creditors moved in, setting up a Commission of Public Debt with commissioners to oversee the country's revenue and expenditure. Ismail's sale in 1875 of his shares in the Suez Canal Company to the British government through the intermediary of Rothschilds was only the most spectacular of the desperate expedients to which he was compelled to resort in an effort to find the interest due on the consolidated debt. In 1878 an Englishman was made Minister of Finance and a Frenchman Minister of Public Works. Four years later Ismail's policies produced their logical conclusion, and with the battle of Tel el-Kebir seventy years of British occupation of Egypt began.

Though Egypt's consolidated debt had by 1876 reached the then astronomical figure of £91 million this had by no means all been wasted. True, Ismail was never able to make a distinction between private and public expenditure, but as well as building himself palaces and entertaining foreign royalty with reckless generosity, travelling abroad in regal state and marrying off his children no less splendidly, he built railways, roads, bridges and new canals. He gave Alexandria a new harbour and made Suez a new town. He created a merchant fleet, set up a telegraph system and enormously expanded education. Ismail's trouble was that for him Europe proved to be an irresistible lure. European manners he found as hard to resist as European money and adventurers. This was to be his undoing.

Sadat too was convinced that Egypt properly belonged with the forward-looking West, not with the backward East. Though frugal in his personal habits he was surrounded by people who had no time for frugality, and he was ready to indulge them. When he took over, the President's salary was still fixed at £E900 a month. In addition the President had at his disposal a special fund of £E1 million a year which was part of the intelligence budget, which in turn came under the Ministry of Defence and was not itemized in the overall budget. In Nasser's day this £E1 million was under the control of the Minister for Presidential Affairs, and more than half of it (£E650,000) went on caring for the many Arab refugees who had sought sanctuary in Egypt. The balance was devoted to matters of national importance and properly audited accounts kept for its disbursement.

When the last Minister for Presidential Affairs under Nasser resigned in May 1971 there was a balance of £E1,850,000 left in the Office of the President, as well as six thousand sovereigns which had been returned to Cairo, the balance left from a sum which had been distributed on Egypt's behalf by King Saud among the Yemeni tribes. These had been left in a suspense account, pending a decision on what should be done with them.

After the dismissal of the 'centres of power' in May 1971, the official who was put in charge of the office took everything he found there, cash and gold, to the President's house in Giza and asked for instructions as to what should be done with it. He was told to leave it all with the President's secretary, Fawzi Abdel Hafez.[1] Sadat also ordered that in future maintenance of the Arab refugees should be a charge against the main intelligence budget. Although this meant that the President now had a clear £E1 million a year at his disposal for which no accounts need be kept, so many demands were made on this account that it soon proved insufficient and had to be doubled.

Frugal though he was in some ways, Sadat greatly enjoyed the trappings of his office. When he saw Nixon's presidential plane, Air Force One, he was immediately anxious to have one like it, but the cost seemed to be prohibitive. Fortunately the Saudis came to the rescue and ordered a Boeing as fully equipped as Nixon's Air Force One at the cost of $12 million which they presented to the President as a gift.

Sadat's restlessness has already been mentioned, and this was to involve further expenditure. He retained his house in Giza, and used Tahra Palace in Cairo as an office, while the rest house at the Barrage was enlarged to become an official presidential residence. The original house at Mit Abu el-Kom was completely rebuilt and air-conditioning installed. In all these places a command post with an elaborate communications system was set up, in anticipation of the impending battle with Israel. A little later a new Mercedes 600 was bought and converted into a mobile command post at a cost of over $700,000. This happened before Sadat and I had disagreed, and I asked him why a mobile command post was necessary. 'Suppose something was to happen while I was moving from one fixed command post to another,' he said. 'I must be able to get in touch by telephone with Hafez el-Assad or Ghadaffi to coordinate.' This reminded me of an

---

[1] A former police officer, who had been attached to Sadat from soon after the revolution and who was to be severely wounded with him on 6 October 1981.

occasion when he was still Vice-President and turned up at a meeting of the Socialist Union wearing a khaki outfit. He was asked what this signified and his answer was that war might break out at any time and it was necessary to be prepared. This exchange was mentioned in the account of the meeting published in *Al Ahram,* and Nasser rang me up after he had read it. 'Is that what our readiness for war amounts to?' he asked, laughing. 'Wearing khaki?'

A presidential means of transport rather less up-to-date than a Boeing or a Mercedes, but one which Sadat found no less attractive, was the yacht *Mahrousa,* originally built for Khedive Ismail. When the formal re-opening of the Suez Canal in 1975 was being planned, Sadat toyed with the idea of travelling through the Canal on this occasion in the *Mahrousa.* I heard of this, and begged him not to do so, because I felt that everyone would make the connection with Khedive Ismail and that this could be unfortunate. I suggested that instead one ship of the Egyptian navy should be renamed the *10th Ramadan* (equivalent to 6 October, the day of the crossing) and that he should make his way down the Canal in that. He liked the idea, and when the day came a cruiser, duly renamed the *10th Ramadan,* entered the Canal with the President aboard. But the yacht *Mahrousa* followed it. Also on board was the Iranian Crown Prince. Sadat had invited the Shah to attend, but being unable to do so he sent his son instead. In a letter to the Shah, Sadat said he hoped this would prove an opportunity for the young man to receive training in the affairs of state.

It is impossible to make any exact comparison between Egypt's indebtedness in the times of its two big spenders, Ismail and Sadat; much more than the value of money has altered in the course of more than a hundred years. However, it is useful to compare Egypt's debt at the beginning and the end of Sadat's presidency.

In 1971, when Sadat became the effective as well as the nominal President of Egypt, debts to the Soviet Union (excluding military supplies) amounted to $380 million. This included payment due for construction of the High Dam, industrial projects and so on. Debts to the United States amounted to $205 million, mainly connected with wheat shipments between 1958 and 1965. Italy was owed $122 million, West Germany $106 million, and Kuwait $130 million. Debts to Japan, East European countries, private banks etc. brought non-military debts to a total of $1,300 million. On top of that Egypt had a military debt to the Soviet Union of $2,200 million, of which $500 million had been paid, leaving a balance of $1,700 million which it had been decided not to pay.

It is worth looking a little closer at the Soviet Union's aid to Egypt. During the period when relations between the two countries were closest, 1955-67, Soviet non-military aid to Egypt totalled $1,839 million. In the same period aid to India totalled $1,975 million, and in a comparable period (that is, over the twelve years before the rupture) China received $1,750 million. This meant that per capita Egypt received from the Soviet Union fifteen times as much as India and twenty times as much as China, the reason being that the Russians appreciated the political and strategic importance of Egypt, and recognized the skill with which Egypt's leaders made use of their position.

Egypt had, in fact, become in a real sense the capital of the Third World. Thus it was no accident that one year, 1964, saw an Arab summit meeting in Cairo in January, in May Khrushchev's long visit for the opening of the first phase of the High Dam, in July an African summit meeting in Cairo, in September another Arab summit, this time in Alexandria, and in October a non-aligned summit in Cairo. The Russians were suitably impressed by all this, and although Egyptian negotiators often found them infuriating people to deal with they never drove a bargain which encroached on Egyptian sovereignty. The accusation which Dulles and others made, that Egypt had mortgaged its principal crop, cotton, to foreigners, in the same way that Khedive Ismail mortgaged the Egyptian customs, was completely untrue. Moreover, what Egypt received from the Soviet Union went into investment for the long-term benefit of the country.

It is extremely difficult to get an exact picture of what happened in the next ten years. Each new Minister of Finance started off his period of office by saying what a shock it was to him when he was shown the figures. Sadat echoed their surprise. But it was not until Husni Mubarak took over the presidency that some definitive figures emerged. These showed an accumulated civil debt of $19,500 million and a military debt of $5,700 million – in other words a total indebtedness of about $26,000 million, just about ten times as great as at the beginning of Sadat's presidency.

But a great deal of confusion in the national accounts persisted.

There was never a clear picture of what Egypt received from Arab governments, from Europe, or from commercial banks, so that, for example, it was possible for the Kuwaiti Minister of Finance, Abdel Latif El-Hamad, to give the figure of $22,000 million as an estimate of the total amount Egypt had received between 1971 and 1980 from the Arabs, whereas such an authoritative figure as Abdel Munim Kaisouny, former Minister of Finance, could put the figure at $14,000 million (admittedly his estimate covered the years 1971 to 1977, but little came in after the Jerusalem journey at the end of that year).

Before 1973 the main source of Arab money for Egypt had been the £120 million (sterling) which the oil-producing countries, Saudi Arabia, Kuwait and Libya, agreed at the Khartoum summit in the summer of 1967 to pay annually to compensate for losses through the June War, including the losses caused by the closure of the Suez Canal. But the real flood of Arab money started to come in after the 1973 war. It now became customary to channel aid for Egypt through special funds; thus went into action the Kuwaiti Fund, the Saudi Fund, the Abu Dhabi Fund and so on.

The way in which discrepancies in accounting could arise was illustrated by what happened at the Rabat Arab summit in 1975. There it was agreed that Egypt and Syria should receive a further $1,000 million aid between them because of their losses in the October War, and a subcommittee was set up to distribute this amount between them. The normal procedure would have been for distribution to have been made on the basis of population, but Mahmoud Riad, then Secretary-General of the Arab League, warned that it would be advisable for the Egyptian Foreign Minister to attend this subcommittee's meetings because the Syrians would almost certainly try to get the grant divided on a fifty-fifty basis. Sadat would not hear of this: 'I'm not begging,' he said. The result was as Mahmoud Riad had predicted; with no Egyptian present the Syrians got their way, a half share. Sadat put in a demand that Egypt's $500 million should not be paid into the Egyptian Central Bank but into a separate fund under his control, on the grounds that it should be held for emergency needs and not be treated as part of the ordinary revenue. Some of the contributing governments did as he wished, but the Kuwaitis refused and paid their contribution into the Central Bank. The resulting confusion in the accounts is not difficult to imagine.

Again, some Arab aid simply never went through the central

accounts at all – for example, the money Saudi Arabia donated 'for fighting communism'. Kamal Adhem[1] has described how some African heads of state, Idi Amin for example, used to turn up in Riyadh saying their treasury was bare; they needed cash 'to fight communism', and would then take away a donation in a bag. It may well be that Egypt was at times a beneficiary from this sort of generosity, though Kamal Adhem maintains that Egyptian officials were never paid in cash, only in kind. Certainly there were contributions of one sort or another to Egypt's defence which, because of their sensitive nature, never appeared in the ordinary accounts. Accounting confusion was highlighted by the contrast between the last budget in Sadat's presidency, that for 1981, which showed a surplus of £E1,000 million (£E1 being then approximately equal to $1) and the first policy statement in Husni Mubarak's presidency, less than a year later, which prepared for a budget deficit of £E2,000 million.

Then, of course, there was American aid, and this requires special attention. Most recent American aid has been channelled through what is known as PL480 (Public Law 480), which was enacted in 1954 to enable the United States government to dispose of some of its food surpluses, particularly wheat. Rather than flood the market with these surpluses, which would have depressed prices for the American farmer, it was decided to make them available to foreign countries for sale against local currencies. The aims of the law were said to be the widening of international trade, payment for American overseas commitments, the encouragement of economic development, purchase of strategic materials and support for US policies. As far as the latter aim was concerned, the surpluses obviously represented a formidable weapon in the American diplomatic armoury, particularly useful when dealing with countries such as India and Egypt which badly needed the wheat, Egypt having become once again eligible as a recipient after 1974.

The funds generated in Egypt by PL480 are divided into three categories: the first going to the export–import bank for the financing of local projects, such as rural electrification; the second being used for local American needs, such as the purchase of new buildings for

---

[1] Director of Saudi Intelligence and Special Counsellor to King Feisal.

American personnel, Embassy expenses etc. (which amounted to 20 per cent of the total); the third for encouraging projects in the private sector of the Egyptian economy. The American government retains a firm control over the use to which these funds are put, with the right to follow up and advise on all activities flowing from them and to terminate any activities which may seem undesirable. The Americans also insist on their right to receive full publicity locally for all activities resulting from PL480 – indeed, they have in Egypt been accustomed to receive publicity two or more times over, the media being filled with appropriate pictures and articles both when an overall agreement is signed and whenever a particular project within the scope of the overall agreement is initiated.

There were other general conditions attaching to American aid of every description – that all goods should be carried in American ships, for example, and that American firms involved should, where necessary, be released from the Arab boycott imposed on those of them who traded with Israel. (The Egyptian government was accordingly instrumental in getting Ford, General Electric, and Xerox so released.) The Egyptian government was also made to sign a 'no bribery' clause – no Egyptian was to make any personal profit out of AID money, a condition easier to legislate for than to enforce.

The actual distribution of funds in Egypt has been made through the agency of AID, which has now become a considerable element in the life of the country. What is odd is that, though Egypt and Israel have been made by Congress recipients of roughly similar amounts, the number of officials working for AID in Egypt has been 1,030, whereas in Israel there have been only four AID officials. It is not surprising that Herman Eilts, the former American Ambassador in Cairo, should have expostulated that his fellow-countrymen were running the risk of the same sort of over-exposure in Egypt which had proved fatal to them in Iran.

One aspect of AID's activities can only be regarded as having had a definitely harmful effect on Egyptian national life. This concerns what is called 'research'. In 1981 $45 million were allocated under this heading, and a great many projects initiated which seemed to serve no conceivable purpose except the spending of money. But they have drained away from Egyptian universities, already weakened by the loss of many of their best staff to universities in other Arab countries, academics who ought to be teaching instead of wasting their time on highly paid absurdities.[1] Looking at all this American money it may be thought that Sadat's dream of a Marshall Plan for Egypt had not been in vain. Between 1974 and 1980 Egypt received from foreign aid more than the four principal beneficiaries of the original Marshall Plan – Britain, France, West Germany and Italy – had together received in the four years of the Plan's operation (1948–52).

Other principal sources of Egyptian indebtedness were the International Monetary Fund, of which Egypt had long been a member, and the World Bank. The IMF was keen to see Egypt, like other recipients of its aid, adopt more orthodox financial and economic measures, including devaluation of the Egyptian pound. The World Bank, whose main contribution before the October War had been a $60 million loan for widening the Suez Canal, now came forward on a much more lavish scale – $227 million in 1974–5, $222 million in 1975–6, $267 million in 1976–7 – so that suddenly it was discovered that here was another creditor to whom Egypt owed $1,000 million.

The outcome of all this borrowing became apparent when, at the beginning of 1982, President Mubarak set up a commission to investigate the position, and it was found that it was costing the Egyptian Treasury $2,000 million a year simply to service its debts, this being equal to the revenue coming in from Suez Canal dues and oil, two of the country's main sources of income.

Private American institutions, as well as governmental and international agencies, became increasingly involved in the finances and economy of Egypt. Easily the most important of these has been the Chase-Manhattan Bank and its president David Rockefeller. Rockefeller's application to open a branch of his bank in Egypt had been advised against by Kaisouny in 1973, while he was still Minister of Finance, as all banks and banking had long been nationalized, but Sadat overruled him and allowed it to appear a year later in a slightly disguised form. A new partnership between Chase-Manhattan and the National (Ahli) Bank, to be called Chase-Ahli, was inaugurated, the Ahli Bank providing $510,000 of the $1 million capital and Chase-

[1] There was, of course, an intelligence element in this exercise, the information provided by 'research' being often quite valuable to the American government. Some of those thus engaged were worried by this aspect, and held a meeting at which they tried to lay down ethical guidelines for their work.

Manhattan the rest. In theory therefore Egypt's National Bank retained control, but as Chase-Manhattan met the cost of adminstration, the Americans got a bigger share. In fact, in the first year of Chase-Ahli's trading Chase-Manhattan showed a profit of $4 million, which was quite a handsome reward for a capital investment of less than half a million dollars.

Chase-Ahli's success was largely due to the exemption it enjoyed from restrictions imposed by law on other banks. Nationalized banks not only had to pay all local taxes but had to observe the regulations governing worker participation. Chase-Manhattan was enabled to get round all these. It was allowed to offer local staff whatever salaries it liked, with the result that an Egyptian being paid the legal maximum in a nationalized bank of, say, £E5,000 would find himself offered eight or more times that at Chase-Ahli. And because it could offer much better facilities than the nationalized banks for banking transactions abroad, Chase-Ahli was soon looking after the accounts of a great many wealthy Egyptians. It even managed all the foreign currency funds of the Arab League. Where Chase-Manhattan led, others were quick to follow, so that by 1981 banking in Egypt was so far from being any longer nationalized that no fewer that fifty-six foreign banks were now operating there.

4

FOR RICHER, FOR POORER

IN 1974 John Marlowe published a book in England called *Spoiling the Egyptians,* the subject of which he described as:

> The story of the technical, financial and economic colonization of Egypt by Western Europe. . . .This had come about because of the pressures which an expansionist, technically and militarily superior, industrialized Western Europe, with surplus capital to invest and surplus manufactures to sell, had been able to exert on a defenceless, easily accessible, technically backward, agriculturally rich country with a docile population despotically ruled by men who were not themselves Egyptian and who had been corrupted and seduced by the allurements of the West.

The analogy between Ismail's Egypt and Sadat's has already been made. It is not of course exact in every particular. In the 1970s it was America rather than Western Europe who was 'expansionist, technically and militarily superior'; it was Arab as much as Western countries which had surplus capital to invest; and Egypt herself, though still easily accessible, was no longer defenceless or technically backward. Nor was she ruled by non-Egyptians; nor was her population docile.

Yet similarities are there too, and, indeed, the conditions affecting Egypt were to be found to a greater or lesser extent in most Third World countries. These, being on the whole exporters of raw materials and importers of manufactured goods, were usually at the wrong end of any trading bargain. Thus it was estimated in 1975 that the consumer in the West was paying eight times as much for raw materials the Third World produced. Somebody in the middle was making a very considerable profit. In the case of the raw material for which the Arab world relied for its prosperity, oil, the margin was not so great – in the same year, 1975, the Arabs received for their oil a total of $125,000 million for which the Western consumer paid $1,000,000 million – a mark-up of four hundred per cent. Third World countries have from time to time tried to bring about changes in the conditions governing international trade, but without success.

Nor was the Third World's failure to keep control over its own affairs always the fault of the West. Mention has been made of the creation of special funds through which Saudi Arabia and some Gulf states were to channel their aid to Egypt. In 1975 it was arranged at a meeting in Paris that these were to be consolidated in one general Gulf Fund. Sadat saw Sheikh Jaber el-Ahmed el-Sabah, Prime Minister of Kuwait,[1] and told him that he was 'thinking of asking David to manage the Gulf Fund'. 'Who is David?' asked Sheikh Jaber. 'David Rockefeller,' explained Sadat. 'But we have our own Davids qualified to do this,' said Sheikh Jaber, 'only they have names like Ali and Ahmed.' But it was David Rockefeller and the Chase-Manhattan Bank which won the day, the bank being appointed not only to manage the consolidated Gulf Fund but also to look after the interests of Egypt – in other words, to be in the happy position of representing both parties.

The first impact of Arab oil money on Egypt was relatively controlled. It went on specific projects such as rebuilding the devastated Canal cities, with appropriate names like 'Sheikh Zaid City'. (When King Feisal was being shown round the Canal area by Sadat, and was told that a new township was arising which was to bear his name, he begged to be allowed to decline the honour: 'Please, Mr President,' he said, 'do not do that. Today we are friends, but tomorrow, who knows, we may be no longer. In which case naming a town after me would only be an embarrassment for you.')

But soon the flood of new money, both Arab and Western, began to permeate the whole structure of Egyptian society. Before the revolution of 1952 most of the commercial and industrial life of the country (including of course the Suez Canal) had been in foreign hands or under foreign control. The revolution had changed all that, expropriating most foreign businesses and greatly enlarging the public sector. Now new groups were emerging – it would not be accurate to refer to them as classes – which benefitted from the new conditions. These groups included the families of people in responsible positions, those who had been working outside Egypt in the oil-producing countries and had accumulated wealth there, and those who were able

---

[1] Since 1977 Ruler of Kuwait.

to acquire influence in the banks and other foreign enterprises that were springing up almost daily.

New legislation eased the way for these new groups. In 1974 it became legal for individual Egyptians to act as agents for foreign companies. In June of the same year Law 43 was passed through Parliament which was designed to encourage foreign investment by giving any new enterprise, even if wholly foreign owned, ten years' exemption from taxation. Port Said was declared a free port, the idea being that foreign manufactures would be assembled and re-exported there, but in fact 80 per cent of the goods entering the port found their way into the domestic market.

In fact, anyone who had foreign currency could import anything he liked and sell it to a population hungry for consumer goods – and made more hungry by their constant advertisement on television. A new market for currency developed, one shop in the Zamalek district of Cairo alone offering facilities for the immediate transfer abroad of as much as £E1 million though the rate of exchange for the Egyptian pound grew increasingly poor.[1]

Almost all this flood of new money went on building, contracting, tourism and consumer goods, particularly luxury goods. The official name of the policy was '*infitah*' (opening) and Egypt was as wide open to foreign financiers and businessmen as it had been in the days of Ismail. It was worth trying to sell anything – no licences would be needed, no questions asked. One observer noted that in a single Cairo supermarket no fewer that fifty-eight different brands of foreign shampoos were on sale. Indeed, Egypt was not being transformed from a planned to a market economy but to a supermarket economy.[2]

The disrupting effect which this transformation had on Egyptian society can hardly be exaggerated. The old feudal class which the revolution had got rid of was small and exploiting, but at least its

[1] By the spring of 1982 the dollar was officially worth £E0.48, but any hotel or shop was prepared to give £E1.15 for it.

[2] Official figures show that the *infitah* policies were responsible for the creation of 512 enterprises, employing a total of 28,000 people. These enterprises exported products worth £E2.4 million a year and imported goods to th value of £E550 million, of which half were needed for the purpose of production and the other half were consumer goods for sale to the public.

wealth and ambitions were based on land ownership. Its stake in the soil of Egypt meant that it was never wholly alienated, never devoid of the fundamental patriotism which comes from putting down roots. But the new rich had no roots.

In 1975, in the early days of *infitah,* the Secretary-General of the Socialist Union talked of the 'fat cats' (the Prime Minister at that time, Mamduh Salem, called them 'fat cows'), referring to the estimated five hundred millionaires in Egypt. By 1981 Parliament was told that their number had risen to seventeen thousand – and that in a country where five million families have to live on the equivalent of less than $30 a month.

The public sector was being dismantled, and private enterprise taking over from it. A visible example of this transition was to be seen at the nationally owned aluminium works set up by the High Dam. This was now surrounded by a number of small private companies taking over from it the manufacture and distribution of aluminium products, which they sold at any profit they cared to make, whereas by law the nationalized enterprise was obliged to keep its costs and profit margin low. One of Egypt's oldest industries, the Mahallah textile factory, had products worth £E1,700 unsold in store while foreign textiles of every description were flooding into the country without any restrictions. Other enterprises in the public sector had unsold goods in store of at least equivalent value.

The private sector, by contrast, had never had it so good. The new companies everywhere springing up tended all to follow the same pattern. They would be a family concern, owned perhaps by father and son, or by two or more brothers, and associated with someone from the old Egyptian ruling class, one of the many adventurers from other Arab countries who were flocking into Egypt, lured by the expectation of quick profits, and an Egyptian member of the new 'parasite class', as it had come to be called. The same associates were to be found in foreign-owned companies.

There was of course growing inflation. By 1979 the rate was officially admitted to be between 30 and 35 per cent but was almost certainly a good deal more. Most of the new building was for luxury apartments, office blocks and hotels, many of which were sold before work on them had begun. One of the more ostentatiously extravagant schemes, the Pyramids Oasis Project, which was to create, in the words of its Canadian sponsor, a 'new jet-set watering hole' with a golf course designed in the shape of the ancient Egyptian symbol of life, the *ankh,* had to be abandoned, in spite of the President's early enthusiasm for it, because of the public outcry aroused by what would have amounted to the desecration of an area which all Egyptians regard as an almost sacred heritage.

Not more than 4 per cent of those young men and women leaving schools and universities would find opportunities open to them in this new world inspired by what David Rockefeller called the alliance of Arab money, Egyptian manpower and American technology. What was there left for the rest of them to do? To buy the smallest flat in Cairo would now cost them at least £E30,000; to rent one they would have to pay a deposit of at least £E5,000. They were accordingly faced with the prospect of more or less permanent unemployment and homelessness or emigration. Egypt began to be drained not only of its intellectuals and skilled workers – carpenters, electricians, plumbers and so on – but even of its cultivators, in spite of the fact that no peasantry anywhere in the world is more attached to the soil than the Egyptian *fellahin.* No fewer than a million *fellahin* migrated to Iraq; 250,000 to Jordan, and hundreds of thousands more to other Arab countries. As soon as they could acquire enough money they would return to Egypt and purchase some stake there – a small piece of land, a taxi, a lorry. It is safe to say that wherever in the Egyptian countryside today the visitor sees a newly built house, or a new tractor, these will belong to some *fellah* who has made enough money outside Egypt to come back. Egyptian society had become polarized between the 'fat cats' and their hangers-on, perhaps 150,000 people at most, on one side, and the rest of the population on the other.

Sadat seemed unperturbed by the consequences of the *infitah* policy. On the contrary, he declared publicly and with apparent pride that the increasing value of real estate in Egypt showed that 'Egypt's price in the world was rising'. David Rockefeller put it another way: 'I think,' he said, 'that Egypt now realizes that socialism and Arab nationalism failed to raise the standard of living of its forty million inhabitants. Sadat has appreciated that if he is to help them he must turn to private enterprise. I have discussed this with Israeli leaders, and they agree that Sadat's attitude towards his country is a constructive one. They can see that there is a better chance of ending the state of war if Sadat is helped to reconstruct his country in a proper manner.'

When in October 1975 I met David Rockefeller in his office at the

Chase-Manhattan Bank headquarters in New York he explained to me the difficulties Egypt faced in attracting foreign capital. Egypt, he said, was part of a high-risk area, which meant that the foreign investor would expect a return of more than 30 per cent on his outlay, which was more than Egypt could afford. So it would be better for Egypt to rely on Arab money. But in fact conditions in Egypt were made sufficiently attractive for all investors. Once again, the Egyptian scene was as it had been described by a Minister of Finance, Abdel Galil el-Emary, in the days before the revolution: 'a cow grazing the pastures of Egypt, with its udders being sucked dry from outside'.

5

LEGITIMACY CRACKS

SO ONCE AGAIN, as in the time of Ismail, Egypt was drowned in debt, and once again her creditors moved in to assert their control.

On 16 October 1976 Paul M. Dickie, the representative of the IMF in Cairo, sent a confidential memorandum to Dr Zeki Shafei, the Minister of Economics, which he called 'Some thoughts about economic reform'. In this he outlined the need, as he saw it, for radical measures, including a devaluation of the Egyptian pound and drastic reductions in the subsidies which for years the government had been paying out on staple foodstuffs such as rice, lentils and sugar, on fuel and clothing – in short on all the basic essentials of life for ordinary men and women. These economic recommendations carried with them political overtones. An Egypt whose economy was controlled from outside, in effect from Washington, would be isolated from the rest of the Arab world, and oil money would be used simply to keep Egypt afloat rather than allowing her to exercise her natural role as leader of the Arab world.

But Mr Dickie's proposals filled Dr Shafei and his Cabinet colleagues with alarm. They pointed out that Egypt had become an importing rather than exporting nation, and that to devalue would only mean increasing the bill for imports. They could only shudder when they thought of the implications of a cut in the subsidies. Dr Kaisouny, an orthodox economist with long experience of negotiations with the West, was at this time Deputy Prime Minister responsible for economic and financial affairs and head of the special group of Ministers concerned with the economy. He did his best to challenge the measures proposed by the IMF, but it quickly became apparent that they were commands rather than recommendations. When news of what was in the wind leaked out there was an outcry in the Assembly, but it was unavailing. Yielding to almost irresistible pressure, the Cabinet agreed that the price of subsidized commodities should be – to use the preferred euphemism – 'rationalized'.

The announcement that there were to be price rises in about

twenty-five essential commodities was made on 17 January. The Prime Minister at that time was Mamduh Salem, a former policeman who had been Governor of Alexandria and Minister of the Interior. He took the precaution of moving into the capital additional forces both of the ordinary police and the highly equipped and specially recruited Central Security Forces. Early on the morning of 18 January the eruption came, first in Alexandria and then in Cairo. Tens of thousands of men and women poured into the streets, people for whom life had long been almost unbearably hard but who knew that now they were going to find it impossible.

From Alexandria and Cairo the rioting spread spontaneously to all the other major cities. Sadat himself was at this moment in Aswan, his favourite winter resort, preparing to welcome there President Tito, and strangely enough it was not until 4 o'clock in the afternoon that he heard of what was happening. He was then in the rest house near the old Aswan dam, where he was staying, and was giving an interview to a Lebanese lady journalist. Suddenly he stopped speaking, and she saw that he was staring at something in the direction of Aswan Town. She turned round and saw a column of smoke rising from the town. 'What's that?' said Sadat. 'Perhaps the rioting in Cairo has spread here,' she said. 'What rioting?' asked the astonished President.

He was not to be left much longer in ignorance. His personal guards had been busily occupied all day in preparations for Tito's visit, moving between the airport and the hotels where the visitors were to be accommodated to check on all the arrangements. Now, because of their uniforms, they found themselves set upon by the rioters; some of their cars were seized and set on fire. Then the Governor of Aswan burst into the rest house: 'Mr President, you must leave immediately!' He warned Sadat that the mob was making for the rest house and that in half an hour the road to the airport would be impassable. The President was obliged to make a hurried departure, leaving all his possessions and papers behind. It was a humiliating exit which he never forgot.

Mamduh Salem wanted the army brought in. He did not think that when the rioting was resumed the next day, as it was bound to be, the police would be able to control the situation. He contacted General Abdel Ghani el-Gamasy, Minister of War and Commander-in-Chief, who reminded him of the pledge that had been given after the October War – that the army would never be used against the civilian population. 'I cannot let you have any of my men,' he said. The Prime Minister reported this to the President as soon as he arrived back from Aswan. Gamasy saw him too, and told him that, while without doubt the army would be able to control the situation, and would do so if ordered by the President, he must make it a prior condition that the cuts in the subsidies should be withdrawn. Unless this was done, he said, he could not guarantee the behaviour of the troops if they were asked to enforce martial law and the curfew which had now been imposed. Meanwhile the presidential plane was standing by at Abu Soweir airport ready to take Sadat and his family to Tehran, and a helicopter was waiting outside his house in Giza to lift them to the airport. The mob surged past his house, chanting abuse, and, which made it even harder for him to bear, praising Nasser and flourishing his photograph.

The next day, 19 January, there was more violence everywhere, and a good deal of looting and destruction of property some of it no doubt the work of criminal elements, always ready to exploit such a situation, but mostly still the expression of a people's misery and exasperation. Then the army moved in and it was repeatedly announced on the radio that the President had 'ordered the recommendations of the economic committee to be cancelled'. When it was all over, at least 160 people had been killed.

If the régime in a Third World country finds that ordinary political measures fail, and that even the new methods of persuasion it exercises through the radio and television have no effect, with the result that it is forced back to such desperate expedients as martial law, curfews and calling in the army, then it must be recognized that its legitimacy is broken. Sadat realized the extent, if not the nature, of the crisis. He began to seek advice from almost everybody – including me, though by this time I was out of favour. I thought the prescription that should be followed must depend on diagnosis of the disease. If he believed, as some people were arguing, that it was all a conspiracy got up by Communists and Nasserites, then he should treat it as a conspiracy. But if, as others argued, the explosion was the consequences of deeper social and economic causes – and this would seem to be the case since he had withdrawn the proposed economic measures – then political solutions were required and I would be willing to help in finding them.

Sadat spent a couple of days in consultation with the National Security Council, wavering between these two points of view. He was bitterly hurt by what he saw as his rejection by the people. He felt that his part in the October War was forgotten, the image of the national leader, the father of his people, which he had tried to project to the world, had been destroyed in a matter of hours. To make matters worse, at that very moment a new and unknown figure was entering the White House. For the second time, it seemed to him, the American electorate had let him down. First they had forced the resignation of Nixon, a man with whom he had established excellent relations – and what an unforgivable way that was to treat a President! – and then, just when, thanks to Kissinger, he had got on good terms with Ford, they had got rid of him too. What he heard of the new President inspired him with no confidence. And not only was Sadat rebuffed by the Americans, but ever since the second disengagement agreement in 1975 his relations with most other Arab countries had been distinctly cool. Now he had been made to look foolish in front of all his smart new friends – the Pahlavis, the Rockefellers, the Onassises. He felt himself spurned and isolated, and almost in despair.

Once again Sadat's reaction was to be a flight, if not a flight into fantasy, at any rate a flight into the unknown. There is a direct link between the food riots in January 1977 and the Jerusalem journey in November.

But first was to come a more usual expedient – a plebiscite. Having come down on the side of those who maintained that the food riots were simply the result of a conspiracy engineered by Communists and other evil-minded people, Sadat presented the electorate with eleven propositions on which they were asked to express an opinion. Did they think twenty-five years' hard labour was suitable punishment for people who planned or took part in demonstrations aimed at overthrowing the constitutional bodies in the state? Did they think twenty-five years' hard labour was suitable for those who took part in strikes aimed at damaging the national economy, or who staged sit-ins in factories? And so on. The verdict of the plebiscite was predictably unanimous.

Sadat could not pretend to himself that the plebiscite was any real reflection of the mood of the country. Something more was needed.

But what? It was his first meeting with President Carter that was to provide the next link in the chain. In spite of Sadat's misgivings his meetings with Carter in the first week of April went well. The new President reminded him of the strategic agreement that Sadat himself had proposed to Kissinger, and that it included a step-by-step policy leading eventually to direct negotiations with the Israelis. Was he ready for another major step? Sadat said he was.

What Sadat was contemplating was negotiation with Shimon Peres. Like almost everybody else, he assumed that at the impending general election Peres would be returned as the new Prime Minister of Israel, and there had already been indirect contacts with Peres through various intermediaries, including Kissinger, King Hassan, Nicolae Ceausescu, the Romanian President, and Bruno Kreisky, the Austrian Chancellor. Sadat thought a secret meeting between Peres and himself would be a distinct possibility.

On 4 May in Rabat Sadat saw King Hassan, who had himself met Peres only a week before. On 11 May Ceausescu was in Cairo, and discussions were carried a stage further. But everyone was still waiting for Peres. Then came the thunderbolt. Begin, not Peres, emerged as Israel's new Prime Minister. All the planning and plotting had to be scrapped, because Sadat regarded Begin and the Likud Party as the last people with whom he would be able to arrange any accommodation.

On 15 July it was the turn of the triumphant Begin to visit Washington. Carter told him of his talks with Sadat (Begin of course being aware of the strategic agreement with Kissinger) and passed on to him the fears Sadat had been expressing about Begin's intransigence. Begin retorted that, on the contrary, he would be just as prepared to come to some arrangement as Peres was – that, in fact, he might be able to do some things that Peres could not do.

At the same time Sadat was getting signals from Tel Aviv that the new government was not prepared to continue dealing with Egypt clandestinely through third parties, as had been recent practice, with the Moroccans, Iranians or Americans usually performing the role of intermediary. It was hinted that the Israelis had news of a plot against Sadat but that they would only give details about it directly to an Egyptian official. So the Director of Military Intelligence was sent to Morocco, where he met the Director of Israeli Intelligence (Mossad) who produced an implausible story about a conspiracy to assassinate Sadat being hatched by Ghadaffi. But Sadat took it seriously enough to order what amounted to a brief war against Libya. For nearly a week Egyptian planes bombarded targets just over the frontier, the excuse urged being that the Russians had been providing the Libyans with such quantities of arms that an invasion of Egypt must be imminent.[1] In fact, as Sadat admitted in an interview later in the year, the purpose of this mini-war was purely punitive, to teach Ghadaffi a lesson. But the real sufferers were the quarter of a million Egyptians working in Libya, whose livelihood was put at risk. One of Egypt's leading surgeons, who was then working in the Central Hospital in Benghazi, found himself having to operate on Libyan civilians wounded by Egyptian bombs. Later he told me that he was weeping so much over this unnecessary tragedy that he was almost unable to see what he was doing.

On 1 August the US Secretary of State, Cyrus Vance, came to Cairo to give Sadat a report on the Carter–Begin talks. He brought with him a hand-written letter from Carter in which he expressed his conviction that if it came to direct negotiations the Egyptians would find Prime Minister Begin prepared to be generous and genuine in his desire for peace. Sadat should not believe all he had been told about Begin's hawkishness. Carter said he felt the moment was ripe for a settlement and that he was prepared to play a part in achieving one.

Meanwhile, back in Israel Begin and his Foreign Minister, Moshe Dayan, had reported to the special committee of the Cabinet and it had been decided that they would conduct their own search for possible intermediaries. On 14 August Dayan made a secret journey to New Dehli (India never having had diplomatic relations with Israel) during the course of which he saw the Prime Minister, Morarji Desai, at his home. But, to Dayan's annoyance, Desai expressed the opinion that the Palestinians represented the crux of the problem and showed no wish to become involved.

Eight days later Dayan was in London, and took the opportunity of King Hussein's presence there to ask for a secret meeting with him. He did not tell the King all that was in the wind, simply asking him if he would be willing to transmit a message to Sadat. But Hussein also was

---

[1] When, in the summer of 1982, President Mubarak protested to Israel about its actions in Lebanon, Begin wrote him a letter in which he reminded him that his predecessor had exercised his right of self-defence by bombing targets in neighbouring Libya after the Israelis had informed him of a Libyan-based plot against him.

reluctant to become involved, though he did report Dayan's approach back to Sadat.

Dayan was more successful with King Hassan. Thanks to the Moroccan intelligence's close connection with other intelligence services through the Safari Club, King Hassan had from time to time met Israelis, but never one quite so highly placed as Dayan. In the first week of September Dayan was in Morocco and met the King, as a result of which meetings between the Israeli Foreign Minister and Hassan Tuhami, a Deputy Prime Minister, were set up in Rabat and Fez, directly sponsored by the King. Unfortunately neither of the parties really understood what the other was talking about, though Dayan played his cards skilfully. The message brought back to Sadat was that he could have no idea of the concessions the Israelis were prepared to make if it came to direct negotiations.

Sadat was still uncertain about the best way to proceed. Leaks had begun to appear in various foreign newspapers about a secret meeting between Dayan and 'a prominent Arab' widely reported to be an Egyptian. He was afraid that if more news of what had been going on leaked out everything might be undone.

It was his visit to Romania that was to prove decisive. He arrived in Bucharest on 29 October and the Romanian President, who had his own close contacts with the new Israeli government, was able to give him assurances on the two questions of fundamental importance which he put to him – did Begin really want peace, and, if he did, would he be able to deliver his side of the bargain? Ceausescu had no doubts on either score. He said that, being known as a hard-liner, Begin might be able, like de Gaulle over Algeria, to impose a settlement which would be rejected if coming from a more moderate politician. Ceausescu suggested that Sadat might like to meet Begin at some secret location near Bucharest, but this was not at all the sort of thing Sadat wanted. He did not think the secret would be kept for long, and when the news came out it could prove disastrous.

It was, as he later revealed, in the plane on his way back to Cairo from Bucharest that Sadat resolved to go in person to Jerusalem – and before, so he said, the plane had reached the Bulgarian frontier, which means a flight of not more than twenty minutes. He had originally been toying with the idea of an international conference in Geneva, at which the five governments with vetoes in the Security Council – the United States, the Soviet Union, China, Britain and France – would be represented, as well as the directly interested parties. But this would pose problems. It would mean bringing back the Russians into the picture, not to mention the Syrians and the Jordanians. Now he saw all the apparent advantages of a Jerusalem journey by himself. It would end all the clandestine meetings with their risks of exposures and misunderstandings. It would take matters out of the hands of go-betweens and leave him the sole arbiter and the undivided focus of attention. Dayan had told Tuhami when they met in Morocco that he thought the real obstacle to a settlement was a psychological one. Very well then, it would be resolved by a psychological bombshell. With one immensely dramatic stroke he would transfer the negotiations from maximum security to maximum publicity. It would be a *coup de théâtre* after Sadat's own heart.

The only person outside Egypt who knew anything in advance of his intentions was the Shah of Iran. Sadat was in Tehran on 31 October and told the Shah, who was enthusiastic about the idea. But when on his way back to Cairo Sadat stopped off in Saudi Arabia he was less explicit. He simply told Prince Fahd that the Americans were pressing him to get into some form of direct negotiations with the Israelis and that he was considering ways and means of doing so. To this vague statement Prince Fahd produced a vague rejoinder, wishing him well in his endeavours.

Then came the President's address at the opening of Parliament on 9 November. When he told the deputies that he was 'ready to go to the ends of the earth, and to the Knesset itself', to talk about peace to the Israelis, most people at home and abroad thought this was a rhetorical exaggeration. The Prime Minister's own office instructed the newspapers not to concentrate on that sentence in the President's speech, and Ismail Fahmy, the Foreign Minister, went even further, advising that the sentence should be omitted altogether. The result was that when Sadat saw the first edition of the Cairo papers he was extremely angry, and gave orders that the front pages should be remade, giving the 'ends of the earth' offer fullest prominence.

One of those who heard the speech, and who undoubtedly did take the Knesset offer seriously, was Yasser Arafat. Sadat had made certain that the leader of the PLO should be present in person when the offer was made. Yasser Arafat was in Tripoli, trying to patch up relations between Ghadaffi and the Egyptians after the frontier bombardment. Sadat sent the presidential plane to Tripoli to fetch Arafat, telling him that he was going to make an announcement which he particularly wanted Arafat to hear. Arafat was predictably furious, both at the Knesset offer and at the trick that had been played on him. 'Sadat put a turban on my head,' he said, using the Arabic expression for being made a fool of. He walked out of the Parliament and has never been in Egypt since.

Once it was realized that Sadat meant what he said about going to Jerusalem, he found himself the most sought after political figure in the world, and further negotiations began to be conducted through the medium of television, mainly American, in which he was the star. President Carter, who had been pressing for direct negotiations, was of course delighted by the course events were taking. He had been thinking in terms of getting Sadat and Begin to New York to address the UN Assembly, and while they were there inviting them to meet each other at the White House. But this was even better. He had high hopes that other Arab governments could be persuaded to join in, particularly the Saudis. But in this he – and Sadat too in so far as he shared these hopes – made a serious misjudgement.

The day of the actual journey which for the first time brought an Arab leader to Israeli-occupied Jerusalem happened to be the day of the *Eid el-Adha* (the Feast of Sacrifice) when the ruler of Saudi Arabia goes to the mosque in Mecca and unlocks the door of the *Ka'aba*. King Khaled was later to say:

> I have always before gone to the *Ka'aba* to pray for somebody, never to pray against anyone. But on this occasion I found myself saying, 'Oh God, grant that the aeroplane taking Sadat to Jerusalem may crash before it gets there, so that he may not become a scandal for all of us.' I am ashamed that I prayed in the *Ka'aba* against a Moslem.

He added that never again would it be possible for him to put his hand in Sadat's. If political necessity ever made contact unavoidable that would have to be done by his brother, Prince Fahd[1] – 'But for me – never. Sadat has made himself a scandal for all Arabs and all Moslems.'

When the Egyptian people heard Sadat's offer to go to Jerusalem their first reaction was amused incredulity. This, they thought, was

---

[1] Since 1982 King of Saudi Arabia.

another example of Sadat the actor being carried away by his own words and not to be taken seriously. But as he went on repeating the offer, and as they saw preparations for the journey actually being made, their mood began to change. They began to watch their President with fascination, like the crowd in a circus watching a trapeze artiste prepare to perform a particularly dangerous act. Could he do it – or would he break his neck?

There was a special element in this absorbed fascination. In thirty years Egypt had fought four wars with Israel (five counting the attrition war), and the Israelis had become creatures of mythology as much as of reality. Legend invested them with almost supernatural powers; they were regarded with a mixture of awe and fear, tinged perhaps, surprisingly enough, with a touch of admiration. So that when Sadat landed at Ben Gurion airport, and was to be seen on television actually walking and talking with the demons who had hardly hitherto seemed real flesh and blood – with Dayan and Golda Meir, with Bar-Lev and Sharon – the absorption of the Egyptian people in the spectacle unfolding before them became total. They were not ashamed of what they saw. All of them glued to their television sets, they were not observers of what was happening, but participants.

Every family in Egypt was watching a superstar at work – a superstar of their own – and they could not but hope that his incredible performance was going to benefit them all. Sadat was going to bring Egypt not only peace but prosperity. There would now be no need for all the money to be spent on armaments, no need to maintain such a large army. The Americans were certain to be generous, and so would the Jews everywhere – and were not they the richest people in the world? Prices were now sure to come down. A new life was about to begin.

But alas! Sadat's greatest personal triumph would be shown to be based on nothing. Even when Jerusalem was followed by Camp David all it brought was Sinai, which the Israelis had never really coveted. They had always been ready to return Sinai, provided Egypt agreed to stay within its borders, concentrate on Africa and forget about its Asian links. Now Sinai was to be returned on terms which safeguarded the interests of America and Israel at the expense of those of Egypt. Sinai, in effect, became an integral element in an American-planned and organized Middle East security system.

Part III

MOSLEM FUNDAMENTALISM

Any of you who sees evil should change it, by his hand if he can, by his word if he can, by his heart if he can; and this is the least in faith.

Prophet Mohamed

I

THE IRON FIST

THE ATMOSPHERE IN EGYPT at the beginning of 1978 was confused and uncertain. Something was still hoped for from 'the initiative', as Sadat's Jerusalem journey was now generally called, though it became increasingly difficult to know exactly what. The Americans and most of the rest of the world were still enthusiastic and full of congratulations for Sadat's courage, but concrete benefits were slow to materialize. No other Arab government had joined 'the peace process'; indeed, they had vied with each other in denouncing it, and almost all Arab aid in cash and kind for Egypt had dried up.

The government urgently needed some material gains from the new policy because the underlying grievances which had led to the riots a year before were still there. Life for the ordinary Egyptian men and women was no easier; inflation was no lower; the rich were still rich and the poor still desperately poor. True, the subsidies on basic commodities had not been cut off as threatened, but this had shown up the weakness of the government and the political strength of the governed.

There had been other indications that the Egyptian people's reputation for docility could no longer be counted on. Three years before, in 1975, there had been a dispute between management and workers in one of the factories in the industrial town of Mahalla el-Kubra in the course of which workers had staged a sit-in, taking over the factory and announcing that they would be responsible for maintenance of the machinery. The trouble was, of course, officially blamed on the Communists, but it transpired that the workers' leaders were ex-servicemen. The authorities had forgotten that between 1967 and 1974 two million young men had passed through the army, and that most of them had undergone a rigorous training programme which included commando methods and survival techniques as well as how to use the most modern weapons. When these young men returned to their towns and villages they did not forget the lessons they had learned, and it was known that after the October War large quantities of weapons had found their way from the battlefields on both sides of the Suez Canal into private hands all over Egypt. What should have been a warning that these hidden weapons could be used came during the 1980 elections. The authorities made a display of force in an effort to prevent the re-election for the el-Badary constituency in Assiut of the popular opposition deputy, Mumtaz Nassar, but were met by seven thousand armed men demonstrating in his support. The police were prevented from removing the ballot boxes, the crowd insisting that the counting of the votes should take place on the spot. To avoid a pitched battle the police were obliged to consent.

Sadat himself remained convinced that the initiative had been a success – that the consequences flowing from it would solve all Egypt's problems, internal and external. On his return from Jerusalem he had summoned one of Egypt's leading newspapermen,[1] and told him: 'All you journalists are going to find yourselves with nothing to do. You've lost the one theme which has been keeping you going all these years. Now everything has been solved. It's all over. You poor people – you'll have to find something else to write about.' The editor said he could understand the President's optimism over Sinai, but what about the Palestine issue – the West Bank and Gaza? 'Oh – that's all finished too,' Sadat protested. 'Arab Jerusalem, Mr President?' asked the editor. 'In my pocket!' said Sadat.

He genuinely seemed to believe that this was so. Thus, although the Saudis had made their total dissociation from the Jerusalem initiative abundantly clear, Sadat sent Hassan Tuhami, a Deputy Prime Minister, to Geneva to meet King Khaled there (no Egyptian representative could any longer be received in Riyadh). The King was told that Tuhami had a very important message to give to him and that it concerned Jerusalem. After a lot of persuasion the King agreed to receive Tuhami, but told him that if he wanted to talk politics this should be done with Prince Fahd. So Tuhami said he only really wished to give the King greetings and inquire after his health. But on the way out he had a brief conversation with one of the King's counsellors, Rashad Faraon, in the course of which he said, 'We have been given a written pledge from the Israelis about the return of Arab

---

[1] Ahmed Bahaeddin. He had been appointed editor of *Al-Ahram* in 1975 by a decree signed by Sadat, only to be dismissed some months later following a telephone order from Sadat to the Minister of Information, Dr Kamal Abul Magd.

Jerusalem to Arab sovereignty.' As Jerusalem must always be a matter of outstanding concern to the Saudis, who consider themselves custodians of the Holy Places, the counsellor asked if this could be put in writing, so that he could show it to the King. So Tuhami wrote: 'We have a letter from the Israelis confirming that Arab Jerusalem will be restored to Arab sovereignty.' But there was no foundation for this statement. The Israelis had made their conditions perfectly explicit – Jerusalem was not negotiable as the undivided and external capital of Israel, there could be no return to the pre-1967 frontiers, no Palestinian state, and no talking with the PLO.

How little the Israelis were prepared to concede could no longer be concealed. The Jerusalem initiative was to be followed up by further meetings between the two sides, and before this could happen Sadat had to prepare a team of negotiators. He still lacked a Foreign Minister, Ismail Fahmy having resigned in protest against the proposed Jerusalem journey, and his deputy, Mohamed Riad, promoted in his place, having also resigned the same day. For the time being there was only an Acting Foreign Minister, Butrus Ghali, who had accompanied the President to Jerusalem. Ghali was prepared to take on the job for a number of reasons. He belonged to one of the oldest Coptic families, but one whose most prominent member in recent history was almost universally regarded as a traitor – that other Butrus Ghali who had presided over the Denshawai trial and later been assassinated.[1] Educated in France, a former editor of the Economic Review of *Al Ahram*, and married to a member of the well-to-do Jewish Nadlar family, Ghali combined ambition with a realistic feeling that there was little prospect for a man like him in the normal context of Egyptian politics. 'What have I to lose?' summed up his attitude.

In the forthcoming negotiations Ghali was supposed to look after his opposite number, Moshe Dayan, while an ex-Prime Minister, Dr Mustafa Khalil, an engineer educated in the States, was detailed to look after the Israeli military with Ezer Weizmann at their head. To Hassan Tuhami was allotted responsibility for watching the Labour

---

[1] See p. 149.

Party politicians, such as Golda Meir and Shimon Peres, and the millionaire contractor Osman Ahmed Osman was available to help him.

But though the men had been lined up, the policies had not, nor had the machinery. Sadat talked confidently of following up Jerusalem with a conference in Cairo at which all interested parties would be represented, but no Arabs were prepared to attend and even the Americans were lukewarm about the proposal. However, December saw a conference of sorts in the Mena House Hotel at the foot of the Pyramids, but the only active delegations present were those of Egypt, Israel and America. The Israeli delegation was headed by Eliahu Ben-Elissar, Director of the Prime Minister's office and a Mossad (Intelligence) man. He immediately demonstrated that the Israeli attitude was to be one of arrogance not of conciliation. Flags of all the invited delegations were in position round the conference table, whether they were expected to be present or not (and most of course were not). But when Ben-Elissar saw the Palestinian flag among them he said his delegation would not enter the room until it had been removed. After a good deal of wrangling it was agreed to leave only the flags of the delegations actually attending. Then Ben-Elissar said he had noticed what he called 'a strange flag' (the Palestinian) among those flying outside the hotel – again, all those who had been invited being represented there. This presented a more awkward problem, for although the public would not know everything that went on in the conference chamber they would be aware if one of the flags on public display was removed. So after more wrangling it was decided to take down all the flags outside the hotel.

This meeting turned out to be a pure waste of time. The Israelis continued to insist that they must have 'security guarantees' – thus presenting the strange spectacle of a nuclear power demanding guarantees from a non-nuclear power. But it proved impossible to pin them down on any specific points. Nor were the Americans much help, being anxious not to involve themselves too deeply in the negotiations, which would be bound to prejudice their relations with the Saudis and the Jordanians, and perhaps with the Syrians too, with whom they wished to preserve some links.

The abortive Mena House meeting was followed by the Ismailia fiasco. On Christmas day, 1977, Sadat's fifty-ninth birthday, Menahem Begin, the Israeli Prime Minister, arrived in Egypt. But on the eve of this historic occasion Sadat reshuffled his negotiating team in a characteristically impetuous manner.

He realized that Brutus Ghali was politically too controversial to be in charge of the Egyptian Foreign Office. There was need for a proper Foreign Minister, and he decided to appoint the Ambassador in Bonn, Mohamed Ibrahim Kamel, to the post. Kamel was one of those who had been, like Sadat, accused of complicity in the murder of Amin Osman, though they came out of the trial with no very high opinion of each other. They had only met a couple of times during Sadat's presidency, and Kamel, who was in Cairo at the time in connection with some discussions he was having with the Federal German government, was astonished to hear on the radio that he had been appointed Foreign Minister. He was summoned to Ismailia, being shown into Sadat's room just half an hour before Begin and the Israeli delegation were due to arrive. Sadat explained that at a critical moment like this he wanted someone in charge of foreign affairs with an impeccable nationalist record. He knew that the Israelis were suspicious of the Foreign Ministry – they had in fact been complaining that some of the position papers prepared at the Ministry on matters like the rights of the Palestinians reflected what they called a 'pre-initiative mentality' – and he wanted to reassure them. 'So,' he explained to Kamel, 'I have asked the principal members of the Israeli delegation, Begin, Dayan and Weizmann, to attend the swearing-in ceremony of our new Foreign Minister.' Kamel protested: 'Please, Mr President, don't do this. It would be signing my death warrant. It would prejudice all the negotiations.' Sadat eventually agreed to drop the idea, but he regarded Kamel as extremely pusillanimous.

At the opening meeting Begin returned to the charge about the saboteurs in the Egyptian Foreign Ministry, though in fact they were only professionals doing their job of trying to supplement the President's vague generalities with memoranda which could be used as a negotiating basis. Then he got onto the subject of the Israeli settlements in Sinai, and took out of his briefcase a book on international law from which he quoted a passage purporting to show that the acquisition of territory by one side in a war was permissible if the other side had been guilty of aggression. 'Didn't the Egyptians concentrate their forces in Sinai for an attack on Israel in 1967, Mr President?' he asked. Sadat puffed at his pipe and gave an affirmative grunt. 'And didn't Nasser threaten us, Mr President?' Sadat grunted again. 'And weren't there a lot of voices in the Arab world demanding that Israel should be thrown into the sea?' Sadat nodded. When one of the Foreign Ministry Officials in the Egyptian delegation tried to interrupt to point out that nobody had in fact said anything about throwing Israel into the sea, Sadat shut him up. 'So, Mr President,' concluded Begin, 'you agree that you in effect started an offensive war in 1967, and that this makes us legally justified in keeping the territory we conquered.' However, he was prepared to consider restoring legal sovereignty over Sinai to Egypt, provided the settlements remained and the settlers maintained their own armed guards, 'otherwise they will not be able to sleep peacefully in their beds.' When Begin began to talk about 'Judea and Samaria', Sadat thought it better to bring the open session to an end and move to private and personal negotiations with Begin alone, but these proved no easier.

Then came the disastrous press conference at which Begin made Sadat read out the points on which agreement had been reached and the points on which they still disagreed. They had agreed, said Sadat, that the October War was to be the last war between their two countries, and that peace was the aim of both of them. As for disagreements, the Israelis, said Sadat, 'had maintained their position on Judea and Samaria, and we shall continue to discuss the question of the West Bank and Gaza.' All this was said in front of the television cameras, and the sight of their President reading from a paper a statement about 'Judea and Samaria', with Begin and Dayan with his famous eye-patch in chairs just behind him, had a shattering effect on most Egyptian viewers.

Sadat had said publicly that if the initiative failed he would resign, but though by the end of the Ismailia meeting it was obvious that his gamble had not paid off there was no more talk of resignation. Yet something must be done. He realized that time was no longer on his side. Disillusionment was spreading, and the memory of the January food riots was still fresh in the public mind. Although most of the five thousand people arrested after the riots had by now been brought to trial a great many had been released because of lack of any evidence against them or given very light sentences, and at the beginning of 1978 there was a particularly damaging court judgement which declared that the rioters, whatever crimes they might have committed, had been reacting to almost intolerable provocation in the form of the threatened abolition of the subsidies. So, in the face of mounting difficulties, Sadat decided that the only remedy was to crack down on all opposition. His policy would have to be that of the iron fist.

Those who had been acquitted by the courts could be kept in prison under the emergency regulations (some indeed were still in prison when Sadat died). But what about those still at large? It was not enough simply to identify them as 'Communists and Nasserites', though that was the label attached to all those who criticized the Jerusalem initiative, just as it had been to those who demonstrated against abolition of the subsidies. To deal with them Sadat refurbished one existing weapon and created another new one.

In 1971 a new post had been created, that of the Socialist Prosecutor. There had been such an official in the Soviet Union in Stalin's time, though after his death the post had been abolished. But Sadat had introduced the Socialist Prosecutor into the 1971 Constitution as a way of dealing with the 'centres of power'. Not having seen the evidence which proved that they had been plotting a *coup d'état*[1] he needed some other way of getting at them. So the Socialist Prosecutor was authorized to take action against anyone who was threatening the 'socialist gains' made on behalf of the people since the 1952 revolution.[2]

---

[1] See p. 40.

[2] I myself fell foul of the Socialist Prosecutor. During eleven lengthy sessions during July and August 1978 I was questioned by him and his two top assistants about my opinions, my beliefs and my record. They interrogated me about articles I had written as much as twenty years earlier. An article which particularly interested them was one I had written in 1970, which they claimed was judged by 'information experts' to be defeatist in attitude. I asked whether they were referring to the experts of 1970 or the current ones. They said the 1970 experts. I pointed out that when this article was written I was not only editor of *Al Ahram*, but also Minister of Information, Acting Minister of Foreign Affairs, and a member of the National Security Council, and so could probably claim to be as much an expert on information matters as anybody else in Egypt at that time. So they changed their minds and said that the experts they referred to were anonymous contemporary ones.

Though prevented from travelling abroad, and of course from writing anything in my own country, I was not otherwise penalized. But I believe my escape was more due to the interest the case aroused abroad than to the clemency of the Socialist Prosecutor and those in authority over him. I should perhaps add that some of those who questioned me were obviously torn between their respect for legal procedures and judicial standards and the instructions which had been given to them personally by the President on the basis of the Law of Shame.

The new weapon was 'The Law of Shame'. Any behaviour which an Egyptian villager regards as improper he will call shameful (*a'ib*), and 'The Law of Shame' was Sadat's own name for one of the most comprehensive pieces of legislation ever produced in any country.

Article 1 of the law laid down that 'the prosecution of the basic values of society is the duty of each citizen.' Article 2 defined 'basic values' as including 'the genuine traditions of the society of the Egyptian family'. Article 3, which describes criminal actions under the law is worth giving in full:

> A citizen committing any one of the following acts shall be held accountable:
>
> 1. Advocating any of the doctrines which imply a negation of divine teachings or which do not conform to the tenets thereof.
> 2. Advocating opposition to, hatred of, or contempt for the state's political, social or economic systems, calling for the domination by any one social class over others or for the liquidation of a social class.
> 3. Allowing children or youth to go astray by advocating the repudiation of popular religious, moral or national values or by setting a bad example in public places.
> 4. Broadcasting or publishing false or misleading news or information which could inflame public opinion, generate envy and hatred or threaten national unity or social peace.
> 5. Broadcasting or publishing gross or scurrilous words or pictures which could offend public sensibilities or undermine the dignity of the state or of its constitutional institutions.
> 6. Forming an organization not authorized by law, advocating the formation of such an organization, joining or hiding behind any organization whatever be its nature when the aim of any of the above is to threaten national unity or social peace.
> 7. Broadcasting or publishing abroad false or misleading news or information which could disparage the state's political system or its economic position or affect its relations with other states.

Penalties laid down for those breaking this law included deprivation of civil rights, withdrawal of passports, forced residence in a specified area and sequestration of property. The Socialist Prosecutor was charged with enforcement of the law, which in effect gave him unlimited authority over the thoughts as well as the actions of every citizen.

Since private enterprise on the American model had replaced socialism in Egypt, the Prosecutor had nothing to do with maintaining socialism but everything to do with suppressing those critics who complained that the Arab socialism pursued under Nasser had been abandoned. Needless to say, the new legislation was duly referred to a referendum and almost 99 per cent of the voters were officially reported to have expressed their approval.

Sadat was now isolated from the rest of the Arab world. His flirtation with Israel was totally rejected and those Arab governments which called themselves socialist were shocked by his dismantling of socialism in Egypt. He decided to make political capital out of his rejection by appealing to Egyptian nationalism.

Two years earlier Sadat had created what he called 'tribunes' – more or less political parties in embryo. There were 'tribunes' of right, left and centre, and they took part in the 1976 elections. When Sadat went to open the new Parliament, he told the deputies he had decided to convert the tribunes into political parties, because he had seen that the elections were fought along party lines. 'There is no need to hide it,' he said, 'so let us call them parties.' He chose the centre for himself, becoming Supreme Guide (since he was theoretically above parties as head of state) of what was now called the Misr (Egypt) Party. It had slogans such as 'Egypt first and last', 'Egypt is and always has been Egypt'. He appointed the Prime Minister of the time, Mamduh Salem, head of the party, which was not a happy choice since, whatever his other merits, Mamduh Salem was known essentially as an efficient former policemen, and while it may be appropriate to put a policeman in charge of the government in an emergency he is not likely to be the best man to run a fledgling political party. The right was allowed to form a Liberal Constitutional Party under an ex-officer, Colonel Mustafa Kamil Murad, while the left was put in charge of Khaled Mohieddin, one of the survivors of the original Free Officers and a Marxist, who headed the National Progressive Unionist Party.

But it was not long before Sadat came to the conclusion that something more was needed than the Misr Party and Mamduh Salem. He declared his intention of returning personally to what he called 'the political street'. He was going to start another new party – the National Party. Or rather, this was not to be a new party but an old one revived. The name was deliberately chosen to indicate that he was going back seventy years to the days of Mustafa Kamel and Mohamed Farid. Zaghlul, the Wafd and Nasser were alike ignored, and it was Mustafa Kamel who was now declared to have embodied the purity of the national movement in Egypt. This was a strange reading of history, for although a superb orator Mustafa Kamel was essentially a romantic figure, now principally remembered for his remark, 'If I had not been born an Egyptian I would have wished to be an Egyptian.' But to make certain that nobody missed the significance of what he was doing, Sadat established the headquarters of the new National Party in the same building which had housed the old party. Unfortunately this turned out to be in a dilapidated condition and in an unfashionable part of Cairo, so Sadat decided to take over the building which had been allocated to the Misr party, and which in its turn had previously been the headquarters of the Socialist Union.

Probably Sadat's idea was that the two parties, Misr and National, should continue side by side and somehow develop separate characters, while both of course remaining loyal in their support for the régime. But this was expecting too much. As soon as the President had re-entered 'the political street' and created a new party with himself at the head of it, all those who had enlisted under the banner of the Misr Party abandoned it for the National Party. The Misr Party more or less evaporated, being represented only by two or three deputies in Parliament who had genuinely thought that something useful could be made of it. One of these was the Minister of Irrigation, Abdel Azim Abu el-Atta, a distinguished engineer, one of the builders of the High Dam and Assistant Secretary-General of the party. He was later to find himself in the same cell in Tora prison as myself, and to die there from a heart attack in front of our eyes, with no doctor or equipment brought to save him.

Though Sadat continued to insist in the frequent interviews he gave in the press and on television that 99 per cent of the people backed him, the extreme measures taken to deal with any hint of criticism belied this claim. So Egypt came to conform to a pattern seen in many Third World countries where the ruler has decided to adopt the iron fist of repression. On the surface there is a façade which presents the recognizable attributes of a state – a President, a Prime Minister and a Cabinet, probably a Parliament which meets and even political parties. But none of these represent the real political life of the country.

To find that it is necessary to look behind the façade, to go below the surface. It is in the underground that the genuine political movements are to be found; it is here that discontent becomes articulate and that the mechanism to express and remedy grievances is being forged. So it was in Iran in the last years of the Shah. So too it was in Egypt in the last years of Sadat.

2

GOING UNDERGROUND

THE FAÇADE which Egypt presented to the world was undoubtedly impressive. Here was to all appearances the most important country in the most sensitive area in the world bustling with new commercial activity and presided over by a statesman of international renown who could be guaranteed to capture the headlines whenever he opened his mouth. The reality was very different. A mood of deep disillusionment had overtaken people in every walk of life.

But to be fair to Sadat, this was not wholly attributable to the manifest failure of the Jerusalem initiative; its origins went further back, even to the time of Nasser. Nasser achieved so much that he created dreams which were incapable of fulfilment. The generation which had grown up to watch the monarchy overthrown, seen the Suez Canal nationalized and two of the great powers, Britain and France, humiliated in their efforts to undo this nationalization, seen Egypt acknowledged as the architect of Arab unity and of a new and juster social order which could serve as a model for all Third World countries, might well believe that nothing was beyond its capacity. Then had come the disaster of the 1967 war. For a time everything seemed lost, all the achievements of the past negated.

It has to be admitted that in 1967 Nasser failed in one of the fundamental duties of any ruler – he failed to defend the borders of his country. By that failure the legitimacy of his régime was flawed, just as Sadat's legitimacy was flawed by the food riots of January 1977. Yet there was an essential difference between the way the two men reacted to the crisis. The defeat of 1967 did not mean the end of the world. The battle continued; the confrontation with Israel moved into the War of Attrition; the army was rebuilt and re-equipped. All the same, the postwar feeling of frustration boiled over in the student demonstrations of February 1968. Nasser's reaction to this evidence of discontent was to try to understand the reasons for it – hence the so-called 'March 30 programme' which promised greater personal and political freedom for all. But Sadat's reaction to popular discontent was to draw still further away from the people, offering them circuses instead of bread, and the iron fist instead of more freedom.

So political life in Egypt moved underground. Who was to be found there? Obviously the Nasserites formed one group which now had no chance of a legal existence above ground, but their trouble was that they were leaderless. Not only had many of Nasser's closest associates been imprisoned since May 1971, but the rank and file had always, not without reason, looked on themselves as the true heirs of the 1952 revolution, so that when, after the 1977 food riots, some in their turn found themselves in prison, they were unprepared physically or mentally for this change in their fortunes. Members of groups with a long experience of underground activity, like the Moslem Brotherhood or the Communists, were much better equipped. Within twenty-four hours their members who had been arrested were being supplied with food and lawyers and their families were being looked after, while the imprisoned Nasserites could only protest that they belonged to the régime which had put them inside. Some organizations of what were known as Nasserist Thought Clubs continued to exist more or less openly in the universities, but they were incapable of providing the necessary leadership.

Even before the 1977 riots the Nasserites had been uncertain how far they could or should cooperate with the régime. Some of them had joined Khaled Mohieddin's National Progressive Unionist Party, as did some Communists who wanted to appear respectable in the eyes of the rest of the Arab world. But more Communists went underground – not that there had ever been very many of them, and from the earliest days the movement had been beset by quarrels and factionalism.

Whether over or under ground, Nasserites and Communists were officially branded as enemies of the régime. It seemed logical therefore to Sadat and his associates that if they needed allies these should be sought on the right – and not just the political right but also the religious right.

The religious forces in Egypt were already receiving substantial encouragement from other governments than their own. In 1971, by what amounted to a unique treaty between state and a foreign religious institution, King Feisal of Saudi Arabia had offered Sheikh Abdel

Halim Mahmoud, Rector of Al-Azhar, $100 million to be spent on a campaign against atheism and for the triumph of Islam. (In fact only the first instalment of $40 million was paid, and as the Prime Minister of the time, Mamduh Salem, was in need of hard currency, he diverted this to the Treasury and gave the Rector of Al-Azhar Egyptian currency instead.) The Rector embarked on a lavish programme of publicity. He himself wrote books attacking Communism, and he arranged for the publication of an Arabic version of *The God that Failed*, in which a number of European and American ex-Communists had explained the reasons for their recantation. New mosques were built and a lot of travelling done by religious dignitaries.

Another way in which King Feisal hoped to encourage religion in Egypt was by effecting a reconciliation between President Sadat and the Moslem Brotherhood. By now the Brotherhood included a number of different elements. There were still a few who thought mainly in terms of violence and terrorism, but they were either in prison or leading an underground existence. Then there were those who had left Egypt, either for political reasons or because they preferred to work abroad, and many of these had begun to do well for themselves. Finally, there were those who remained in Egypt and tried to adjust themselves as best they could to the existing order of things.

With this end in view King Feisal in the summer of 1971 arranged for some prominent members of the Brotherhood to be given a safe conduct for their return to Egypt so that they could have discussions with Sadat. The meeting was held at the Janaklis rest house, in conditions of strict secrecy, the representatives of the Brotherhood being led by Said Ramadan, who had lived in Saudi Arabia for some years and was at this time living in Geneva in charge of a Saudi-sponsored organization called the General Islamic Movement. In the course of their discussions, Sadat argued that he and they were confronted by the same enemies, atheism and Communism, not to mention surviving Nasserist ideas. He said that, if they were prepared to come out in the open and give him their support, he was ready to make a pact with them. But the Brotherhood was undecided how to act. They were suspicious of Sadat's good intentions, and the whole direction of Egyptian politics since 1952 had been antipathetic to them.

So matters continued for some years, though naturally the Moslem

Brothers, like everyone else, were aware of the increasing emphasis on religious matters both at the official level and underground. Meanwhile some of them had found a new patron in the person of the man who was closest to the President, Osman Ahmed Osman.

Osman Ahmed Osman, one of the richest men in Egypt and probably one of the richest men in the Arab world, belongs to a family which had its origins in El-Arish, the capital of Sinai. He came to Ismailia where he built up a contracting business which prospered even in the days when Egypt was in fact as well as in name a socialist country. Ismailia was the home of the Moslem Brotherhood. It was here that the first Guide, Hassan El-Banna, had founded the movement in 1928. Proscribed by the Prime Minister, Ibrahim Abdel-Hadi, in 1949, and ruthlessly crushed after the attempt on Nasser's life in 1954, the Brotherhood had seen many of its leaders executed or imprisoned while others sought refuge abroad. Osman's contracting business branched out into other Arab countries and brought him into contact with the exiled Brethren, whom he was prepared to employ. Some of them prospered and came back to Egypt with the money they had made. There they found Osman in a position of great authority, still friendly to them, and anxious to persuade them that they no longer need lead the life of conspirators. He had the President's own assurance on this score, he told them.

But the Brethren thus approached remained sceptical. They found Sadat's Westernizing policies even less to their liking than the progressive policies of Nasser. And after Sadat's Jerusalem journey they totally rejected the rapprochement with Israel, both because it appeared to involve the sacrifice of Jerusalem and because of their mistrust of the Jews as a people, which has always been a fundamental aspect of the thinking of the Brotherhood. All the same, some of the leaders were willing to strike a bargain with the authorities. One of them, Omar el-Tilmsani, had for some time been editing and distributing his magazine *El-Dawa* without any interference by the police. Now a splinter group of the Brotherhood was encouraged to produce another magazine called *I'tisam*. On their side the Brethren made a number of conditions as the price of cooperation, one of which was that the presidential guard should be withdrawn from Nasser's tomb, because they claimed that implied official endorsement of Nasser's ideas. Sadat accepted this condition and the guard disappeared. But the partnership was not an easy one, and much was going on in the underground which was to make it more uneasy still.

3

ORIGINS

As the term implies, Moslem fundamentalism is a movement which aims at a return to the basic ideas and practices which characterized Islam in its earliest days. The Prophet Mohamed had instituted not only religious beliefs and observances but a whole code of behaviour by which society was to be organized. Islam defined both man's relationship to God and man's relationship to his fellow-men. These institutions were not just for his own people and his own age, but for all peoples and all ages. A believer must assume their universal validity.

Under the first four Caliphs the armies of Islam humbled the two great empires of the day, Byzantium and Persia, and created a new and much greater empire of their own, stretching from the Pyrenees to the Indus. But victory brought with it the seeds of decay. Byzantium, though defeated, strongly influenced methods and manners of life under the Umayyads, as did Persia life under the Abbasids. The luxury of the cities replaced the simplicity of the desert. And although Islam was the great unifying force in this new and dynamic superpower, it was unifying many peoples – Egyptians, Syrians, Mesopotamians – with long and rich histories of their own, which they could never forget or reject.

It was at a time of the Abbasid empire's greatest splendour that a theologian emerged in Baghdad denouncing the luxury of the court and preaching the need for a return to the original purity of Islam. This was Ahmed ibn Hanbal (780–855) who, by becoming responsible for the so-called *Salafy* (ancestral) movement, can be regarded as in a sense the ancestor of modern Moslem fundamentalism. It was, he asserted, adherence to certain basic principles which had made the first generations of the Moslems great. These principles, he said, are as valid in the present, and will be as valid in the future, as they were in the past. If there is to be greatness again it can only be achieved by the same means which produced the original greatness. Ibn Hanbal was also the founder of one of the four principal schools of Islamic law.

From the ninth century onward the Abbasid empire was in decline, and as the original Arab impulse in it grew weaker that of other races grew stronger. The Seljuk Turks took control over the Caliphate of Baghdad in the middle of the eleventh century, and two hundred years later came the final catastrophe when in 1258 the Mongol leader Hulagu Khan sacked Baghdad and ordered the execution of the last *fainéant* representative of the house of Abbas.

These warrior races from the lands of Central Asia posed problems not only for those who tried to protect the frontiers of Islam but also for those who were interpreters of its doctrines. Sooner or later most of the invaders came to call themselves Moslems. But what sort of Moslems? Was it enough that they should make the profession of faith, that there is no God but Allah and that Mohamed is his prophet? Did being a Moslem mean no more than the repetition of a formula?

One of the refugees from Baghdad after Hulagu's conquest of the city became a professor of Hanbali law in Damascus. When he died he was succeeded in this office by his son, Ahmed ibn Taimiya (1263–1328), who almost as much as ibn Hanbal himself inspires the thinking of today's fundamentalists. Ibn Taimiya's career was divided between Damascus and Cairo, sometimes in favour with the authorities, sometimes out of favour and in prison. He preached the *jihad* against the Mongols, declaring that though they professed themselves Moslems they could not be accepted as such; they were tyrants, he claimed, abusing the real nature of Islam. When the Mongol armies laid siege to Damascus, and raised the Koran on their swords in an attempt to display their piety, ibn Taimiya denounced this as a fraud, an attempt to mask their true purposes under the cloak of religion.

Among those who in recent times have been much influenced by ibn Taimiya are two of the most important thinkers in the Arab world of the nineteenth century, Jamaleddin el-Afghani and Mohamed Abduh. Afghani urged the need for a regeneration of Islam and was prepared to use violence against those policital leaders whom he saw as obstacles to this aim. He was widely believed to have inspired the assassination of Nasreddin Shah of Persia, and certainly made no secret of the satisfaction this event gave him. His Egyptian disciple, Mohamed Abduh, an educator and reformer, looking back to the early days of Islam as a golden age, was also prepared in his youth to advocate the use of violence when he felt it to be politically necessary. And from time to time in the eighteenth and nineteenth centuries the outside world was reminded of the effect that a call to return to the primitive purity of Islam could have by the movements connected with the names of Mohamed Abdel Wahhab in Arabia, Mohamed Ahmed (the Mahdi) in the Sudan, and Mohamed el-Senussi in Libya, though eventually all these movements became identified with a tribal grouping which developed into a monarchy or a political party.

In Egypt the intellectual debate stirred up by revolutionaries and reformers like Afghani and Abduh and by the influence of Western thinkers branched out in a number of directions. Mohamed Rashid Ridha, the disciple and biographer of Mohamed Abduh, was influenced by the teachings of Hanbal and ibn Taimiya and welcomed the conquest of the Holy Cities in Arabia by the Wahhabis. In his periodical *Manar* (*Lighthouse*) he reprinted a number of ibn Taimiya's writings, as well as his own extensive commentaries on religion and politics. But he lacked the understanding and originality of his predecessors, and his stereotyped religious teaching in *Manar* shed increasingly little light on the problems of the day.

By contrast the secular, liberal movement produced writers and thinkers of the calibre of Ahmed Lutfi el-Sayyid, equally a friend and disciple of Abduh, and Taha Hussein who, though never decrying religion or its essential role in society, became more and more involved with the struggle for national independence which dominated almost every aspect of Egyptian life in the first three decades of the nineteenth century.

By the 1930s, however, political nationalism in Egypt had begun to lose some of its original sincerity and thereby some of its earlier appeal. Either through collaboration with the imperial power it was supposed to be fighting, or by succumbing to the temptations of such positions of authority as were open to it, the mainstream of nationalism had become corrupted – and not in Egypt alone, but in Syria, Iraq and in other Arab countries.

So, once again, a vacuum both of thought and action was being created, and something was bound to fill it. The deficiency was to be made good by Hassan el-Banna, founder and first Guide of the Moslem Brotherhood, who came from Ismailia. It was no accident that Ismailia should have been the birthplace of the Moslem Brotherhood, for it was the most Europeanized of all Egyptian towns, headquarters of the foreign-owned Suez Canal Company and surrounded by all the camps and installations of the occupying British army. A reaction against this alien environment was inevitable, though ironically there were those who argued that it must be the British, so strong in Ismailia, who were building the Moslem Brotherhood up to be made an alternative to the Wafd.

Hassan el-Banna was a teacher who had been influenced by the writings of Rashid Ridha. He was quickly to prove himself a dynamic preacher, a first-rate organizer and a truly charismatic personality. His message was simple – 'The Koran is our constitution, and the Prophet is our leader' – thereby implicitly rejecting the 1923 Constitution under which Egypt was theoretically governed, the leadership of the Wafd under Nahas Pasha, and in fact the whole political scene as it existed when the Brotherhood first came into being in 1928.

Hassan el-Banna moved from Ismailia to Cairo. The Moslem Brotherhood expanded in the capital, then throughout Egypt, and eventually into almost all the Arab world. It was obviously a power to be reckoned with. Not surprisingly the Wafd viewed this new rival with grave misgivings, as did the Palace. Hitherto the Palace had always regarded organized religion in the country as being under its patronage, and therefore its ally. But here was a religious organization which owed the Palace nothing.

For all his shrewdness and ability, Hassan el-Banna was to find the complexities of the Egyptian political scene too much for him. Some military men as well as politicians naturally began to look on this new force as a potential ally rather than an enemy – men, for example, like General Aziz el-Masri, General Saleh Harb, Ali Maher and Abdel Rahman Azzam. Even before the birth of the Arab League in 1944 and the growing feeling of solidarity among the Arab countries, men such as these had been looking eastwards, to the Moslem countries of Asia, as an area where Egypt might find friends and be able to play a useful role. All these had contacts with the Brotherhood, and Ali Maher was prepared to make use of it on behalf of the Palace. It may be that in the difficult circumstances of the war Hassan el-Banna was not unwilling to fall in with Ali Maher's ideas.

The aftermath of the war, with the proliferation of nationalist movements of every sort, made it harder than ever for the Brotherhood to steer a consistent course. There could be no denying the electrifying appeal it had to the rising generation – 'monks of the night and cavaliers of the day' as Hassan el-Banna called them. The contingents which they sent to fight in Palestine in 1948 acquitted themselves with distinction, and at one time or another many of the Free Officers, including Nasser, found much to admire in the Brotherhood and contemplated throwing in their lot with it. If in the end they all drew back this was mainly because they felt that, apart from its generalized religious and ethical principles, the Brotherhood lacked a programme capable of meeting Egypt's needs. When Hassan el-Banna was asked about a programme he would say, 'Our programme is the Koran,' or 'Our programme is Islamic government.' If pressed to explain a bit more what this meant he would confine himself to saying: 'When we achieve power we will consider what it is necessary to do in the light of existing circumstances. Until that time we are not going to be pinned down by details.' This was hardly good enough. No effective political movement could be constructed on so nebulous a basis.

Hassan el-Banna was well aware of the dangers surrounding him. He knew that he had many enemies who would like to see the movement liquidated, and he accordingly organized a secret wing of the Brotherhood known as the Special Order, which was armed and trained to carry out terrorist acts, not only against the British but against any opponent who might be identified. Initiation into the Special Order was by solemn ritual. The neophyte was taken into a darkened room where he was confronted by a Koran and a revolver. On these two objects he had to swear to observe the principles of Islam and to give absolute obedience to the Supreme Guide of the Brotherhood.

In the wake of the first Palestine war tension between the government and the Brotherhood increased. The loyalty of many of the rank and file weakened under official harassment, but the Special Order remained intact and began to assume a commanding position in the movement. There were outbursts against what were considered symbols of decadent and un-Islamic influence – bars, department stores, nightclubs, cinemas. In March 1948 a judge who had passed sentence on some members of the Brotherhood convicted of terrorist acts was assassinated. Nokrashi Pasha, the Prime Minister, decided that the Brotherhood represented a direct challenge to the constituted authorities and that the time had come to crack down on it.

This he did. On 8 December an order was issued dissolving the

Brotherhood and confiscating all its considerable funds and properties. Three weeks later Nokrashi himself was assassinated by a member of the Special Order disguised as a police officer.

Originally Hassan el-Banna had sanctioned the death sentence on Nokrashi, but later had second thoughts, realizing that the murder of a Prime Minister could not be allowed to go unavenged and that he himself would be the most likely target for official vengeance. But it was too late; the Special Order went ahead and Nokrashi was shot. Ibrahim Abdel Hadi became the new Prime Minister, and, as he had feared, Hassan el-Banna was not allowed to escape, even though he issued a statement denouncing the murder and insisting that those responsible for it were 'neither Brothers nor Moslems'. The attack on him was planned and carried out by the head of the special police department responsible for the safety of Ministers (*haras el-wizarat*). With two policemen from his department in civilian clothes he ambushed and killed Hassan el-Banna in Cairo's Queen Nazli Street at 9 o'clock in the evening of 12 February 1949. The Abdel Hadi government was uncompromising in its suppression of what was left of the Brotherhood.

However, after the elections of January 1950, which brought the Wafd back to power, the Moslem Brotherhood gained a temporary reprieve. Seeing his old enemy Nahas in office again, Farouk cast around for potential allies, and the Brotherhood was one obvious candidate. It was accordingly granted a limited existence under a respectable new Supreme Guide, a judge by the name of Hassan el-Hodeibi. At the beginning of 1952 the alliance was publicized by a summons to Hodeibi from the Palace, after which he made a statement to the waiting journalists which he and the Brotherhood found hard to live down. It had, he said, been 'a gracious visit to a gracious king'.

When the revolution came in July 1952 the Brotherhood continued to enjoy a measure of toleration. Although all political parties were banned the Free Officers could not forget their past connections with the Brotherhood and allowed it to function more or less openly. Hodeibi tried to play a part in the post-revolutionary political scene, but proved as little able to define his political programme as his predecessor had been. He still insisted on 'the full application of Islamic principles', whatever that meant, and though some members of the Brotherhood broke ranks and accepted an invitation to join the government, the reconciliation between the RCC and the Brotherhood was short lived. The Brotherhood felt it was being made use of, and the Free Officers, who after all now constituted the government, felt that the Brotherhood was trying to tell them what they should and should not do. Moreover, the Special Order continued to exist and Hodeibi was powerless to control it. Nasser was well aware of this small but ruthless organization – and indeed knew some of its members – and could not countenance it.

Once again, in January 1954, the Brotherhood was officially dissolved, and once again a nucleus went underground. It was known that the remaining Brothers opposed the negotiations with Britain for the final evacuation of British troops which were conducted during the spring and summer of that year because it allowed for the maintenance (by civilians) of a military base in the Canal area, and on 26 October a plumber belonging to the Brotherhood tried to assassinate Nasser as he was addressing a meeting in Menshia Square in Alexandria. A special 'People's Court' was set up to try those accused of conspiring against the régime, Sadat being one of its three members. Severe punishments were handed out, including six death sentences and several long terms of imprisonment.

After 1954 Egypt ceased to be the centre of Moslem fundamentalist thought or organization. A new centre arose – in Pakistan. A member of the Moslem Brotherhood in Karachi, by the name of Abu el-A'ala Mawdudi,[1] started a newspaper called *Turjiman-i-Koran* (*The Interpretation of the Koran*). This reflected the teaching of the Brotherhood on the need to return to the basic teachings of Islam, but with a difference. The situation in Pakistan was, after all, very unlike that in Egypt. Whereas in Egypt and its neighbouring Arab countries the political emphasis had all been on unification, in Pakistan the emphasis was on separation – political separation of Pakistan as a state from India, and religious and cultural separation of the Moslems from the Hindus. The only reason for the existence of Pakistan as a nation, as a state, was the religion of its inhabitants.

---

[1] Mawdudi was arrested and sentenced to death, but largely owing to pressure from other Islamic countries was reprieved. He was released from prison on the fall of Ayub Khan and died, his tomb becoming a focus of pilgrimage for fundamentalists from many countries.

Mawdudi made one important contribution to fundamentalist Islamic thought. He distinguished between two stages of development in contemporary Islamic communities – the stage of weakness (*istidhaf*) during which Moslems would have to withdraw and prepare themselves, and the stage of action (*jihad*) when they would be strong enough to accomplish their aims. The first stage he compared to the period when the Pròphet Mohamed was regrouping his forces in Medina, and the second stage to his return to Mecca and the triumph of Islam.

Mawdudi also discussed at length the question of *hakimiya*, the authority by which men should be ruled. For him the only legitimate authority was God, and the ruling agency must be the text of the Koran. The Koran was naturally almost all the Arabic Mawdudi knew. He was not able, as an Arab theologian *(faqih)* would be, to analyse and interpret the meaning of the Koran. For him the text stood by itself, self-contained and self-explanatory. So apart from any other considerations he was, for linguistic reasons, inevitably a fundamentalist. Because of this, and because of Pakistan's origins as a state and its relations with its neighbour, India, Mawdudi wrote a great deal about questions of political change, revolution and the use of force. His ideas found a ready audience over the border, in Iran, as events were later to demonstrate.

Mawdudi wrote a small book called *The Four Expressions* which was to have a considerable influence on the course of events in Egypt. The four expressions he dealt with were, first, *hakimiya*, and he contrasted the rule of God with all other forms of rule by men; second, *uluhiya*, contrasting the godliness of God with attempts to make gods of, or endow with divine qualities, any human beings; third, *rabaniya*, lordship, contrasting enslavement to the Lord with enslavement to individuals or systems; and finally *wahdaniya*, the oneness of God, contrasted with attempts to dissipate that unity. He insisted that in all these there was no room for compromise. It was either the *hakimiya* of the Koran or a negation of the Koran; either the *uluhiya* of God or a blasphemous challenge to it; either enslavement to God or to a false god; either the oneness of God or the infidel wish to become a partner with God.

This book made a strong impression on a man who was to become the foremost exponent of fundamentalist ideas in Egypt, Sayyid Qutb. He had originally been an exponent of liberal ideas, and a poet, but had then joined the Moslem Brotherhood and been imprisoned, with so many others, in 1954. While in prison a copy of Mawdudi's book was smuggled in to him. He read it with enthusiasm and disseminated its ideas among his fellow-prisoners. Eventually Sayyid Qutb and others were released, and he wrote two books of his own reflecting Mawdudi's views about *hakimiya* and about the two stages of development, *istidhaf* and *jihad*. These books were called *In the Shadow of the Koran* and *Marks on the Road*.

The Moslem Brotherhood could never really accept the true nature of the Egyptian Revolution. They objected to its egalitarianism, quoting the text from the Koran which says 'We have created you class upon class.' They regarded the RCC as a secular authority interfering in matters which they believed should not be its concern. They thought the Communists exercised an un-Islamic influence on government policies and disapproved of the country's friendly relations with the Soviet Union.

In 1965, after evidence had accumulated of a conspiracy against the régime, there was another crackdown on the Brotherhood. Many of those who had been released were imprisoned again, and some, including Sayyid Qutb, were hanged. The result was that, by the time Nasser died and Sadat took over, an entirely new fundamentalist underground had come into existence. Its members regarded the old Brotherhood, and the ideas of people like Hassan el-Banna, as completely out of date. They had suffered in prison and been hardened by suffering. Their mentors were Mawdudi and Sayyid Qutb, who in their eyes was a martyr (*shahid*). His books became their Bible. They accepted his absolutist teachings, that there could be no compromise between two systems, two sorts of society, two beliefs. In their eyes everybody had to choose between Islam or pre-Islamic *jahiliya*, ignorance, between good and evil, right and wrong, between belief and infidelity, between God and being a renegade (*taghuti*). And as the policy of *infitah* developed, bringing in its wake foreign influences, vulgar ostentation and materialist values, they felt more than ever convinced of the justice of their cause.

4

A FRANKENSTEIN MONSTER

THE RÉGIME showed little or no awareness of the new movements that were fermenting beneath the surface. It still thought of the opposition in terms of those it regarded as its old irreconcilable enemies – Nasserites, leftists, liberal intellectuals, Wafdist survivors. Certainly these did represent a real opposition, and they were now being joined by all those who rejected Sadat's initiative and accommodation with Israel, by those who still believed in Arab unity, who resented American interference, high prices, inflation, the country's mounting foreign debts, and the whole sordid vulgarity of the *infitah* profiteers. It was all these malcontents that the régime felt it would have to combat. But how?

Nobody had any illusions about the effectiveness of the official institutions – Parliament and the tame political parties created and fostered by the régime. Neither the Misr Party nor the new National Party represented anything except the patronage they were able to exercise simply by being in power. Half the deputies in Parliament were time-servers who changed their opinions with every shift of government policy – who were socialists when it seemed wiser to join the Socialist Union and capitalists when the door was opened to foreign capital; who were friends of the Soviet Union when that appeared to be in order, but just as ready to switch their friendship to the Americans; who would clamour for war or peace with Israel with equal enthusiasm. Most of the rest, apart from a handful of active and energetic deputies who deserved the label 'independent', were people who had genuine reasons for supporting the régime because they had gained much from it and hoped to gain more. Indeed some of the new class proved too indiscreet in their parasitism. One deputy, Rashad Osman, was accused by the Socialist Prosecutor of amassing £E300 million from illegal dealings in hashish, and another deputy was actually arrested red-handed smuggling hashish into the country. The police had to ask Parliament to raise his immunity from prosecution, but found they ran into obstruction. It was only in 1982 that he was eventually convicted.

If Parliament and parties were useless even as safety-valves, what was left? It was no use expecting that the army could be used again, as it had been in January 1977. Yet some other buttress for the régime was clearly needed. So the decision was made to call in religion as an ally.

Religion can take many forms and face many demands and challenges according to the climate of opinion of the time. In Nasser's day religion was never seen as being an obstacle to social progress; on the contrary, strong sympathy was felt with the saying attributed to the Prophet by one of the earliest philosophers of Islam, Abu Zurr el-Ghaffari: 'There are three things which belong to society as a whole and which cannot be claimed by any individual – fire, grass and water,' a principle which by many centuries anticipated the doctrine of the nationalization of the means of production. Now there was a complete change. All the emphasis was to be on those aspects of religion which stressed the need for the ruled to obey the ruler and on the transcendental as opposed to the practical teachings of Islam.

The consequence of the régime's decision to call in religion as an ally soon became apparent. A separate radio programme, called the Koran station, wholly devoted to readings from the Koran and programmes connected with it, was greatly expanded. No doubt there was an audience which welcomed such a programme, but much more was to come. All ordinary programmes, on radio and television, now had to be interrupted for the call to prayer five times a day. Whatever was going on – a thriller, a love story, a comedy, the news – the programme would be abruptly interrupted so that the voice of the muezzin could be heard. The régime's new devotion to religion was to be given demonstrative backing at the highest level. Sadat was now not only officially known as 'the pious President', but was to be seen on television every Friday going to a different mosque to pray – an occasion which, since journalists were always informed in advance of where he would be going, provided him with a useful opportunity to give a press conference.

Special attention had to be given to the universities. Hitherto the dominant influence in the student unions had been either Nasserite or leftist, and this was obviously not to be tolerated. But it was admittedly difficult to know what to do about the situation. One attempted solution was to create a new post, that of Minister of Youth. For this position Sadat chose a graduate from the Faculty of Medicine, Dr Abdel Hamid Hassan, who had been one of the student leaders with whom Nasser had held discussions after the demonstrations which followed the defeat of 1967. Considerable funds were put at his disposal, but the appointment proved ineffective. Making a man a Minister does not necessarily put him in the position of being able to speak for the young or to influence them.

In addition Sadat decided on a more direct approach. He would invite the student leaders to the presidential rest house at the Barrage, and there in front of the television cameras he would employ his arts of diplomacy and persuasion to effect a reconciliation. But it did not work out that way. One of the student leaders began to complain about the privileges enjoyed by certain favoured classes and Sadat lost his temper. Viewers were presented with the unedifying sight of the President shouting at the young man: 'Be careful of what you are saying! Stop that! Remember you are talking to the head of the family – you are talking to the President!' The experiment was not repeated.

The authorities refused to recognize that new forces were at work among the students and beneath the surface everywhere. They continued to assume that as far as religion was concerned the people they had to deal with were either simply the unorganized mass of Moslem believers or known organizations like the Moslem Brotherhood. Yet they had been warned that much more was involved, if only they had been willing to read the warning properly.

Back in 1974 a young doctor of philosophy called Saleh Sarrieh had led a small group of young men, many of them students, in an attack on the Military Technical College, collected volunteers and arms from it, and marched on the building of the Central Committee of the Socialist Union. Their declared objective was to assassinate Sadat and the other members of the Central Committee and seize power for themselves. It was obviously a hopeless venture, quickly crushed. Several people were killed in the course of it and later the leader was hanged. The escapade was attributed to a group nobody had ever heard of, calling itself the Islamic Liberation Party, and no more was thought about it.

Two years later a former Minister of Waqf (Religious Endowments), Sheikh Mohamed el-Dhahabi, was kidnapped from his house in Helwan, a Cairo suburb, by a group of men wearing the uniforms of police officers. The conditions given for his release included a public declaration by the authorities over the radio that the country was not being governed according to Islamic principles and that these would be adhered to in future. This demand was refused, and the victim killed. Subsequently some of the kidnappers were arrested, and as a result of what came out during their interrogation the police gave them the name '*takfir wa hijra*', meaning that they saw themselves as living in an infidel society, comparable to that in Mecca before the Prophet's migration to Medina. The group totally rejected the society in which they found themselves, and would have nothing to do with it. They proposed to withdraw from it to the mosques and to the mountains, there to regroup until they felt strong enough to return and destroy that society. But their time was not yet. They had only broken their rule of withdrawal in the case of Sheikh el-Dhahabi because he had once been a sympathizer but, while a Minister, had given a *fetwa* (ruling) against them. This made him in their eyes a traitor who had to be punished. But once again, after the appropriate punishments had been handed out, the authority preferred to regard the affair as just another isolated incident.

Still acting on the assumption that he had only to deal with religious organizations of a familiar nature, Sadat decided that during Ramadan in 1980 he would have a meeting each week with some Moslem body. One week it was the turn of the Al-Azhar *ulamas*, and at the last moment he asked Omar Tilmsani to attend, representing that section of the Moslem Brotherhood which was on the whole willing – except for the accommodation with Israel – to go along with the régime and so was tolerated by it. Of course the proceedings were to be shown live on television, and in spite of the mishap over his meeting with the student leaders Sadat calculated that he would be able to say anything he wanted without fear of contradiction.[1]

---

[1] He had once said on television, in the presence of Khaled Mohieddin, 'I was responsible for bringing Khaled into the Free Officers Movement.' Khaled Mohieddin was unable to contradict this rewriting of history and could only sit in silent fury.

After talk with the *ulamas* had gone on for some time, Sadat turned to Tilmsani and said: 'Omar, I am still allowing you to go on publishing *Dawa*, but I know what the law is. You have been going too far in what you write, and I could close you down tomorrow if I wanted to.' Tilmsani was a wily old man, so he said: 'Mr President, you put me in a very difficult position. How can I make any answer to you, situated as you are in all the splendour of your position at the head of your government and your official functionaries? I can only complain to God.' Sadat saw that he was in danger of being upstaged, and hurriedly said: 'No! You must not complain to God. I fear God. Do not complain to God!' But Tilmsani refused to be silenced. 'Mr President,' he said, 'why should you be afraid? I am complaining to the author of all justice, and if you have no sin you need fear no punishment. Why are you afraid, Mr President?' Next day this exchange was the talk of the whole town.

5

TRUCE WITH THE MONSTER

IT BECAME increasingly apparent that those who profited from the new order of things in Egypt were doing their best to drown criticism in a tidal wave of religion. Huge sums of money were coming from abroad, much of it being channelled to that part of the Moslem Brotherhood which was prepared to lend its support to the régime. Osman Ahmed Osman and Osman Ismail, Governor of Assiut and Secretary-General of the Socialist Union,[1] were supporting several Islamic groups with arms and money. Much money was also going to the universities, where lavish exhibitions of religious literature were frequently staged. Societies were promoted to provide students with what was described as 'Islamic costume', veils for the girls and *galabiyehs* for the boys. (There was indeed a real benefit for poorer students in the adoption of this uniform dress, which effectively masked all social distinctions.)

But most energy was devoted to ensuring that the students were correctly represented in their unions. To give just one example: in the elections for student unions in Alexandria University at the beginning of the academic year in the autumn of 1978 candidates from the Islamic Association won all sixty places in the Faculties of Medicine and Engineering, forty-seven out of forty-eight in the Faculty of Law, forty-three out of sixty in the Faculty of Pharmacy. These new student bodies quickly began to assert themselves. They insisted that the sexes should be separated in classrooms and in cafeterias, and that each day's programme of study should start with prayers. Their demands were granted. They forbad the celebration of secular national holidays, and declared Mother's Day an atheistical feast.

Knowing that they had the support of higher authority, the Islamic students began to behave as if it was they who were running the

---

[1] Dismissed by President Mubarak in the summer of 1982.

universities. They decided what subjects were suitable to be taught, forcibly preventing, for example, lectures to be given on Darwinism. They put a stop to the traditional celebrations given to a professor when he retired or was moved to another post, because these usually took the form of a party with music. They took upon themselves to decide what food should be permitted on the campuses and what forbidden – what was 'Islamic food' and what not.

Any students who openly disagreed with the Islamic groups were liable to severe disciplinary action. Boys and girls seen walking together were beaten up. One day in Cairo Univeristy hundreds of members of the Islamic Association suddenly appeared with knives in their hands – all the same pattern of knife, shaped like the horn of a gazelle. A few who were arrested for inflicting wounds with their knives were released on orders from above.

It was clear that the religious students were not simply tolerated by the authorities but actively encouraged by them. No longer content with simply dominating the university campuses, they began to extend their activities outside. They took over some of the big mosques in Cairo, and invited everyone to join them in prayers on the occasion of the principal Islamic festivals. At the Eid el-Adha in 1980 a crowd estimated at 400,000, mostly young men, assembled for prayers in Abdin Square, in front of the presidential palace. A congregation of this size could never be assembled without the connivance of the authorities. So overbearing had the Islamic societies become by the beginning of 1981 that the Socialist Prosecutor went to see Sadat in his winter rest house in Aswan to protest about them. He said their activities had become quite intolerable, and they should be halted before it was too late. Sadat not only brushed aside his complaint but ordered the release of twelve of the students who were then under arrest.

The students were not alone in their religious zeal. Most of those profiteering from the *infitah* policies were equally ardent in an outward show of religion. New mosques were springing up everywhere, endowed by the government or wealthy individuals. In the new luxurious apartment blocks proliferating in Cairo and Alexandria it was common to find that the basement housed a mosque. As mosques enjoyed exemption from taxation, this device secured the builders protection both against demonstrators and against the tax collector.

Consciously or unconsciously the régime seemed determined to put to the test Marx's dictum that religion is the opium of the people. The trouble was that they did not know the sort of religion with which they were dealing. In fact the new strain of Moslem fundamentalism which was being so recklessly encouraged was largely superficial, concentrating on the visible attributes of religion and the letter of the law but ignoring the real lessons of history. This was not an attempt to understand and recover the high ideals of the early days of Islam, as ibn Hanbal and ibn Taimiya had done, but a rough and ready attempt to mask political and social problems beneath the *galabiyeh* and the *chador*. Other strains of fundamentlism were at work elsewhere, unseen and uncontrolled by the authorities. The régime and its backers were creating a monster, and one day, sooner probably than they expected, it was going to turn and rend them.

Part IV

THE COPTIC CHURCH

I shall go softly all my years in the bitterness of my soul.

Isaiah 38:15

I

CHRIST AND CROSS

'It was Egypt who invented eternity.' The speaker was André Malraux, and this epigram was produced in the course of a long conversation which I had with him in Paris in December 1970. There is much truth in it. Certainly the idea of eternity plays a large part in ancient Egyptian literature and art, as anyone with the slightest acquaintance with Egyptian antiquities must have been made aware. Sinners, for example, would be threatened not with physical punishment in the after life but with the 'loss of their eternity'.

The religion of ancient Egypt cannot be regarded as one of the cults, like those of Mithras or the Druids, which have vanished without leaving any significant trace behind them. The beliefs and symbolism of ancient Egypt are particularly close to the beliefs and symbolism of Christianity – the death and resurrection of Osiris, the representations of the mother goddess Isis with her son Horus on her lap, the symbol of life in the form of a cross, all evoke parallels to be found in every Christian church building and every Christian service. Nor is this connection necessarily accidental.

Christianity came early to Egypt, brought there, according to immemorial tradition, by the evangelist St Mark, himself said to have been of Egyptian origin, only a few years after the crucifixion. Tradition also records that it was while on his first visit to Egypt, accompanied by St Peter, that Mark wrote down the Gospel which bears his name. No part of the Roman Empire had therefore more reason to be proud of its Christian origins than Egypt, the land in which the Holy Family had sought refuge from the persecution of Herod.

Christians in Egypt were to face many more persecutions, particularly under the emperors Decius, Valerian and Diocletian in the third and early fourth centuries AD, until Constantine issued his edict of toleration (AD 313). During the early centuries of its existence the Church in Egypt developed in two ways which were to become permanently characteristic of it. The first was monasticism. Almost from the beginning individual Christians had sought a life of solitude and prayer in the desert, but it was Anthony, the son of wealthy Christian parents who, in about the year AD 268, heeding Christ's advice 'go and sell that thou hast, and give to the poor', was to become the father of monasticism. So many enthusiasts followed St Anthony into Nitria (Wadi Natrun), his desert retreat south of Alexandria, that some years later fifty monasteries containing five thousand monks were counted there, as well as the cells of many individual anchorites, so that one Christian writer could boast that the number of monks in Egypt equalled the whole of the rest of the population.

The second characteristic of the Church in Egypt was its close association with the national life of the country. Since its conquest by Augustus (30 BC) Egypt had been a province of the Roman Empire, but its people never forgot that they were heirs to more than two thousand years of independence. Alexandria, at the time of the Roman conquest, was the greatest city in the world, both as regards trade and learning. When Christianity came the Patriarch of Alexandria was in authority at least the equal, and in the eyes of many the superior, to the other patriarchs, those of Jerusalem, Antioch, Rome and Constantinople. With this heritage it is not surprising that the Egyptians should have been bitterly resentful of outside interference, whatever form it might take. They rejected imposed dogmas as much as imposed taxes.

It was the reign of Constantine that was to see the appearance of the greatest of all those who have occupied the partiarchal see of Alexandria. Athanasius was still a young man when in 326 he was elected to succeed Patriarch Alexander, whose secretary he had been. He was to occupy this exalted position for over forty-six years, and to do more than perhaps any other theologian to ensure the doctrinal lines along which Christianity, both of East and West, was to develop. A man of untiring energy, of unshakable faith and dauntless courage, persuasive in speech and writing, his whole career was devoted to combating the heresy of Arius which, by diminishing the divinity of Christ ('there was a time when He was not') destroyed the essential Christian doctrine of the Trinity.

For twenty years of his life Athanasius was in exile or hiding, for six of them, during the reign of Constantine's son and his successor Constantius, a hunted man with a price on his head. But all this time, flying from one refuge in Egypt to another, hidden by peasants and monks, he was never betrayed, though many of his protectors suffered martyrdom on his behalf. Not for the first or the last time the Patriarch of Alexandria became the symbol of Egyptians' resistance to all attempts by non-Egyptians to dictate what they should believe or to whom they should give their allegiance.

When, under the Emperor Theodosius the Great (380-95), Christianity became the official religion of the Empire this brought disadvantages as well as advantages to churchmen. A state religion must find itself liable to state control, and the emperors were anxious to ensure uniformity of belief as well as uniformity of laws. Doctrinal arguments, mainly about the relationship between the divinity and the humanity of Christ, for long distracted the Church. The creed to which Athanasius gave his name has become the symbol of Christian orthodoxy, but a century later at the Council of Chalcedon (451) his successor, the Patriarch Dioscorus, was excommunicated. Because the point of difference on which the split occurred was the single incarnate nature of Christ, God and man, on which Dioscorus would admit no compromise, the Church in Egypt became known as Monophysite, as it is today. This heresy, if heresy it was, became adopted as a badge of nationalism.

> When the news that their Pope had been deposed and excommunicated reached Egypt, the indignation of the nation knew no bounds. With one voice they refused to acknowledge the decision of the Council. If their Pope was excommunicate, they were content to remain excommunicate with him; what he declared to be the true faith, that was enough for them, whatever a Byzantine Emperor or Roman Pope might decree. To them it was a question of national freedom, and the doctrinal question a mere difference of expression, except in so far as the formula which their own Pope had sanctioned became to them a national watchword. The line between the Byzantine residents in Egypt and the native Egyptians became more sharply marked than ever. Those who were proud of their pure Greek descent sided with the Byzantine Church, but the vast majority were still Egyptian in feeling as well as in blood. It became a point of honour, as a true patriot, to reject the decrees of the Council of Chalcedon.[1]

The emperors continued their efforts to bring the refractory province to heel, but without success. Justinian (527-65), who from Byzantium reconquered much of the empire in the West that had been

---

[1] *The Story of the Church of Egypt* by E. L. Butcher. London, 1897, Vol. I, p. 301.

lost by his predecessors, tried in vain to persuade Patriarch Theodosius to adhere to the doctrines of Chalcedon. A rival patriarch was brought to Alexandria with a powerful military escort, but the effort to install him was followed by a riot and massacre. The only lasting result was that henceforward there were to be two rival patriarchs in Egypt, one based in Alexandria and supported by imperial arms, and the other usually to be found in one of the Nitrian monasteries and enjoying the support of the mass of the people. Significantly the imperial Church became known as Melchite, meaning the church of the king, or emperor, while the Coptic Church derives it name from the same root as the word for Egypt.

The year 623 saw the elevation to the patriarchal throne of a man who was to have almost as long, and certainly as stormy, a pontificate as Athanasius. Like Athanasius, Benjamin, belonging to a wealthy family from Farshut, had been secretary to the Patriarch (Andronicus) and nominated by him as his successor. His election took place during the brief interval when Egypt was under Persian rule. He was to see Roman rule restored, but only for an equally brief period, to be finally swept away by the victorious armies of Islam led by Amr ibn el-As.

Benjamin was a zealous and reforming Patriarch, who seems quickly to have won the affection of his people. Their loyalty was soon to be put to a severe test. Heraclius, the Emperor whose remarkable campaigns eventually succeeded in expelling the Persians from Syria and Egypt, formed the worthy design of reconciling the religious differences which had divided Christianity in the East since the Council of Chalcedon by a new formula. Unfortunately, like so many well-intentioned compromises, it only antagonized those it was intended to reconcile. The Copts regarded it

> as treason to their faith and religious independence. It was this last point on which their passion centred. National independence they had never known, and such an ideal can scarcely have entered into their dreams; but for religious independence they had struggled and fought incessantly every since the Council of Chalcedon. That ideal they cherished at all times in their hearts, and for it they were prepared to sacrifice all else whatever. In this lies the key to all their history.[1]

The great mistake Heraclius made was to attempt to force his

---

[1] A. J. Butler, *The Arab Conquest of Egypt*, Oxford, 1902, p. 181.

compromise formula on the Copts through an alien nominee, Cyrus, whom he appointed to the combined offices of Melchite Patriarch and Viceroy. Cyrus made no attempt at an accommodation with Benjamin, and ten years of savage persecution of the Monophysite Copts followed, during which Benjamin, like Athanasius before him, was a fugitive in his own country, for most of the time in Upper Egypt. It was not surprising that when a new conqueror appeared on the scene most Egyptians were prepared to welcome him as a deliverer.

The Prophet Mohamed had died in Medina in June 632. The armies of Islam reached the Syrian capital, Damascus, in September 635, and the Caliph Omar entered Jerusalem in January 638. Little more than a year later Amr ibn el-As and a small force of between three and four thousand horsemen were poised for the conquest of Byzantium's richest province, Egypt.

The Arabs were no strangers to many Egyptians. Nomad tribes of semitic stock were to be found in the deserts surrounding the Nile valley. Reports had been received by the Egyptians that the Arab conquerors of Syria, though inspired by their new religion, were not persecutors. No doubt the story had been received of how the Caliph Omar had prevented one of his attendants from spreading his prayer mat on the floor of the Church of the Holy Sepulchre in Jerusalem, on the grounds that if this was done his followers would want to turn the church into a mosque and so cause grave offence to the Christians. So he prayed outside the church. On their side the Arabs in the invading army regarded Ishmael as their progenitor, and he was the son of Abraham by his Egyptian wife Hagar. Nor could they forget that the mother of the only son born to the Prophet, though he did not live long, had been a Coptic woman, Maria.

All Arab historians agree that the Copts welcomed the Arab armies as deliverers from an intolerable tyranny and were glad to cooperate with them. The sermon which Amr is reported to have preached in the mosque which bears his name on the Friday of Easter week, 644, helps to explain why. 'Go forth with the blessing of God to your cultivated land,' he told his hearers, 'and enjoy its benefits – milk and flocks and herds and game: feed your horses and fatten them, guard them and better them, for they are your defence against the enemy, and through them you gain booty and wealth. And take good care of your neighbours the Copts. Omar, the Commander of the Faithful, told me that he heard the Apostle of God say: "God will open Egypt to you after my death. So take good care of the Copts in that country; for they are your kinsmen and under your protection." '

Although the numbers which took part in the original Arab conquest of Egypt were small, the country was to become Arabized in a surprisingly short time. In the eighth century Arabic became the official language of the state, and subsequently the language of learning and science, replacing Greek. By the eleventh century Arabic had become the vernacular of the great mass of the inhabitants of Egypt, Coptic having retreated to the monasteries. Though church services continued to be in the ancient tongue, the sermon was in Arabic. It is a remarkable fact that, whereas almost a thousand years of Roman and Hellenistic culture had failed to force conformity on the country, within less than four centuries Egypt had become completely Arabized.

As it had been under the Romans and Byzantines, Egypt when part of the empire of the Arabs remained a rich province and therefore a rich prize for whoever governed it. Thus it is not surprising that under the Umayyads there were thirty-one *walis* (governors) of Egypt, or an average of a new *wali* every three years, and under the Abbasids no fewer than seventy-four *walis*, or a new one every year and a half. Many of these simply came to extract what gain for themselves they could from the province, and on numerous occasions the people rose in protest, only to be bloodily suppressed.

All the same, when the Crusaders appeared in the area after five hundred years of Moslem rule and Arabization the Copts showed little inclination to cooperate with their fellow Christians. Partly no doubt this was because they remembered the other conquerers who had come from the northern shores of the Mediterranean, Romans and Greeks, and who had brought them no liberty, but also because the Catholic Crusaders regarded the heretic Monophysites as almost worse offenders than the Moslems. Copts were not allowed any more than Moslems to go on pilgrimage to Jerusalem while the city was in Crusader hands. When, in the course of the Fifth Crusade (1219), Damietta fell into the Crusaders' hands all the small children were bought up by the zealous Bishop of Acre (a Catholic of course) and baptized. And when thirty years later the saintly King Louis IX of France once again captured Damietta, though he was scrupulously correct in his treatment of the Coptic inhabitants, he offended them by appointing a Catholic prelate as Patriarch of the city. A final footnote to the Crusades came in 1365 when King Peter of Cyprus made a successful assault on Alexandria, but his troops were only interested in plunder, looting and murdering Christians as freely as Jews and Moslems. A few years later Peter himself was assassinated and four hundred years were to pass before another intruder from the West appeared off the harbour of Alexandria.

Napoleon landed in Egypt in July 1798. After the battle of the Pyramids and the occupation of Cairo he tried to set up institutions of local government, and in this, like the Mamluks he had defeated, he found it necessary to make use of the Copts as tax collectors. The senior Copt, nominated Intendant General, was Moallem Girges el-Gohary, who also advised on most other matters of administration such as customs and irrigation. A martial Copt was found in the person of a certain General Ya'acub, who formed a Coptic Legion which he put at the service of the French. He became joint commander, with General Desaix, of the force which pursued Murad Bey into Upper Egypt, but his activities were disapproved of by the Patriarch. Ya'acub tried to enter the patriarchate building on horseback, accompanied by some armed troops from the Legion, but his followers would not support him and he was obliged to withdraw. He later married a Frenchwoman and sailed back to France with the remnants of the French army in 1801, but died on the voyage.

Napoleon's invasion brought the winds of change into Egypt. Even before he appeared rumours of the heady new doctrines of equality and nationalism had begun to penetrate the barrier which, in the name of Islam, the Ottomans had erected round their possessions. Now was to begin a period of profound self-questioning among Moslems and Christians alike in most areas of the Sultan's dominions, and nowhere more than in Egypt.

But Napoleon's expedition did more than that; it drew the attention of Europe, and particularly of Britain, to the sea and land routes to India and the Far East. And it drew the attention of a body of men and women who were to play a vital part in Western penetration of the East – the missionaries.

Some British missionaries arrived in Egypt in 1815 but left soon without achieving anything. Forty years later it was the turn of the American Presbyterians, already established in Lebanon and now branching out into Upper Egypt where, as in Lebanon, a long-established Christian community was to be found. Both British and Americans had originally hoped that their mission field would be among the Moslems, but finding conversions there almost impossible turned their attention to more promising opportunities among the Copts.

Unfortunately for it, the Coptic Church in the mid-nineteenth century was in no way equipped to meet the challenge from overseas of new ideas and new men. For centuries the Copts had lived side by side with their Moslem neighbours; sometimes the relationship was easy, sometimes stormy, but all alike regarded themselves as Egyptian – indeed the Copts felt themselves to have a better claim to the name of Egyptian than the rest. In almost all Egyptian villages the same pattern could be seen repeated; the *omdah* (headman) would be a Moslem, and by his side but subordinate to him would be the *sarraf* (tax collector) who would always be a Copt. The *omdah* would fear no rivalry from the *sarraf,* who could never aspire to supplant him.

Not all Copts by any means could read and write. Most priests were ordinary fellahin, working daily barefoot in their fields, opening up on Sundays one room in their house to conduct the ritual of a service which they had learned by heart in a language which they did not understand. Even the patriarch's throne was no more than a rush mat spread on the floor of his dwelling.

The Patriarch Kirollos IV (1854–62) appreciated the dangers facing the Coptic community. Rita Hogg, daughter of one of the American missionaries, John Hogg, wrote a book in which she described how her father tried to persuade Kirollos to lift the ban which he had imposed on foreign missionary activity among the Copts. John Hogg had brought with him to the interview the American Consul-General, to lend weight to his plea, but the Patriarch was firm. He had other ideas for improving the lot of the Copts. He bought a printing press, the first equipped to print books, and had it brought into his church while the congregation sang the hymn 'Ob-Oro', used to greet the entry into the church of some eminent personality. It was an appropriate welcome for the first indication that the Copts were ready to face the challenge.

A story is told of a meeting between Kirollos and another Consul-

General, that of Russia. It was pointed out to the Patriarch that the Orthodox Church, like the Coptic, did not accept the doctrines of Chalcedon. Would it not be appropriate if he were to place his community under the protection of the Czar of all the Russias? Kirollos in reply asked one question – would the Czar die? The Consul answered that, of course, eventually, like all other men, the Czar would die. 'Then,' said Kirollos, 'why should I put myself and my people under the protection of someone who is mortal rather than under the protection of someone immortal?'

2

WINDS OF CHANGE

KIROLLOS was known as the Reformer, not simply because of his printing press but also because of the schools which he opened, for girls as well as boys, in Cairo, and for his rebuilding of the cathedral church in Cairo. He was followed by the Patriarch Demetrius, and after his early death there was an interregnum, during which the Metropolitan of Alexandria, Marcos, acted as Vicar-General.

By now Ismail was Khedive, and the winds from the West were blowing through Egypt with almost gale force. The Copts were as much affected as the Moslems, and for the first time the lay members of the community felt that they ought to play an active part in church affairs. The reformers' original idea was that in every diocese there should be a council consisting of two houses, one of clergy and the other of laymen, the latter being elected for a five-year term by general suffrage and to be charged with supervising the financial and civil affairs of that diocese. This proposal was supported by Marcos, and in 1874 developed into the creation of a new body, sanctioned by law, to be known as the Mejlis Melli (a communal council, such as existed in the Ottoman Empire to look after the domestic affairs of each religious community). This was to be headed by the senior Copt in government employment, who would normally at that time be an under-secretary in one of the ministries.

A year later, in 1875, a new Patriarch was chosen. He was a monk from the monastery of Beheira, where he had become known as Yuhanna the Scribe because he had spent much of his time in copying and preserving ancient manuscripts. He took the name Kirollos V. For a time relations between the Patriarch and the reformers were cordial, but friction eventually arose, partly because of arguments over who should have control of the Church's *waqf* funds (religious endowments). The conflict between an authoritarian Patriarch, resisting what he saw as an illegal challenge to his authority, and the reformers who felt that too much was at stake to be left to the individual control of a single monk, grew increasingly bitter. Butros Ghali Pasha, chairman of the Mejlis Melli, tried to restore peace by calling on the intervention of the Khedive and by forming a new society to be known as the Council for Coptic Conciliation. His efforts were unavailing, and in 1892 the reformers appealed to the new young Khedive, Abbas II, asking for Kirollos to be deposed. The Russian Consul-General made an attempt to mediate, but in vain. One bishop, Athanasius of Sanabu, sided with the reformers, but Kirollos proved too quick for him. He sent the Bishop of Beni Suef to the station to meet Athanasius and greet him with the message that, because he had exceeded his authority and proved disobedient, he had been excommunicated. Athanasius all the same proceeded to the cathedral but found the doors barred against him. However, in spite of the manifest popular backing he enjoyed, Kirollos was for a time exiled to Nitria. It was a Moslem Prime Minister, Riadh Pasha, who protested about this action to the Khedive, pointing out that he had no power to send anybody into exile without an order from the court, let alone a religious leader whose status was comparable to that of the Pope of Rome.

Kirollos V was to return to take his part in the revolt against the British occupiers in 1919. Much had changed for the Copts as a result of the opening up of Egypt under Ismail and the growth of national consciousness culminating in the brief revolt of Orabi Pasha, which in its turn led to the occupation of the country by the British. Increasing wealth and status had enabled some of them to become landowners and they began to occupy many senior posts in the government, particularly in the Ministries of Finance and Irrigation, in Posts and Telegraphs and Railways. Inevitably this aroused some jealousy, but what more than anything else compromised the position of the Copts was the choice made by the British of Butros Ghali Pasha to preside over the court which, in June 1906, tried the villagers accused of attacks on British army officers after the shooting incident at Denshawai in the Delta. The savage sentences passed, including four executions, hard labour and flogging, caused a wave of patriotic indignation and have never been forgotten. In February 1910 Ghali was assassinated by a Moslem nationalist, Ibrahim el-Wardany.

The British authorities tried to make use of the Copts, on the old principle of divide and rule, as did other foreign diplomats and business houses, who tended to regard them as harder-working and more adaptable than the Moslems. Alarmed by the implications of

Ghali's assassination, a General Coptic Congress was convened in Assiut in March 1910 at which an attempt was made to formulate their rights as a minority. This was answered by a Moslem Congress which met in Cairo the following year. The British tried to compensate for Ghali's murder by persuading another leading Copt, Yussef Suleiman Pasha, to accept the premiership, but on the advice of the Patriarch he declined. An approach was later made to yet another leading Copt, Yussef Wahba Pasha, to take over the post, and though the advice of the Patriarch was again negative he accepted. A Coptic nationalist, 'Erian Sa'ad, volunteered to assassinate Wahba, arguing that to avoid the dangers of a communal outburst the deed should be done by someone of the same faith as the renegade. He did in fact throw two bombs at Wahba, who escaped with his life. But he had been sufficiently warned to abandon the idea of becoming Prime Minister.

This was in 1919, when the debate about the form which the Egyptian renaissance should take seemed to have been decided in favour of a unified struggle aimed at the single goal of political independence. Earlier Mustafa Kamel and his National Party had shown clearly that they thought of Egypt as essentially a Moslem country, and as, with the defeat of Turkey at the end of the First World War, the Caliphate was obviously on the verge of collapse, and there was a real possibility that the King of Egypt might inherit the office, the Copts felt themselves threatened. But secular ideas triumphed. The revolution of 1919 proclaimed the unity of Crescent and Cross. The Copts appreciated that British rule was no more than a temporary phenomenon, and that though only one-tenth of the total population it was their destiny to live side by side with their Moslem brothers. The interests of the expanding bourgeoisie, Moslem and Christian alike, united them more than any religious differences could divide them. Both Moslems and Copts felt that such differences as they had were being exploited by the British as a means of retaining their power. They were determined that this attempt should not succeed, and as a demonstration of solidarity sheikhs could be found preaching in Coptic churches and priests giving the Friday sermon in the mosques.

Sa'ad Zaghlul was very conscious of the communal problem, and it is to a great extent thanks to his leadership and to the success of the 1919 revolution that, following it, the problem appeared to have been resolved. In the preparatory discussions from what emerged as the

Constitution of 1923 a subcommittee on minorities was appointed, with both Moslems and Christians represented on it. To its great credit this committee rejected the idea of a fixed proportion of seats for minorities in Parliament, on the grounds that this would tend to emphasize divisions between what were essentially all parts of one nation.

In the Wafd, first under Sa'ad Zaghlul and later under his successor, Mustafa Nahas, many of the leading spirits were Copts, such as Wissa Wassaf and Seynout Hanna. Nahas's deputy, and also the most able Minister of Economics Egypt had produced, Makram Ebeid Pasha, was a Copt. Makram also showed more awareness than any other leading politician at that time of the country's social needs. It was he who, in the middle of the Second World War, declared: 'It is our duty to liberate Egypt from foreign domination, but it is also our duty to liberate the people of Egypt from social slavery.'

So, politically, economically and socially the Copts were becoming integrated in the mainstream of Egyptian life. But inside the Church another picture was emerging.

3

A NEW GENERATION

AT THE BEGINNING of this century there was a certain official in the patriarchate by the name of Habib Girgis. His special concern was education, but his interests ranged far and wide over every aspect of the community's life. He was very conscious both of the Coptic Church's inheritance and of the challenges now facing it, from foreign missionaries, from secularism, and from the Islamic element in political movements like Mustafa Kamel's National Party. He was the author of many books and pamphlets, in one of which he wrote, 'We, as Copts, ought to be proud of the leading part which we have played in the development of Christianity. If one of us was to go, for example, to Finland he would find that Christianity had only been introduced there in the eleventh century, whereas it has been here from the very earliest times. We helped to form the fundamental tenets of the Church.' Girgis was the first to use the expression 'the Coptic nation', meaning by that something much wider than the Church and its members. He also started a campaign to revive the use of the Coptic language. In some ways his efforts on behalf of his fellow-religionists were parallel to the re-examination of the place of Islam in society which was simultaneously being carried out by Jamal el-Afghani and Mohamed Abduh.

When Girgis contemplated the condition of the Coptic Church he was acutely conscious of its shortcomings. In theory its structure was as it always had been. The archpriest (*kummus*) in the church conducted the services, helped by assistant priests (*kasees*) and by deacons (*shemmas*). The latter were supposed to be occupied full-time in Church work, but owing to lack of funds were more often part-time volunteers. The country was divided into dioceses, the boundaries of which were fixed by the Holy Synod. Each diocese was presided over by a bishop (*uskuf*) who was invariably drawn from among the monks and was therefore unmarried (deacons and priests were allowed to marry). The Holy Synod was composed of the bishops and of the heads of the principal monasteries. It was the Holy Synod which elected the supreme head of the Church, the Patriarch.

Such was the theory, but the practical state of the Church left much to be desired. As has already been mentioned, the village priest was usually still an illiterate fellah who recited the liturgy in a language which neither he nor his congregation could understand. Such education as there was was left to an *areef* who would instruct a few boys in the traditional prayers and hymns. The *areef* would receive payment for his services in kind – perhaps a chicken or some eggs or dates in season.

But times were changing. British and American missionaries had built hospitals and orphanages. Of wider impact was the introduction of Bibles from Lebanon. These were in Arabic and were hawked around Assiut, the main centre of Christian population, on donkeys and handcarts for as little as half a piastre (about a halfpenny). There was more printed material which the missionaries were zealous to distribute, and their efforts met with a fair measure of success, some Copts being converted to various Protestant denominations or to Catholicism (for the Catholic missions were active too).

Some attempt at self-help was made with the creation of an association which called itself 'Friends of the Holy Book', but Girgis showed much more enterprise. Thanks largely to his initiative, a theological college (Madrasa el-Eklerikiyeh) was founded in 1910, catering mainly in the first instance for the sons of priests, who might be expected to have at least some grounding in religious matters. To begin with the only qualification needed was primary schooling, but Girgis later amended this so that candidates had to have passed their baccalaureate. After his death the college received the status of a university.

Girgis was also instrumental in getting Sunday Schools started. The idea was a Western one, but its application in Egypt was to do much to preserve the Coptic Church from being overwhelmed by Western proselytizers. American Protestants had in fact introduced Sunday Schools at their missions in Upper Egypt. Now, thanks to Girgis, boys in Coptic churches could be taken away from the main service to another room, usually a basement, where they would be taught the Bible and the history and traditions of their Church. Indeed, the combined effect of the theological college and the Sunday Schools was to create what amounted almost to a cultural renaissance among the

Copts, and, as is so often the case, it became a cultural renaissance with political overtones.

The first generation from the college and schools emerged in the 1930s and early 1940s. This was a time when the young everywhere were eagerly seeking political solutions to pressing social problems, and when extreme movements such as the Moslem Brotherhood attracted many. But though some Copts joined the small Egyptian Communist Party, or formed Trotskyist cells, of much more significance was a development which came rather later, at the end of the Second World War, and which was virtually without a parallel elsewhere – university graduates, from the faculty of engineering as well as from those of law, philosophy and literature, began presenting themselves to the monasteries and asking to be received as postulants. Their reasoning was logical. The Church was still the main element in the life of the Coptic community. Control of Church affairs was in the hands of monks who, either as heads of monasteries or as bishops, made up the Holy Synod. Power in the Church, and so power in the community, lay through the monasteries.

Then, in July 1952, came the revolution. To begin with its advent was welcomed as much by Copts as by Moslems. True, there were many wealthy Coptic landowners who, like everyone else associated with the *ancien régime*, had reason to feel themselves threatened. But their numbers were relatively small. The mass of the people, whatever their religion, had been exploited and not exploiters. But then came doubts. Copts could not help remarking that they were not represented in the Revolutionary Command Council, which had become in effect the government of the country. True, nobody could expect an underground movement to operate a *numerus clausus*, and in any case Coptic officers, coming from a minority, would have been extremely reluctant to involve themselves in any clandestine activity. But, as all the old political parties were now banned – and in some of these, notably the Wafd, Copts had been prominent – there was a sense of deprivation.

After a time the revolutionary leaders tried to make amends by appointing Copts as Ministers, but the men chosen, though admirably qualified for the posts they were to fill, were in all cases technocrats, without any particular standing among their fellow-religionists. The Patriarch and other community leaders tried to use these new men as a channel of communication with the government, but they were very conscious that it was not like the old days. These were bureaucrats chosen by the Revolutionary Command Council because of their specialized qualifications, not men who had risen to prominence through services rendered to the community.

Land reform and nationalization followed, which together broke the power of the upper Egyptian bourgeoisie. The Copts were hit particularly hard, because in several sectors of business and commerce they had come to be disproportionately well represented. In foreign policy the new régime gave first priority to the encouragement of Arab nationalism and Arab unity, and though the Copts, like the Maronites in Lebanon, subscribed to these ideals with genuine enthusiasm they could not but be aware that there was a distinct Islamic element in both of them. With business opportunities severely curtailed, and political activity reduced almost to zero, the Copts began to contemplate the future with anxiety. The only field for their activities seemed once again to be the Church.

⁂ 4 ⁂

A CHURCH AT LARGE

IN THE LATE 1940s a secret organization which called itself 'The Movement of the Coptic Nation' was founded. This was an extreme group, with ideas about autonomy for the Copts, as its name implies. In 1954 a certain Ibrahim Hillal, who belonged to the movement, thirty-four years of age, went with five of his followers in the early hours of the morning to the partriarchal headquarters in Sharia Clot Bey in Cairo. They were armed, and forced their way inside, the Patriarch's attendants being too astonished to offer any resistance. Entering the Patriarch's bedroom, they presented him with two documents which, at gunpoint, they insisted on his signing. One was an act of abdication, and the other an order convening the Synod and ordering it to prepare for the election of a new Patriarch under new rules. Having extracted signatures from the totally bewildered Patriarch they cut the telephone wires and carried their victim off with them to one of the monasteries in Wadi Natrun. It was still early in the morning when the monks were roused by a violent knocking at the gate of the monastery, and when they saw the figure of the Patriarch they assumed that he had come to pay them a surprise visit. However, it quickly became obvious that he came as a prisoner. Back in Cairo the kidnappers circulated copies of the documents they had compelled the Patriarch to sign. But the whole affair was too absurd to have any chance of success. The government intervened, the kidnappers were arrested, and the Patriarch released and reinstated.

In the 1950s many young Copts began leaving Egypt, most of them seeking a new life in the United States, Canada, or Australia where Christians with good professional qualifications found a ready welcome. Some members of the wealthier Coptic families sought a refuge for themselves and for their money in Switzerland. One result of this emigration was that branches of the Coptic Church were formed overseas, still in touch with the Mother Church in Egypt, sending financial aid back to it and, not surprisingly, expecting to have some influence in its affairs. They also began to act as an indirect pressure group on the Egyptian government, being very vocal in their complaints about anything they regarded as discrimination against their fellow-religionists back home.

These developments coincided with increasing attention being paid in the West, particularly in America, towards Churches in other parts of the world. The World Council of Churches was formed in 1948, in the early days of the Cold War, and reflected the belief held by many that religion could be made to play a useful part in the struggle against what, with increasing frequency, was being referred to as 'atheistical Communism'. It was not inappropriate that at the inaugural meeting of the Council in The Hague one of the Presidents chosen should have been John Foster Dulles. It was Dulles who was later responsible for the maxim that 'to preach Christianity is to preach Western civilization', and it has now come out in Congress that the Council received financial support from the CIA, the head of which was at this time Dulles's brother, Alan.

The new head of the Coptic Church was Kirollos VI, who was elected in 1959. He had been backed by the young university graduates who had chosen to become monks, because whereas most of the other monasteries had refused to accept such unusual postulants he had been shrewd enough to welcome them. Now he had his reward. But these young militants had nothing in common with the official representatives of the Coptic community, the bureaucrats who had been promoted to senior positions in the government. Indeed, one of these officials described the militants as 'our Moslem Brotherhood'. After the attempt on Nasser's life in 1954 the Moslem Brotherhood was banned, and the Movement of the Coptic Nation was banned at about the same time following the attempt to kidnap the Patriarch.

However, Nasser and Kirollos VI got on well together. They admired each other, and it was well known that the Patriarch could come and see Nasser whenever he liked. Kirollos, always anxious to avoid a confrontation, made use of this friendship to resolve any problems facing the community. One such thorny problem concerned the building of new churches. This was a matter still governed by the old Ottoman rescript which was based on the principle that religions other than Islam might be permitted to exist but not to expand. But, in spite of emigration, the Copts were increasing in number and new churches were needed. Obtaining permission to build them was a long and complicated process, the applicants encountering perhaps more than the usual bureaucratic delays. So some more adventurous spirits tried to find ways of circumventing the regulations. Some trustworthy member of the community would buy a piece of land, on the perimeter of which shops would be erected. In the centre a room would be built to serve as a school, and on Sundays there would be a Sunday School and a sermon preached. Then one night an altar, a cross, a chalice and the rest would be smuggled in, and the new church would be a *fait accompli*. But then the police would get to hear of it, declare that the law had been broken, and the trouble would start.

It was understandably humiliating for the Patriarch to find that any applications for building permits he made got lost in the labyrinth of the Ministry of Interior. So he approached Nasser on the subject. Nasser was sympathetic, and asked how many new churches the Patriarch thought he needed. The answer was between twenty and thirty a year. Right, said Nasser, and immediately gave him permission to build twenty-five new churches a year.

Another problem concerned the building of a new cathedral. This was something very close to the Patriarch's heart, but he did not want to look abroad for the finance for it. Nor did he like to approach Nasser directly on the matter, because he did not see how the government could reasonably be expected to intervene. Little financial support was forthcoming from the local community now that there were no longer a few rich Coptic families ready to foot the bill, and the big monasteries had lost most of their estates under the land reform. The new overseas communities were not yet in a position to be generous. So the Patriarch asked me for my advice. I spoke to Nasser, who decided that the government would contribute £E500,000 towards the new cathedral, half to be paid in cash and the other half in the form of work to be done by contracting companies in the public sector. So the cathedral was built, and Nasser attended the service of its dedication. He felt it appropriate that the Church of St Mark should be worthily housed. Nasser was also able to help the community when it came to elections for the Socialist Union, the only permitted political organization. Not enough Copts were returned in the constituency voting, but the President had the right to nominate ten members of the Assembly, and a majority of those he nominated were Copts (to have chosen all Copts would have been a bit too obvious).

By now the new activists in the Church were pressing the Patriarch for some return for the support which they had given him and which had helped to secure his election. They wanted bishoprics, and thereby a voice in the Holy Synod. But episcopal vacancies do not occur every day, and so the Patriarch took the significant step of appointing new bishops, for the first time without territorial dioceses. This reflected the increasing sophistication of the Coptic Church and its contacts abroad as well as the ambitions of individual members of it.

Three of these new bishops at large were of particular note and destined to play important roles in the affairs of the Coptic Church. The first was Sa'ad Aziz, who took the name Bishop Samweel. He was made responsible for relations with other Churches – the Vatican, Canterbury and so on, and of course the World Council of Churches – as well as with Coptic Churches in other parts of the world. He was in effect the Coptic Church's Minister for Foreign Affairs.

Bishop Samweel was also responsible for the Church's finances, and in the 1970s he showed considerable skill in fostering its fortunes and the fortunes of individuals in it. Some of the old well-to-do families found new opportunities thanks to the policy of *infitah* and it was through Bishop Samweel that some of them became managers of the local branches of the American and German banks and other Western companies. After Bishop Samweel had been killed while on the reviewing stand with Sadat on 6 October it was found that he had £11 million (sterling) on deposit in a Swiss bank account. He left a will which stated that all this money belonged to the Church, and that none of it belonged to his own family.

Another of the new bishops was Anba Gregorius, born Waheeb Atalla. He had a doctorate in philology and was put in charge of scientific research. He also created a Higher Institute for Coptic Studies, and set up a committee charged with editing a complete Bible and preparing a Coptic Encyclopaedia. This committee has an endowment of several million pounds. Together with an assistant called Muftah, Atalla has been active in an attempt to record for posterity all the hymns and liturgies of the Coptic Church.

A third bishop at large was Anba Shenouda, born Nazeer Gayyed. Before becoming a monk he had been a journalist and a poet. He was made responsible for education, and so was in charge of the Sunday Schools and the theological colleges. He started the practice of giving once a week in the cathedral what was called the 'lesson of Friday' (*dars el-guma'a*), reminiscent of the 'lesson of Tuesday' which Hassan el-Banna used to give when he was Guide of the Moslem Brotherhood. This proved enormously popular and was normally attended by as many as ten thousand people. Shenouda became the idol of the Coptic youth. But one of the new bishops preferred to stay in his monastery. This was a young man called Yussef Iskander, who took the name Matta el-Miskeen.

Kirollos was growing old, and though he had originally welcomed and indeed encouraged the new men and their new ideas, the pace of developments began to alarm him. He felt that Sunday Schools and theological colleges were becoming increasingly political, and so he told Shenouda to stop his Friday lessons and go back to his monastery in Wadi Natrun. But this provoked so much opposition that he was obliged to let Shenouda return to Cairo.

Kirollos also quarrelled with Bishop Matta el-Miskeen, who was turning his monastery of Abu Makkar near Alexandria into a huge agricultural enterprise. (Kirollos said he ought not to be called Miskeen, which means poor, but Miskoon, which means possessed.) Large amounts of WCC money were coming into the Middle East from Europe, particularly from West Germany, and much of this found its way to Bishop Matta who was importing Friesian cattle by air. Kirollos ordered him to leave his monastery and retire to the desert, which he did, but thanks to the intervention of a special envoy sent by the Vatican the quarrel was patched up and Miskeen allowed to return to his monastery.

But the dispute was not simply between the older Patriarch and the young militant bishops. There were deep divisions among the bishops themselves. One school, led by Shenouda, argued that the Church was an all-embracing institution which could provide a solution to all problems and an answer to all questions, temporal as well as spiritual. The other school, represented by Miskeen, insisted that religion was essentially a matter for the individual conscience, and should have nothing to do with politics. It was, in fact, the argument which has divided churchmen of all denominations and all ages. But as Shenouda was still responsible for education he was able to organize classes not only for young men, but also for young women and even for children and church servants, in which not only was the Bible studied but discussions were held on social problems of every description, such as the role of the family, relations between the classes and so on. And then , in 1971, Kirollos died.

5

MILITANT MONK

In Nasser's time, when the technicians who had been given ministerial appointments were the official representatives of the Coptic community, a new regulation had been adopted that the Patriarch must be over forty years of age. This was aimed at preventing the election of one of the new generation of militant monks, but time had passed, and now most of these young men had reached the qualifying age. So the election of a new Patriarch was going to present problems.

The method of election had been changed, so that now it was by the Holy Synod, but with the aid of the Divine Will. The names of the three candidates enjoying most support in the Synod would be written on pieces of paper, which would then be put into a box and the box placed in a darkened room. A child would be brought into the room and told to withdraw one piece of paper from the box, and the name on that piece of paper would be that of the new Patriarch. God, through the agency of an innocent child, would have spoken. One dignitary, Anba Gregorius, had argued, at the time that the new regulation was being debated, that this made the field too narrow. It was possible, he said, that God would not approve of any of the names submitted, and a fourth piece of paper, left blank, should be added to allow for His disapproval to be made manifest. But this objection was over-ruled.

Quite by chance I happened to take part in a discussion about the approaching election which took place in President Sadat's house in Giza shortly after the death of Kirollos. Also present, besides President Sadat, were the then Minister of Interior, Mamduh Salem, and the Deputy Prime Minister, Mohamed Abdel Salam el-Zayyat, a man with an excellent legal mind and very close to the President (though this did not prevent his being arrested, with so many others, in September 1981). There were two main contenders for the patriarchal post, reflecting the main divisions in the Church at that time. One was an elderly monk of the old school, and the other Anba Shenouda.

Most of the discussion was between the President and the Minister of the Interior, but when I was asked what I thought I suggested that it would be better to go for the older man, on the grounds that if there was any trouble a man of seventy-five (which was his age) was unlikely to be around for long, whereas a man in his forties was probably going to be in office for quite a time. But Mamduh Salem was definite. 'I can guarantee Shenouda,' he said, 'but I can't guarantee the older man.' Sadat accepted this argument, and when the piece of paper was drawn from the box in the darkened room Shenouda's name was found to be on it.

Sadat knew little about the man with whom he was going to have to deal. Shenouda was the outstanding representative of the new generation of militant monks, determined to change the Church from an isolated and backward institution into something more in tune with the contemporary world. In this endeavour he was now able to call on moral and material support from the outside world, and this gave him a certain freedom of action vis-à-vis the government which his predecessors had not enjoyed. Shenouda had a colourful personality and a varied experience, both secular and religious; as well as spending twelve years in a monastery he had been a member of the press syndicate. He was capable of proving a formidable opponent.

It was not long before Sadat was made to realize this. Only six months after the new Patriarch's election Church and state came into conflict. A new church had come into being in the Cairo suburb of Khanka in the manner already described – the land bought, the surrounding shops erected, the central room serving first as a school and then by degrees converted into a church. The police moved in and knocked the church down. The day after this had happened Shenouda ordered bishops and priests to go to the ruins of the church and celebrate mass there, even if they risked being shot at and killed. The police tried to stop them, and there was a struggle.

Sadat was dismayed to find that the man he had regarded as his own nominee was prepared for such an open challenge. He determined to have a showdown. He rang me up in my office at *Al Ahram* to tell me he was proposing to go to Parliament and bring the business of the Church into the open. 'I am not going to take any more,' he said. 'The man Shenouda has gone beyond everything. I can't carry on with this time-bomb ticking away underneath me.' This was of course at a time before the October War when what was seen as Sadat's procrastination laid him open to a great deal of criticism, so that his position in the country was difficult. But I told him that I didn't think the right way to deal with the Coptic problem was through confrontation and asked if I could come and see him about it.

When we met I explained to him the arrangement about the construction of new churches which had been arranged between Nasser and Kirollos and told him I was afraid that, probably owing to obstruction on the part of some bureaucrats, this had been allowed to lapse. I told him I feared that if there was a head-on collision we risked opening Egypt to a sort of communal strife that had been seen in Lebanon. Sadat was still extremely angry and wanted to go to Parliament and, as he put it, 'open the wound', in other words, make a direct attack on the leadership of the Coptic Church. I suggested that it would be better to make it the subject of a parliamentary inquiry. He could send a letter to Parliament explaining what had happened, emphasizing that such incidents threatened the unity of the nation, and asking Parliament to consider what, with the best interest of the whole nation in mind, it thought should be done. I also suggested that a committee of Parliament might be set up to look into the matter. Sadat gradually calmed down and agreed to my proposal. A letter was duly sent to Parliament, and a committee was appointed under the chairmanship of Dr Gamal Oteifi, one of the Deputy Speakers of the House.

Oteifi was also legal adviser to *Al Ahram*, and he mentioned his work on the committee to me. I told him I thought the best outcome of its deliberations would be for it to report that after a full investigation it had not been found possible to allocate blame for what had happened to any particular person or persons and that the problem clearly needed the attention of the one man who was responsible for the unity of the nation and the guardian of national values. This was in fact the form which the committee's report took, and when he had got it Sadat telephoned me to say 'Mohamed! They have simply returned the ball to me!' I said I thought this was as it should be, and went round to see him. I told him that in my opinion the heart of the problem was the question of new churches, and suggested that a return should be made to the Nasser–Kirollos formula. If Shenouda was enabled to establish a certain number of new churches each year it would enhance his position and make him feel he really was the effective head of the Church. Sadat asked how many new churches Nasser had allowed

Kirollos, and when I told him twenty-five he said he thought this was much too high a figure.

Feelings at this time were running high among Moslems as well as Christians, so it was decided that the President should go to Al-Azhar to meet the *ulema* and to the patriarchate to meet Pope Shenouda and the Synod, and that his message to both of them should be that what the country most stood in need of was schools and hospitals, and that if there had to be any rivalry between them both religions should compete in the building of these. He would remind his audiences that the country was still preparing for war, so that national unity was more than ever essential.

So Sadat went first of all to Al-Azhar, where he had a cordial discussion with the *ulema*. Then he went to the old patriarchate building where he met Shenouda and the Synod. He had expected to find their attitude reserved, if not actively hostile, but was delighted to be greeted by them as 'father of his people' and in other complimentary terms. However, no doubt to reassure the Moslems that this was indeed the 'pious President', he made a point of observing the noon prayer while he was in the patriarchal chamber, and of being photographed doing so, with his astonished hosts in the background. I saw Sadat on his return from this visit and asked him how it had gone. 'Excellently,' he said. 'I told him he could have fifty new churches a year!'

Shenouda was not appeased by this gesture, and he had an opportunity to capitalize on the new overseas Coptic community when he was invited to visit the United States and Canada in April 1977. This was just a month after Sadat had gone to Washington for his first meeting with President Carter. Shenouda arrived in New York on 14 April, and was greeted by a big demonstration. He was due to go on to Washington and was invited to the White House – an invitation which he was naturally eager to accept, but he insisted that he should be accompanied on this occasion by the Egyptian Ambassador. Bishop Samweel came along too.

The first visit to America by a reigning Coptic Patriarch received, as was to be expected, a great deal of publicity, and the White House meeting set the seal on it. Carter told Shenouda that he had heard a lot about him from President Sadat, who had spoken very highly of him. They then discussed the history and observances of the Coptic Church, particularly the Flight into Egypt by the Holy Family and,

Carter being himself a Baptist, the baptismal ceremonies of the Copts. Shenouda presented Carter with an icon made by a modern Egyptian artist containing three panels portraying the virgin and child, the baptism of Christ and the resurrection. In accepting the gift Carter said he would be happy to pass on the information he had received about baptism in the Coptic Church to members of his own Church. Carter asked Shenouda about Jerusalem, knowing that the Coptic Church had its own views about the problem. According to the account published in the official Church magazine, *Al-Karaza*, after the meeting Shenouda's reply was that the Jews could not be regarded as a people specially chosen by God, because this would mean that the Christians had not been so chosen. 'As for political questions,' he said, 'we only talk about general principles, and leave details to the politicians.'

After this exchange of courtesies representatives of the press and television were admitted, and Carter told them, 'I am glad to introduce to you the leader of the seven million Copts in Egypt.' This was something of a bombshell because the latest quinquennial census in Egypt had given the number of Copts as two million out of a total population of forty-one million, and while this estimate was certainly too low the figure produced by Carter was no less certainly too high. However, for many Copts a figure which had received the *imprimatur* of an American President must be correct – he had probably got it by satellite.

Part V
GATHERING STORMS

I am a millionaire. That is my religion.

G. B. Shaw *Major Barbara*

I

THE ILLUSION OF POWER

BY THE BEGINNING OF 1981 Sadat was an isolated man. He was isolated in his own country, and he had isolated Egypt from the rest of the Arab world. It was a strange and tragic paradox that just at the moment when the Arab world as a whole had become more important – economically, politically and strategically – than ever before, Egypt should have opted out of it. Over the past generation Egypt had devoted much of its energies in the cause of other Arab countries, assisting them to achieve their independence, to gain the recognition due to them, and to obtain control over their own resources, particularly their own oil. Even the Yemen war, so often criticized as a blunder, did have the effect of causing the winds of change to blow through the Arabian peninsula. It was directly responsible for the abdication of King Saud and his replacement by his brother, King Feisal, who tried to convert Saudi Arabia from being the private fief of one family into a properly organized state.

Geography has dictated that Egypt must always be a regional power. Some countries – America, Russia, China – are really continents and so can be self-sufficient. But Egypt, because of its large and concentrated population, its pioneering struggle for independence first from the Ottomans and then from the British, its leadership in education and the arts, must be the centre of the region in which geography has placed her, or be nothing.[1] The Russians realized this, which is why they devoted to Egypt so much of their time and treasure. The Americans realized it too. But Sadat turned his back on the Arabs whose help he needed, staking all on the friendship of the Americans.

[1] When the Arab League was founded in 1945 not only was it unanimously agreed that the League's headquarters should be in Cairo and its Secretary-General an Egyptian, but Egypt contributed 37 per cent of the League's budget.

Even in financial terms this was a poor exchange. Before the Jerusalem journey of 1977, America had been giving Egypt aid to the amount of $1,000 million a year, but four years later this figure had not been increased in spite of inflation and the falling value of the dollar. By comparison the wealthy Gulf states had, since terminating their contributions to Egypt, given Iraq no less than $22,000 million to help to finance the war with Iran – a sum which was almost exactly equivalent to the total of Egypt's external debt; Egypt of course having received from the same source in the meanwhile only a trickle.

True, Egypt had had other sources of revenue – from oil and from remittances from Egyptians living and working abroad. But Egypt's limited oil deposits are a capital asset which cannot be replenished, while the position of Egyptians in other Arab countries was jeopardized by the hostility Sadat's policies had aroused everywhere.

Even at his own valuation, as the architect of an overall peace settlement for the Middle East, Sadat had by now been proved ineffective. It was already apparent that Begin had not the slightest intention that the autonomy promised the Palestinians by the Camp David agreements should have any real meaning. On the contrary, the West Bank was to be Israel's reward for handing back Sinai. Nor had Egypt been able to prevent Israel's annexation of Jerusalem. Israel's creeping annexation of the West Bank meant that Egypt's vital link with Arab Asia was being irrevocably cut.

It is often said that Sadat had at least for the first time given Western public opinion a proper understanding of the Arab world and its problems. That is unfortunately not true. What the West was watching was the performance of a superstar; the public in the West appreciated the posture of one man, not the problems of millions. Nor was there any realization of the price at which superstardom had been bought. There is a story told of Helmuth von Moltke, brought by the Sultan to train the Turkish army before the 1914 war. He saw a Turkish officer on manoeuvres giving some extraordinary orders and called him over: 'Who do you want to get your medals from?' he asked the officer. 'From your own people or from the other side?' It is always important to watch where the medals are coming from. It is not the mark of a good general to capture a new position at the cost of losing his own base.

* * *

Sadat could not admit to himself that the 'initiative' gamble had failed – that he had staked everything and lost. So once again he took flight into a world of illusion. He became increasingly restless, travelling continually around the country, usually by helicopter, which encouraged the sense of unreality. From a helicopter Egypt looks so calm and prosperous – the lush green fields, the compact villages, the spreading towns, all strung along the blue ribbon of Nile water. But the real Egypt and the real Egyptians can only be known by someone who is prepared to move among them; and this Sadat no longer did.

The daily routine which Sadat now followed seemed almost designed to insulate him from the harsh realities of the world outside. He usually woke late, between 9.00 and 9.30, and on waking would be given a spoonful of mixed honey and royal jelly and a cup of tea. He would read the papers in bed, paying particular attention to all the items concerning himself. Then came massage from his personal masseur,[1] some physical exercises and a bath. This would be followed by a light breakfast, consisting probably of a piece of cheese and some calorie-free toast (all his cereal requirements were made from calorie-free flour imported from Switzerland – even his sweet pastry *kunafa)*.

Sadat had found that vodka was a helpful stimulant, besides having the advantage of being not only colourless but, as he believed, odourless. Two or three vodkas would be taken, so that by 12.00 or 12.30 he was ready for the day's interviews and appointments. After a couple of hours of this he would be complaining of the burden of business ('They are killing me with work'), and would adjourn with a friend for perhaps some more vodka, followed by a light lunch of cold chicken or meat and salad. At about 4.30 he would retire to bed and sleep soundly till 7.00 or 7.30, when he would wake hungry. A mint tea would be followed by dinner, consisting of perhaps grilled meat and calorie-free macaroni. Then there would be talks with some officials or telephone conversations with foreign politicians and Cairo editors. At around 9.00 he would ask to be given a list of films that were available (all films brought into Egypt from abroad as well as all Egyptian films were sent to the President before being passed to the

---

[1] His masseur travelled everywhere as part of the presidential entourage. An Egyptian ambassador, on one of the President's European tours, was surprised to find that the unknown personage seated next to him at dinner was the President's masseur.

censor), and by 10.00 he would be watching the first film in his private cinema. Before midnight there would be a nightcap of whisky and a second film, but during this he would begin to doze off, though encouraging his guests to sit up with him until well after midnight. And so to bed.

Sadat was capable of making a virtue of his isolation. When he had to make a decision there would be reports in the papers that the President was going into retreat, to the Barrage or to Mit abu el-Kom, 'to ponder the problem' – as if the right decision was more likely to be brought by a messenger from heaven than by consultation with the presidential advisers. His only contacts outside the small circle of his cronies came when he attended official receptions, when he would be applauded by the specially invited guests. He began to believe the figures of the plebiscite results, insisting that 99 per cent of Egyptians supported him and that there were not more than five thousand 'renegades' in the country, though he must have known as well as everybody else that the plebiscite returns were filled in by the village *omdahs* without bothering about the formality of counting votes.

Because of his restlessness there was a need for yet more presidential residences. As soon as the first stage of the evacuation of Sinai was completed he built a new rest house for himself at Wadi Raha, the valley at the foot of Mount Sinai where Moses is supposed to have rested after the crossing of the Red Sea. Another rest house had been built on the beach at Mersa Matruh in the western desert, but now this was not enough. He cast a longing eye over the palace where King Farouk had spent his last night in Egypt, Muntazah Palace. (The four royal palaces, Abdin and Kubba in Cairo, and Muntazah and Ras el-Tin in Alexandria, had been taken over after the revolution but used only for state functions, and never lived in.) Now Sadat said he thought Muntazah Palace should be turned into a guest house for the many important foreign visitors who could be expected to arrive. It was to be restored exactly as it had been when it was built in the nineteenth century, but with the most modern kitchens and bathrooms. This was done, at the cost of £E7 million – and at a time when many of the most notable monuments in Egypt were collapsing because of lack of funds to keep them up. Then Sadat decided that the palace was not after all to be a guest house but his office when in Alexandria. As he never had any time for office work wherever he was, this was another illusion. In fact he used the restored Muntazah Palace as an office for exactly one hour of one day.

All this movement created a logistic nightmare. The presidential guard now consisted of a brigade of special troops, equipped with tanks and armoured cars and the most up-to-date communications systems. One battalion had to follow him wherever he went – one day to his old house in Giza, the next day to the Barrage, then to Mit Abu el-Kom and Bourg el-Arab, and so on. He himself travelled by helicopter, but for reasons of security, so that nobody should know which actually contained the President, there always had to be three of them. So three of the five Westland helicopters that Egypt had bought were consecrated to the President's personal use.

Sadat found a new use for another of the palaces, Kubba Palace in Cairo being turned over to the exiled Shah of Iran as a permament residence. From the outset the Iranian Revolution had found no more vehement or consistent opponent than Sadat, in spite of the fact that, whatever might be thought of Khomeini, it was clear the Iranian people had rejected the Shah and that Iran was going to remain an extremely important Middle Eastern country whoever ruled it. But Sadat actually interrupted the Camp David negotiations to telephone his support for the Peacock Throne, and when that throne had collapsed, and the Americans and the Iranian Court were trying to pretend that the Shah was simply leaving his country for a series of state visits and not into permanent exile, Sadat was the only one who was prepared to take part in the charade. (King Hussein refused.) A crowd was assembled to cheer the Shah and the Empress when they arrived in Aswan, and after they had been moved on from Morocco and Mexico and become stateless fugitives, Sadat offered them asylum in Egypt. This was applauded in the West as an act of great generosity, particularly by those countries like America and Britain which had all along been the Shah's staunchest supporters but which had no intention of letting humanity get in the way of the interests of the state. They had no welcome for the exiles, only for the gesture which relieved them of responsibility for doing something for their former friends. It was, of course, no more in Egypt's interest than it was in America's or Britain's to provide asylum, but Sadat saw himself as the embodiment of the state, so his friends must be Egypt's. When the Shah's illness reached its terminal stage it was President Sadat in person who gave to the press the daily bulletins on the state of the ex-monarch's health, and when he died it was Sadat who over-ruled the wishes of the Empress, who wanted a private burial, and insisted on a state funeral to which numerous heads of state and other VIPs were invited, though few, apart from ex-King Constantine of Greece and ex-President Nixon, turned up.

L'état c'est moi. Sadat became increasingly possessive in his references to Egypt; now it was always 'my people, my army, my navy'. But he failed to appreciate that the head of a state can only truly speak in the name of his people in so far as he expresses their legitimate interests and aspirations. If the people he is supposed to lead do not follow he has lost the right to call himself their leader. This was not how Sadat saw it. If anyone criticized him, they were insulting Egypt, and this applied to foreigners as much as to Egyptians. When no other Arab government showed any signs of following the lead he had given by his journey to Jerusalem and Camp David he dismissed them all as of no account – 'pygmies'. He even thought fit to attack King Hussein as the grandson of King Abdullah, but, as King Hussein said to me with his usual courteous restraint: 'It is a little hard for Sadat to denounce my grandfather for his reported contacts with the Zionists when he himself has signed a separate peace with Israel.'

Those now engaged, as they thought, in practical negotiations with Sadat often found the rarified atmosphere in which he moved difficult to cope with. Ezer (or Ezra, as Sadat always called him) Weizmann on one occasion, when trying to discuss specific concrete issues, felt obliged to remind him: 'Mr President, even the men who went to the moon came back' – a reference to the flattering comparison frequently made between the Jerusalem journey and the first moon landing.

Sadat had many new friends besides the Shah of Iran and Ezer Weizmann. There was 'my friend Giscard', 'my friend Schmidt', 'my friends Nixon, Ford, Carter', 'my friend Onassis'. And there were other new friends who, like the Shah, found themselves enjoying Sadat's, and thereby Egypt's generous hospitality. One such was Elizabeth Taylor, preceded by a telegram from her then husband, a senator for Virginia, asking that she should not be the recipient of any gifts 'which would embarrass me'. Nevertheless, the President was there to welcome her when she landed at Ismailia. 'Welcome, Queen!' was his greeting when they met. Elizabeth Taylor's somewhat blank look showed that an explanation was needed. 'Have you forgotten? You are Cleopatra – the Queen of Egypt!' As befitting her royal rank one of the presidential helicopters was placed at her disposal for the duration of her stay in her dominion, and the presidential guard was made responsible for security. 'My God,' said one of the officers on duty at her hotel. 'What are we doing here, guarding an actress?'

Nor was Elizabeth Taylor the only representative of the world of entertainment to be honoured. Frank Sinatra sang at the foot of the Pyramids before a party of four hundred wealthy tourists flown in from the West and prominent Egyptians, but to the outrage of most Egyptians this was followed by a private party in the President's house for a few selected guests on 28 September, the anniversary of Nasser's death. Enrico Mathias from France and Julio Inglesias from Spain, in a televised festival of song at the Pyramids, were others to perform before *'tout Caire'*.

Stars like these were no rivals, for Sadat himself was the superstar and they were his guests. It was a different matter where other Presidents or Kings were concerned. When President Reagan began to talk about 'a Jordanian option', by which he meant involving King Hussein in the 'peace-making process', Sadat registered his disapproval. He wanted no competition – not that there was ever any chance of the 'Jordanian option' amounting to anything.

If King Hussein and the other Arab leaders were 'pygmies', the rulers of the rest of the world – apart of course from the favoured 'friends' – were little better. In the summer of 1981 some members of the parliamentary group of his own National Party had the temerity to express fears about the increasingly obvious American involvement in the affairs of the country. 'Could not a move be made in the direction of non-alignment?' they suggested. Sadat considered. 'There's nobody in Yugoslavia I can talk to on equal terms since Tito died,' he said. 'Unfortunately, towards the end Tito thought he could be my mentor and he sided with the Palestinians and the Rejection Front. But I could always talk to him. And India – Yugoslavia and India were always the non-aligned leaders with Egypt. But now there's Indira Gandhi. She's completely under the thumb of the Russians. She doesn't understand how the world is changing. No, I couldn't talk with her. There's really nobody in the non-aligned world I could have anything to do with.'

Yet, in spite of all his new friends, the applause of the world and the plebiscite results, Sadat instinctively felt that all was not well. There were some, particularly his wife Jihan, who were prepared to confirm this and to urge him to seek a remedy. But what remedy? He was convinced that his course was the right one, that his motives were pure and his arguments irrefutable. It must be that his message was not getting across, and that must be the fault of the press, radio and television. So from time to time editors would be summoned for a dressing-down by the President, after which they would redouble their efforts. It was not uncommon for a newspaper to have five of its sixteen pages devoted to the President – his activities, his speeches, his memoirs – accompanied of course by daily photographs of him.

Radio and television were just as concentrated on the President, and he was, in the months before he died, particularly concerned with the serialization of his autobiography, *In Search of Identity*. He had closely supervised a radio production of the book, and was taking even more care over the version for television, so that in the end he was spending more time with the producer of the programme than with his Prime Minister.

Any happening which could keep attention on the President had to be pressed into service. When it became known that the Prince and Princess of Wales were to spend their honeymoon cruising through the Mediterranean the opportunity was too good to be missed. As an act of courtesy they invited the President to dinner on the royal yacht *Britannia* as it sailed down the Suez Canal, but unhappily the newly married couple were reluctant to have the television cameras record the meal. That, in Sadat's eyes, robbed the occasion of all its point. However, the return flight to London from Hurgadah on the Red Sea provided another opportunity. Sadat determined to make it an official send-off. A battalion of the Presidential Guard in their new Germanic steel helmets were flown into the port and drawn up on the seldom used desert airstrip. Thus supported, the President, his wife, his children, his grandchildren, with their nannies in the background, gave a televised farewell to the young couple whose own television spectacular a few days earlier had even surpassed on the ratings Sadat's journey to Jerusalem.

In contrast to these public occasions there was one private ceremony which Sadat himself supervised at the end of each year. This was a bonfire in which all papers he thought would be better forgotten were destroyed. It took place either at his house in Giza or in Mit Abu el-Kom. The sort of papers involved were any showing how the secret funds at the President's disposal had been disbursed or transcriptions of tapped telephone conversations, for in spite of the destruction he had ordered after the defeat of the 'centres of power' in May 1971 of all tapes in the Ministry of Interior ('symbolic of the restoration to the people of their long-lost freedom'[1]) tapping had greatly increased in volume. When Sadat became President there were taps for a maximum of 1,200 lines; by the end, thanks to the technical assistance supplied by America and Mossad, the capacity had increased to 16,000, and was being made full use of. But any tapes which reflected adversely on the presidential image were not destined for preservation and were consigned to the flames.

A good example of how completely Sadat came to identify his personal interests with those of the state is to be found in his dealings with the Department of Antiquities. One of the buildings which Sadat wanted to take over for presidential use was the rest house at the Pyramids which belonged to the Department. But before the rest house could be suitable for the President certain repairs and improvements would have to be carried out. These were entrusted, not surprisingly, to Osman Ahmed Osman's Arab Contractors Company, and the final bill came to £E224,000. This bill was presented to the Department, which pointed out that, as the total grant for all its activities had been reduced to no more than £E60,000 a year, it was quite unable to pay. The argument was still going on when Sadat was killed, and at the time of writing remains unresolved, though ironically, symbolic of the change of régime, the rest house itself has been demolished.

But what caused the Department of Antiquities real anguish was the President's fondness for commandeering its treasures and presenting them to his friends. True, there had been precedents when, in the Eastern tradition of making gifts, an antiquity had, on very special occasions, been presented to a foreign government or head of state.

[1] *In Search of Identity* p. 224.

Thus, after the first stage of building the High Dam had been completed, Nasser gave Khruschev a marble pot from the Sakkara excavations which was in the Department's storeroom, and other pots were given to the National Museum in Tokyo and to the Vatican Museum. The whole list of official gifts before 1970 takes up only one page in the Department's records. But now generosity was to be administered on a wholly different scale.

In February and March 1971 Tito was given a statue of Horus 47½ centimetres high, and Brezhnev a statue of Isis suckling Horus 22 centimetres high.[1] These came not from store, but had been on show in Hall 114 in the Cairo Museum. On 30 April a necklace of precious stones was sent to the Empress of Iran to mark the celebrations for 2,500 years of the Iranian monarchy. For the first time the order to the Department to release this antiquity was given by telephone and not, as always previously, in writing from the Council of Ministers. A month later a bronze statue of Thoth, the god of wisdom, was requisitioned for the Shah, and a statue of Osiris for his son-in-law, Ardeshir Zahedi, to mark the same occasion. In November 1973 Dr Henry Kissinger was also the recipient of a statue of the god of wisdom,[2] and Mrs Nixon of a necklace made up of twenty-three pieces of gold and seventeen precious stones. The next year it was Nixon's turn to receive a bronze statue of Isis, the eyes inlaid with precious stones, while Onassis, who had attended the wedding of one of Sadat's daughters and brought her a gift of diamonds, received in return the present of a marble pot. President Giscard d'Estaing received a wooden statue of Thoth 34 centimetres high, the legs and head made from bronze. All these were on exhibition, not in store, and the order to hand them over was given by telephone and not in writing.

When the President embarked on his journey to Europe and America in 1975 he did not go empty handed. Another telephone order obliged the Department to hand over two necklaces of precious stones 65 and 59 centimetres long, a wooden statue of Thoth with bronze tail and legs, and twelve smaller statues of Thoth. All these were to be distributed at the President's discretion and there is nothing to show

---

[1] These and following particulars are drawn from the official records of the Department of Antiquities.

[2] A newspaper report in the summer of 1982 stated that Henry Kissinger had returned to Egypt the antiquity which had been given him by President Sadat.

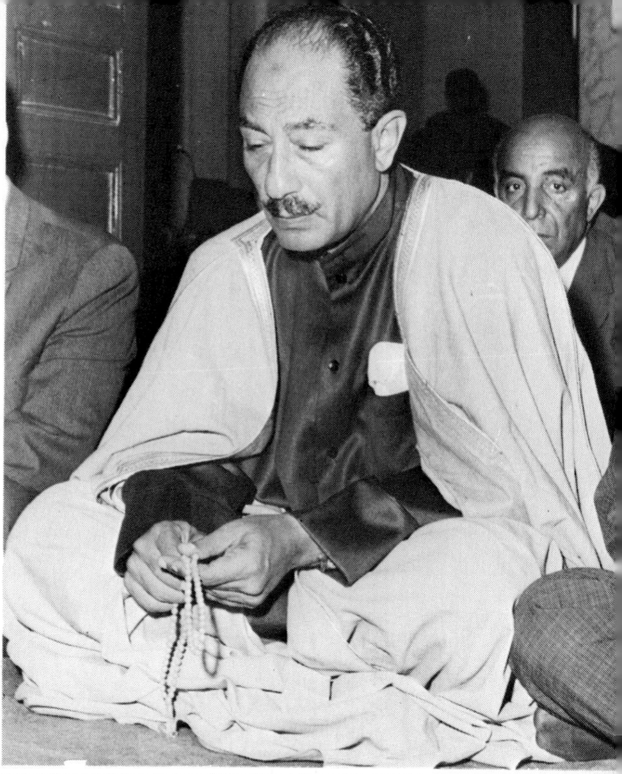

Top left Editor of *Gomhouriyeh*
Top right Sitting in traditional dress before prayer in Mit Abu El-Kom
Bottom Father of the Egyptian family

Top With his wife Jihan at the Mamourah rest house
Bottom Shaving – the cameras were always present

Top With David Rockefeller shortly before the October war: military uniform by Cardin
Bottom Reading a speech as Nixon listens

Top My friend the Shah
Bottom The Sadats and the Begins

Top Plebiscite results: the Minister of Interior, Nabawi Ismail, reads the results to the President in Mit Abu El-Kom – a 99.9 per cent success
Bottom Giving a speech in 'Medinet Al-Salam'

The last parade:
Vice-President
Husni Mubarak
on his right

Opposite
6 October 1981

Top left Lieutenant Khaled Ahmed Shawki El-Islambouli
Top right Mrs Kadriya El-Islambouli, Khaled El-Islambouli's mother
Bottom The funeral: security in evidence

who got them. It is on record, however, that when Jihan went to attend a Women's Congress in Mexico she took with her, as a gift for the wife of the Mexican President, another wood and bronze statue of Thoth 23 centimetres high. The wife of President Marcos of the Philippines was luckier – her statue was 41 centimetres high.

In January 1975 it was the turn of the Shah to be favoured again with an early dynastic wooden head, the eyes inlaid with precious stones, and the following year with a particularly valuable standing figure of Osiris 25 centimetres high. In February 1976 six statues were sent to the President to be distributed as gifts to his friends in the Far East, and in March another six pieces, of which there is no detail, for him to take with him to Europe. Ten days after this first order it was decided that six items would not be enough, and another six were asked for, followed by a demand for another six, making eighteen in all, to be distributed at the President's discretion.

In August 1976 a telephone order was received by the Department for twelve pieces to be sent to the presidency, the most important being a statue 114 centimetres high. A second telephone call the same day asked for another twelve pieces, including a bronze statue of Osiris and a statue of an ox from the Sakkara excavations. Against all these in the Department records is written simply: 'Removed on instructions from the President.'

In November 1976 the Empress of Iran was especially favoured. She received three antiquities – a bronze statue of Osiris holding in his hands the thrones of Upper and Lower Egypt, the eyes inlaid with precious stones, 24 centimetres high; a necklace with a gold pendant 64 centimetres in length, and a marble pot for perfume which had belonged to Nefertiti.

In January 1977 Jimmy Carter received a limestone relief with hieroglyphic inscription representing an offering being made to the gods, Franz-Joseph Strauss a marble bell 94 centimetres high, and in June there was another limestone relief, this time of Amenhotep, for Jimmy Carter. After this the Department gave up. It said it refused to take any more responsibility for what was going on. If the President wanted to take more antiquities he would have to do it himself, without making the Department a party to the transaction.

★ ★ ★

It was not only with Egypt's treasures of the past that Sadat was prepared to be generous when dealing with his new international friends; Egypt's current assets did not escape. In 1978, during his meeting at Schloss Fuschl near Salzburg with Bruno Kreisky, the Austrian Chancellor mentioned in passing a problem facing him. His small country was planning to install nuclear reactors, he said, but did not know what to do about nuclear waste. The experts said that disused saltmines in remote areas were the best repositories for such waste, but unfortunately there were none in Austria. Sadat immediately volunteered to make available the old saltmines to be found in Egypt's eastern deserts, and instructed the Deputy Prime Minister with responsibility for energy matters to draw up and sign the necessary agreement. But when the Ministry of Foreign Affairs heard of what was proposed it insisted that, because of the requirements of the International Atomic Agency, this would have to be the subject of a proper treaty and not a simple administrative order. This meant that, as a treaty, the proposal would have to go before Parliament. When it did there was such an outcry, and not in Parliament alone, that the idea had to be dropped.

Another example of how the President could over-reach himself in his desire to accommodate his new friends came over his offer of Nile water to Israel. After his visit to Haifa in September 1979 Sadat confided to a group of Israeli editors that he was thinking of diverting some of the Nile waters through Sinai to the Negev: 'Why not? Lots of possibilities, lots of hope.' Jerusalem, he said, was a city sacred to the three faiths. What could be more appropriate in the new climate of peace than to supply all the believers in Jerusalem with a new *zamzam*.[1] It may be that Sadat thought such an offer would persuade Begin to be more amenable over the negotiations which were then proving distinctly sticky, but, if he did, he was soon to be disabused. 'Mr President,' Begin wrote to him, 'our principles are not for sale for Nile water. Israel's security and the sacredness of Jerusalem are not for sale for Nile water.'

Another of Sadat's ecumenical ideas was for an edifice to be constructed on Mount Sinai which was to combine a mosque, a

---

[1] The sacred well in the Haram at Mecca whose water is drunk by pilgrims. It was by tradition opened by the Angel Gabriel to prevent Hagar and her son Ismail from dying of thirst in the desert.

church and a synagogue. He suggested that the American people might like to contribute towards its cost and said that he would himself choose to be buried there. But unfortunately only about $50,000 was collected in America, and, as none of the religions involved showed any enthusiasm for this sort of symbolism aimed at masking their fundamental differences, nothing was to come of it.

With his new concern for religion, at home and abroad, Sadat began to apply to himself attributes which are normally reserved for God. He was not only 'the pious President', but also the merciful. 'I will not have mercy on so and so,' he would say, scandalizing those who recognize mercy as God's prerogative. He even applied to himself a verse which in the Koran is applied to God: 'No word can be twisted before me, and I am not unjust towards my slaves' – but he substituted for 'slaves' the word 'people', which in Arabic sound much alike.

To the many decorations on the uniforms which he so often wore, and which were made for him by a London tailor, he now added yet another – the green 'Sash of Justice', a new order created by him and bestowed at his pleasure – worn over all of them. He no longer was seen with his Field-Marshal's baton under his arm but held upright in his right hand, like a pharaoh holding the key of life, and like a pharaoh in a bas-relief he preferred, in the representations of him which were now to be seen in all public places, to be shown in profile – which also had the advantage of not emphasizing the Negroid element in his features.

The more exalted the position, the lonelier it becomes. In the last months of his life Sadat seemed to have only one person outside the family in whose company he could be truly at ease – the contractor Osman Ahmed Osman, now in fact a member of the family by the marriage of his son to the youngest of Sadat's daughters. On one occasion, when the President, accompanied by the Ministers of Irrigation and Tourism, was inspecting Lake Nasser, created by the building of the High Dam, it was with Osman alone that he took his meals in the accommodation provided for the President, leaving the Ministers to fend for themselves outside.

Alone, or with this single companion, he came to spend hours watching on video the filmed record of past triumphs – his address to Parliament after the October War, his journey to Jerusalem, his reception in Cairo on his return, his television appearances in

America. He now lived almost entirely in a world of his own creation, in which he was the continuing star and from which all hostile forces or rivals were effectively excluded.

2

ORGANIZED LOOT

NOT SINCE THE DAYS of Khedive Ismail had Egypt been the scene of looting on such a massive and organized scale as it was during the last years of President Sadat. Corruption spread from the top of the pyramid of Egyptian society to the bottom.

At the beginning of his presidency Sadat had assembled all the close members of his family – brothers, sisters, nephews, nieces – and told them that he had no objection to their engaging in business, but if the slightest whiff of impropriety reached him he would deal ruthlessly with the guilty ones. If in the end this threat was never implemented, that is in part at least due to the President's own failure to distinguish between his public and private capacities. His generosity towards foreign politicians and others has been noted, and it must be assumed that this was not all a one-way traffic; Sadat was a receiver as well as a giver of gifts, but there is no trace of any of these gifts or record of them in any government department. What went out of the country was public property; what came in remained private property. It is therefore not surprising that others should have made the same confusion between public and private. Thus one of the President's brothers was able to tell journalists, while on a visit to Salonika in 1980, that he was proposing to invest $7 million in a textile factory in that town. He was not rebuked, nor were questions asked how someone who not long before had been an employee in a small concern came to have millions of dollars to invest abroad.

Cairo became a city of middlemen and commission agents, men from Europe and America and Japan in their neatly pressed suits and Gucci shoes shuttling between the luxury hotels and government ministries, wheeling and dealing on an ever-increasing scale. Now there were not only the importers of luxury goods but agencies in the public sector, including arms. No longer was the supply of arms a government-to-government matter; 'diversification' opened the door to arms dealers of all nationalities. And now not only was there a proliferation of agencies but a new breed of 'consultants', to be found in every sort of business enterprise, public or private. If Beirut in its boom years had been a caricature of Cairo in the final hectic days of the monarchy, Cairo had now become a caricature of Beirut before it was crippled by civil war.

From time to time some of the seamier evidence of what was going on would come out in the open. In the early days of Sadat's presidency there was the matter of the Boeing contract. Misrair, the Egyptian national airline, was negotiating for the purchase of six Boeing 707s, the technical side of the deal being the responsibility of the Minister of Aviation, Ahmed Nouh, and the financial side that of the Minister of Finance, Mohamed Merzaban. The Kuwaitis had agreed to guarantee the financing of the deal, and the Boeing representative in the Middle East was none other than Kamal Adhem, head of Saudi intelligence and the long-standing friend of President Sadat.

One day in 1972 the Minister of Aviation was in his office engaged in difficult negotiations with officials of the Boeing company when he received a telephone call to the effect that an officer in the Presidential Guard was on his way to the Minister's office and proposed to take him for a confidential meeting with Kamal Adhem. (This officer was at that time engaged to Sadat's elder daughter, though the engagement was later to be broken off.) The meeting duly took place that afternoon, but the Minister was embarrassed to find that, so far from being confidential, the meeting in Kamal Adhem's flat was attended by the same Boeing officials with whom he had been unsuccessfully negotiating that morning. He was a friend of mine, and I, at that time, was still on good terms with Sadat. Ahmed Nouh told me that he felt acutely the awkwardness of his situation, and that this sort of thing might damage the President's position. When I spoke of the matter to Sadat he was extremely angry and told me that the meeting set up for the Minister had been most irregular and that he must on no account allow himself to be subjected to any improper pressure.

Two weeks later the Minister of Aviation and the Minister of Finance both received letters from Fawzi Abdel Hafez, secretary to the President, which said simply: 'Dear Sir, the President has given orders that the agreement with Boeing and the accompanying financial arrangements should be signed immediately.' There was no alternative but to obey, but the Ministers took the precaution of keeping copies of the letters sent to them. Part of the story leaked out; there was an investigation in the course of which the Ministers produced their letters. Later Jim Hogland in the *Washington Post* referred to the story of the Boeing deal, revealing that following it two sums, one of $8 million and one of $750,000, had been deposited in numbered accounts in Switzerland, but without stating who the beneficiaries, one obviously much more useful than the other, had been, though certainly neither of the Ministers were in any way involved.

Then there was the affair of the buses. A fleet of buses had been assembled in Iran under licence from Mercedes, but when the Shah decided he did not after all want them he managed to unload them on the Egyptian government and, by charging very high prices, make a profit into the bargain. A Deputy, Dr Mahmoud el-Kadi, tried to raise the matter in Parliament and demanded a court of inquiry but was effectively silenced.

Another matter which came out concerned steel from Spain, bought at 70 per cent above market price although of inferior quality. This also was raised in Parliament, but though the Prime Minister of the day, Dr Hegazi, a prominent and efficient economist, refused to defend the deal, it too was not investigated.

Yet another matter which was revealed concerned the contract for the complete renovation of Cairo's telephone system, worth $2,000 million which, through the good offices of Chancellor Kreisky, went to a consortium headed by an Austrian businessman called Kahan, even though competing American companies were able to convince deputies that their offers had been 50 per cent lower than the successful one.

In 1973 a shady deal involving the export of cement at a lower price than had been paid for its importation was investigated by Parliament and shown to implicate some who were close to the President. The same smell of corruption was given off by contracts for a Cairo underground system and for a nuclear power station, but nothing was done. In 1981 a deputy was to claim in Parliament, without being challenged, that there were now seventeen thousand millionaires in the country, and that while seven thousand of these might have become rich simply by owning land or other property in an inflationary period, the newly acquired affluence of the other ten thousand could not be legally accounted for. The ordinary Egyptians had a name for the cash in these people's pockets – the first hundred thousand they called *balata,* a tile which gave the owner somewhere to stand, but the first million pounds they called 'rabbits', because they bred so fast.

However, it was not always plain sailing for the owners of rabbits. Sometimes they clashed with each other, as in the famous mineral water war. Egypt being now visited by a million tourists a year it was clear that there was a big opening for the sale of mineral water to people who had probably been told by their guidebooks to beware of the water which came out of Egyptian taps. So one company was formed linked with Evian water and another linked with Vitelle. Soon both were battering on the doors of the Minister for Industry to be awarded a monopoly to the exclusion of the other, but as both were closely connected with some of the highest families in the land he was unable to decide between them. The same dilemma arose over the war between Coca-Cola and Pepsi-Cola, and was resolved so that they both won.

As can be seen, Parliament was not inactive in drawing attention to abuses – or, rather, it would be more accurate to say that there were a handful of deputies who felt it their duty to do so. The most active of these was Dr Mahmud el-Kadi, a prominent engineer and one of the best parliamentarians Egypt ever produced. It was he who raised the question of the buses, steel, cement and other scandals. I was not surprised to find him a fellow prisoner in September 1981.

But probably the best way to give an indication of what commercial life in Egypt had become in the last years of Sadat's *infitah* is to examine the careers and achievements of five individuals – a businessman, a worker, a student, a member of the President's family and a bureaucrat.

The obvious place to start is the empire created by Osman Ahmed Osman. As has already been mentioned, Osman came from a family in El-Arish, had moved to Ismailia and built up a flourishing contracting business with ramifications in the Arab world as well as in Egypt. Although almost all the work on the High Dam was carried out by nationalized enterprises, his firm was given a contract to remove the huge quantities of rock and other debris thrown up by the excavations. Though not an operation requiring any particular technical expertise it was one employing large numbers of men and machines, and Osman showed a remarkable talent for public relations, his budget under this heading even in those days amounting to hundreds of thousands of pounds a year. Newspapers were filled with advertisements and news items about the doings of his firm, the Arab Contractors Company, so that many Egyptians began to get the impression that Osman was building the High Dam almost single handed, without any help from the Russians or Nasser.

More important for Osman's success than his talent for publicity was his friendship with Sadat, who at the end of 1973 appointed him Minister of Construction. He had earlier been called in to make improvements to the President's house on the Pyramids Road, and when Sadat had asked how much this had cost he was told not to bother about that. Sadat insisted on paying, so Osman said: 'All right, shall we say £E80, Mr President?' Sadat paid up. Renovation of the presidential house at Mit Abu el-Kom, with air conditioning and wooden panelling, was carried out by the Arab Contractors Company.

A common joke in Egypt was: 'Who founded the Ottoman Empire?' To which the answer was: 'Osman Ahmed Osman'.[1] It is worth taking a closer look at this network of enterprises which, though the parent company remained nominally part of the public sector, was, through its many private subsidiaries, in effect much more the fief of one family. These subsidiaries included the Arab Contractors for Investment, the Engineering and Industrial Construction Company (Eicon), the Contracting and Specialized Industries Company, Misr Company, Acro-Misr Company, Elio-Misr Company, Sinai Gipsene Company, Osmac Company, the Middle East Land Reclamation Company, Consulting Egyptian Engineers Company, the Group of Specialized Osman Companies and the Engineering Oxygen Company. Full details of the ramifications of all these companies were, after Sadat's death, to be submitted to the Socialist Prosecutor by a former adviser to Osman Ahmed Osman.

After he became a Minister Osman volunteered to step down – or up – becoming honorary president of the Arab Contractors and making the chairman of the company his brother, Hussein Osman. Another brother, Ismail Osman, was general manager. The deputy chairman was his nephew, Salah Hasballah; vice-presidents included

---

[1] Osman I (1258?-1326) gave his name to the Turkish empire of which he laid the foundations.

Abbas Sufieddin, married to one of Osman's nieces, and Yehya Abul Gheib, married to his daughter. The general director at large of the Arab Contractors was a very old friend, Hilmi Abdel Megid. Muhsin Abul Gebba and Mohamed Rifaat, married to nieces (and Adhem Zaid, husband of another niece, until he died), and Hassan Nassef, a cousin, were other directors. A nephew of Osman, Adil Ayad, was secretary of the company.

Osman's son married a daughter of Sadat, and became chairman of a group of specialized companies, including one producing insulating material, and a new company called the General Investment Company. Muhsin Abul Gedda, married to one of Osman's daughters, was made president of the Elio-Misr Company and was on the board of the Eicon Company. Another nephew, Ismail Osman, was the managing director of the Engineering Company, chairman of the government planning commission, a member of the National Development Board, a director of the Federated Contractors Company, and of the Arab-Libyan Contracting Company. Most of these, at the time of writing, still hold the same positions.

There was plenty of room in which the Arab Contractors and its associated companies could operate. In 1981 development projects were allocated a total of £E3,700 million, of which £E1,500 was earmarked for construction work, of which half was given to Arab Contractors. As all development work was considered high priority it was argued that there was no time to put projects out to tender. Instead, work was allocated by a system called 'recruiting', which meant that the Minister of Construction decided who should do what, without the formality of bidding. And, of course, the Minister of Construction happened to be Osman Ahmed Osman, who was in the happy position of being able to feed his companies with contracts and decide the scale on which they were to be paid.

It was a system which did not go uncriticized. Immediately after the October War reconstruction of the devastated Suez Canal towns began. The Arab Contractors had a major share in this work, and questions were asked in Parliament about the shoddy quality of much of the building, but the excuse was made that when things are done in a hurry there are bound to be some shortcomings. Another project which prompted questions in Parliament was that for a tunnel under the Suez Canal at Ahmed Hamdi. The contract for this was given to the Arab Contractors, as nominally part of the public sector, but subcontracted by them to a private Anglo-Egyptian Consortium called Osmac. The agreed cost for the project was £E31 million, but by 1980 it had risen to £E105 million and was still rising.

Then there was the Salhiya land reclamation project. The Arab Contractors were to reclaim 150,000 *feddans*[1] but after only a third had been made productive costs had already risen to £E200 million. There were complaints in Parliament that this meant each *feddan* was costing the country the astronomical figure of £E20,000 to reclaim. But the same day that questions were being asked in Parliament, 6 October 1981, Sadat appointed Hussein Osman, brother of Osman Ahmed Osman and now head of Arab Contractors, Deputy Prime Minister in charge of all land reclamation projects. In a memorandum written to Sadat by Ismail Osman, which reached him the very day he was assassinated, addressing him as 'head of the family' (one of the titles he applied to himself), he referred to his brother's appointment and suggested that the Salhiya project was one which ought to be repeated all over Egypt.

Another coup by the Arab Contractors was the purchase for development of an area of two million square metres known as Jebel Ahmar in Abbasiyeh, outside Cairo, on the site of the old British barracks, for £E1 million. The area used to be part of Nasser City and was publicly owned. As part of the deal the government had to spend £E1 million on preliminary work (roads, drainage, etc.), which in effect meant that the Arab Contractors were getting the land free. The man who had been responsible for the land under public ownership, General Arafa Mahdi, protested against the deal, but was obliged to resign.

Among his other activities, Osman Ahmed Osman launched several banks, including the Suez Canal Bank and the National Development Bank. In all the holdings were the same – one-quarter contributed by the National Bank, one-quarter by the Misr Bank, one-quarter by the Bank of Alexandria, and one-quarter by private subscribers, including Osman himself. He would then boast about the contributions his banks were making to Egypt's prosperity ('The National Development Bank has initiated fifty-nine new projects') without pointing out that three-quarters of the money involved was public money.

* * *

[1] A *feddan* is slightly more than an acre.

Now we come to the example of the worker, by name Rashad Osman. It appears that Rashad Osman came from Qena in Upper Egypt to Alexandria in 1974, where he worked in the port at the then going rate for a labourer of 30 piastres (about 30 cents) a day. At the time of writing (1982) he is under investigation by the Socialist Prosecutor and said to be worth over £E300 million. That is quite a remarkable success story in only eight years. How was it achieved?

When this young man, and so many others like him, arrived in Alexandria they were looking for work in a port bustling with activity. *Infitah* was just beginning, but already ships of every nation bearing goods of every description were crowding the roadsteads and docks. As has happened in other large ports, control of most docking, unloading and warehousing activities in Alexandria had slipped into the hands of about half a dozen shady bosses. The Prosecutor's reports first show Rashad smuggling cigarettes on a fairly small scale, but then moving into the timber business. In fact, Rashad fairly soon became one of the largest timber importers in Egypt, this being a vital ingredient in most construction projects and all supplies of which have to be imported. But it was not only wood that Rashad was bringing into the country, for according to the Prosecutor's account quite a lot of the timber was hollow and its hollowed spaces filled with hashish, an extremely profitable sideline.

Money breeds power. Rashad Osman became head of the government-sponsored National Party in Alexandria, the main financer of the party's election campaign in the city, and one of the principal contributors to the funds of the party's newspaper. He was also put in charge of the government's development plans for Alexandria.

Rashad Osman had arrived. He had a retired general as his secretary and began to take lessons in English and French, though without much success. He also became, as he said in court, the protégé of the empire builder, Osman Ahmed Osman, who advanced him even higher. On 10 October 1980 (and this too came out in court) Osman Ahmed Osman said to his new protégé: 'Come and pray with the President in Ismailia.' So they went, and after their prayers the President was reported as saying: 'Rashad, take care of Alexandria. I put it in your charge. I want it to be a better port than Beirut.' 'Alexandria is in my heart and before my eyes,' was the answer. A photograph was taken of the meeting and appeared in the newspapers.

Money breeds power, and power breeds influence. It appears that

Rashad Osman, in his capacity as a timber merchant, had paid £E5,500,000 duty on imported wood. This, he felt, was unfair. So he wrote to the Minister of Economics urging him that, as wood was such an essential ingredient in most development projects, it ought to be allowed into the country free of duty. The Minister was persuaded, and wrote a letter to the Customs Department instructing it to repay the £E5,500,000 to Rashad Osman. The speed with which the decision was reached, the instructions given and obeyed, must be unparalleled in the annals of Egyptian bureaucracy, as is the sight of the Customs disgorging what it has once swallowed.

Another important friend Rashad Osman had acquired was the Minister of State for Parliamentary Affairs. There was a new block of luxury flats for tourists and summer visitors being built in the Alexandria suburb of Mamourah, and Rashad Osman bought and furnished two of the flats for his friends, one of them being the Minister of State. This also came out in court.

But perhaps the most audacious and successful of Rashad's coups was his dealing in state lands. There is an old law which was designed to encourage the settlement of beduin which says that anyone who settles on state land on the outskirts of a city, and can prove continuous occupation for five years, can apply to have his permanent title to the land registered. It came out that Rashad and other members of his family had made use of this law to lay their hands on nine hundred acres of state lands around Alexandria which were going to be used for private development. It has to be admitted that Rashad was not alone in this. The same trick was being played in Cairo and elsewhere, and not for the benefit of the beduin the law was designed for but for the 'fat cats'. As the official in charge of state lands reported: 'It is time to bring this matter into the open. Those involved are all people with influence – ministers and their relatives, governors, ex-ministers and ex-governors, deputies from both Houses of Parliament, contractors and engineers and leading members of the National Party.' An article in *Al-Mussawar* magazine[1] under the headline 'The Looted Lands of the State', estimated that 53.5 per cent of the state lands round Alexandria with a market value of £E4,000 million had passed into private hands without any payment being made.

[1] Although published by the National Party, *Al-Mussawar* began, after Sadat's death, under a new and energetic young editor, to publish articles such as this, displaying a new critical spirit.

Rahad Osman eventually found himself in court and, temporarily at any rate , in prison, perhaps because the smell of corruption became so strong that someone had to be thrown to the wolves. But in court this tough mafioso character proved extremely difficult to silence. The newspapers of 21 December 1981 carried reports of an outburst in court during which Rashad Osman had shouted: 'May God punish you, Osman Ahmed Osman,' and had then gone on to describe their joint meeting with Sadat. He was asked why he had been removed from the Popular Development Board. 'Because I refused to take part in the corruption going on, Mr President,' he answered, addressing the President of the Court. 'Because I am a nationalist. I appeal to the honour of Gallal Fahmy, the chairman of the Port Authority, as a witness. Why don't you ask me about the Eric Company? Osman Ahmed Osman asked me to cooperate with the Eric Company, but I refused. Please write this down. I don't eat my people or the food of my people.' Seeing that the President of the Court was apparently unable to follow, he went on: 'You don't know about Eric? That is the company of Tewfiq Abul Hai. He is a swindler, and he is the partner of Osman Ahmed Osman. I refused to let the swindlers own the food of the people. I refused, Mr President.'[1]

Now that Eric, Tewfiq Abul Hai and Popular Development have been mentioned, it is time to move on to the third of our success stories, which is indeed that of the student, Tewfiq Abul Hai. After the student demonstrations of 1968 Nasser had a meeting with some of their leaders, and one of the things they demanded was that, instead of the wall newspapers in the universities which was all that they had then, they should be allowed to produce their own weekly. Permission was given, and the weekly *The Student* began to appear. It was still flourishing when Sadat became President, but its comments had become sometimes too critical and he was thinking of closing it down. Among those it criticized was Osman Ahmed Osman, and it so

---

[1] A statement by the President of the Court after this hearing said: 'Although the Court is not competent to rule on some of the accusations made during the course of this hearing, yet it feels that some of those named should be made the subject of investigation, according to article 40 of the Constitution.'

happened that, the newspaper being in need of advertising to help its revenue, one of those engaged in its production, a student named Tewfiq Abul Hai, approached the Arab Contractors Company. Osman was prepared to be generous, and several advertisements extolling the company's achievements appeared in *The Student*.

Then Osman had a better idea. He was by now actively engaged in politics, and he thought that a more effective way of promoting right-thinking among the students than suppressing their newspaper would be to start up a rival to it. So a new magazine called *Voice of the Students* came into being with Tewfiq Abul Hai as its editor. This magazine could be relied on to be complimentary about Osman and his friends and uncomplimentary about his enemies. But *Voice of the Students* was not a success and folded, and Osman, now Minister of Construction, proposed to Tewfiq Abul Hai that he should use his talents in producing a magazine for the ministry, to be called *Construction*. This he did.

In 1976 Osman decided to resign as Minister. Awkward questions were being asked in Parliament and he was altogether being subjected to too much harassment as a public official; he would concentrate on his business affairs. When he left he took Tewfiq Abul Hai with him, and suggested to him that what his experiences now particularly fitted him for was the running of an advertising agency. So was born Eric, the agency which was the target of Rashad Osman's outburst in court. Eric, the directors of which were Tewfiq Abul Hai, his wife and brother, not only dealt in advertising but also in imports, and so in Popular Development.

Popular Development was one of Sadat's brainwaves. He was aware of the discontent caused by the inflationary rise in prices, which not even the subsidies were able to check. Eggs, for example, which could formerly be bought four for a piastre, now cost ten piastres each. The trouble, he decided, was all the fault of the bureaucracy. Red tape and nationalization were creating artificial shortages; if there were alternative channels of import and distribution all would be well. So in 1976 'Popular Development' enterprises, nominally under the auspices of Osman Ahmed Osman and the National Party, sprang up, and one of these was the advertising agency, Eric.

It was suddenly announced that Eric was to be given 152 new outlets in Cairo and Alexandria. Special kiosks were built at vantage points in the city, even on the pavements (which was against the law) so that these new shining examples of free enterprise would be able to fulfil their mission to feed the people.

Then, shortly after Sadat's assassination, the Customs held up a shipment of frozen chickens destined for distribution by Eric. These birds, claimed the Customs, formed part of a consignment which, as was clearly indicated, should be eaten not later than 1974, and it was now 1981. The shipment was confiscated, but inquiry showed that 15,000 tons, which represents six million chickens, from the same consignment had already been received by Eric and presumably sold to the unsuspecting public.

There was a tremendous outcry, and the Prosecutor General ordered the arrest of Tewfiq Abul Hai. But the same day that the warrant for his arrest was issued Tewfiq Abul Hai flew from Cairo on Olympic Airlines, first to Athens and then to Panama, where he established himself on a ranch. Moreover, it came out that in the week before his hurried departure Tewfiq Abul Hai had borrowed £E35 million from banks in Egypt which he had promptly transferred abroad.

'Unfortunately,' the Deputy Prime Minister, Fikri Makram Ebeid, reported in Parliament,

> before slipping out of the country on 20 February 1982, Tewfiq Abul Hai was able to deceive many people. In addition to Eric, which had a capital of £E5000, and the Giza National Company with a capital of £E100,000, he created another company in Panama called 'Excellence' of which he, his wife and two of his sons were directors. Unfortunately this company was able to arrange for the shipment of 105 consignments of chickens, seven of which were intercepted by Customs, but one of which he was able to direct to a cold store in his own village on the pretext that he was awaiting a final report on it from the Ministry of Health. He then telephoned to the Director of the Medical Department in the Alexandria Customs, telling him that he had received a call from the Under-Secretary in charge of legal affairs at the Ministry of Health ordering this consignment to be released. This was a lie. There are always people in every society who can find a way round the regulations.

'Unfortunately,' the Deputy Prime Minister continued,

> Tewfiq Abul Hai was able to obtain £E10 million from the Suez Canal Bank and another £E1 million from the same bank, which is managed by Osman. Unfortunately, he also managed to obtain £E1,033,000 from the

> Mohandis Bank, £E681,000 from the Arab Bank for Investment, and £E435,000 from another bank. Unfortunately, he also obtained an advance of £E870,000 from the Arab Company for International Trade. We must all regret that these loans were given without any proper guarantees or any proper investigation by the companies and banks concerned to prevent this outrageous abuse of public funds.

It certainly was all most unfortunate. When the director of the Suez Canal Bank was asked why the bank had been prepared to hand over such vast sums, and what guarantees they had asked for, his answer was: 'We acted on the basis of his reputation. He was a very prominent figure in the business world.' But it might have been noted that earlier, when Tewfiq Abul Hai had tried to be made president of the municipally owned Heliopolis Lido Club, the Governor of Cairo had declared him ineligible because of his unsatisfactory record, since he had presented cheques which had bounced. Yet this known adventurer was able to retire with his family first to Panama and then to England with £E35 million of public money, leaving behind him millions of stale birds.

The fourth case is that of Esmat Sadat, third of the sons of Mohamed Mohamed el-Sadaty, coming after Talaat and Anwar. He was born in 1925, his education stopping after primary school. He was trained as a mechanic, but remained in obscurity until after the Revolution, when his brother was put in charge of *Gomhouriyeh* and he was given a job on the distribution side of the newspaper. For distribution purposes the country was divided up into a number of districts, or 'lines' as they were called, each 'line' being supervised by an agent who organized daily deliveries by truck to news-stands and other outlets, collected payment and supervised the accounts. Esmat held this job down for some time until he was dismissed on charges of embezzlement. There had been a number of accusations of embezzlement and passing dud cheques against him before this, all for quite small amounts – a few hundred pounds (the largest for £E600) – and though the police had been brought in no prosecution had followed, presumably because of his brother's influence.

After this nothing is heard of Esmat until about 1974, when, with the dawn of *infitah*, he reappears on the scene. Nobody seemed certain what exactly he was doing, but everybody agreed that he was extremely active. There were rumours, suspicions, but nothing open or definite. When an Independent Deputy, Adel Eid, claimed in Parliament that he had specific charges to make against what he called 'members of important families', and that he wanted to give their names to the Speaker, he was shouted down and accused of making unsubstantiated accusations. So the fact that Esmat Sadat was the first name on his list never came out.

However, once the activities of Rashad Osman and Tewfiq Abul Hai began to be aired in court Esmat's name cropped up too often for it to be possible any longer to ignore it. An official investigation was launched, and by September 1982 the Socialist Prosecutor was ready to call Esmat in for questioning. When informed of this President Mubarak pointed out that, while of course he had no wish to obstruct the work of the Socialist Prosecutor, any proceedings had better be left until after 6 October, the first anniversary of the assassination of President Sadat.

So there was a pause. On 6 October President Mubarak called at the former President's house in Giza to offer his condolences. There he found, among other members of the family, Esmat, to whom he gave a warning that his activities had created too offensive a smell in the nostrils of too many people for him to be any longer immune.

Immediately thereafter evidence began to come out from the Socialist Prosecutor's office, building up a picture of corruption and manipulation on a quite fantastic scale. In a curious way the career of Esmat reflects that of his father, Mohamed Mohamed el-Sadaty, he having had four wives and fifteen children. But with one marked difference; instead of all being housed in one slum flat in Kubri el-Kubba, Esmat's wives and children were installed in conditions of maximum comfort in palaces, villas, or luxury flats.[1]

The family was shown to control ten companies engaged in shipping, transport, the distribution of tractors and tractor spares, and contracting. They owned five enormous apartment buildings as well as scores of flats and offices and seaside chalets at Mamourah for use in the summer. Esmat seems never to have experienced any difficulty in getting permits to import anything he or his companies needed, and

[1] His last wife, whom he married in 1980, was a Greek girl called Maria, less than half his age. Together they established a number of companies in Salonika, where she now lives, concerned with shipping, oxygen cylinders, etc.

not to have been above extorting mafia-like protection levies from some of those who, willingly or unwillingly, became his partners. His son, Talaat, is similarly said to have demanded £E2000 from an official in the Alexandria customs if he wanted to keep his job, and to have used the same technique with other officials.

The full extent of the family's fortune is unknown; at the time of writing (October 1982) no fewer than twenty-two investigating committees are engaged in following up all its ramifications. Not altogether unexpectedly, they have found nothing at all in Esmat's bank accounts, he having sent his money out of the country as soon as the cold winds of public criticism began to blow, but the account of his youngest son was found to be over one and a half million dollars in credit.

From the wealth of evidence relating to the activities of Esmat's family which has already emerged, two cases may be quoted as typical. The first concerns an enterprise called the Sun Company for Commerce and Investment. In Egypt it is possible to lay claim to a piece of land, and if, after a period of years, this claim has not been challenged, to apply for permission to purchase it. This is, naturally, normally only done in the case of unused land belonging to the state. But an agreement has come to light, dated 11 December 1980, between the Sun Company and Esmat Sadat and signed by both parties, for the purchase of a piece of land near Cairo Airport, which was not only already in private ownership but was currently occupied by the military police. By the terms of this agreement Esmat undertook, in exchange for payment to him of £E56,000, to arrange for the sale of the land to the company and to clear the military police off it.

The second case involves one of Esmat's daughters, Nadia. She, like some of her brothers, was in the habit of fabricating documents purporting to come from some individual whom they did not know and who did not know them, or who did not necessarily even exist. Armed with such a document they would approach a lawyer and obtain permission to act on the individual's behalf. Nadia in this way became authorized to act on behalf of a certain Hanim Rateb, a member of the well-known Rateb family, who owned a palace in the Cairo suburb of Maadi, which she had vacated and put up for sale. Nadia thus acquired title to the palace, worth an estimated £E5 million. When the Shah arrived in Egypt on his first visit there as an exile, this palace was offered to him as a residence, though for reasons of security Kubba Palace was in the event preferred.

The real owner, Hanim Rateb, got to hear of what was going on and wrote a politely worded letter to President Sadat, addressing him as 'the respected head of the Egyptian family, the pious President, Anwar Mohamed el-Sadat, President of the Republic,' setting out the circumstances and adding that she did not want to pursue the matter through the courts but hoped that it could be settled 'on the mastaba' (the bench outside the *omdah*'s house where village disputes can be argued out).

When his official examination started Esmat was lavish in his denunciation of others, including his brother and Jihan. He claimed that he was really a cleverer man than Anwar, and that the career of the late President had jeopardized his own chances. He was forbidden to travel abroad, caught, ironically enough, by the Law of Shame and the Socialist Prosecutor, and at the end of October 1982 was consigned, with three of his sons, to Tora prison.

The last child of the *infitah* to be looked at is a bureaucrat, Dr Naim Abu Talib. It will be noticed that all five cases overlap and interlock, Dr Abu Talib's activities having been publicly exposed as a result of the trial of Rashad Osman.

Dr Abu Talib was Professor of Engineering at the University of Alexandria, then became a Minister and finally Governor of Alexandria. As Governor he showed a taste for the flamboyant, erecting a stage in the Antoniadis Gardens at the cost of £E90,000, which was supposed to be for festivals worthy of a great port, but which in fact was only used on one occasion, though this was honoured by the presence of Jihan, the President's wife. He also appointed twenty-two public relations consultants, cultural attachés and so on, all on the municipal payroll. Entertaining the Governor's guests cost in one year no less than £E50,000.

It was while he was still Governor that Dr Abu Talib created an enterprise which he called the Maritime Bank. The issued capital of the bank was £E30 million in 600,000 £E50 shares. Banks and other institutions in the public sector were invited – indeed, encouraged or even obliged – to take up shares, and ten companies and the Investment Bank did so, becoming responsible for £E20,600,000 worth of the issued capital. Thus the General Water Authority, which is government owned, found itself in receipt of a direct order to participate, which it did, taking up 18,000 shares, and this in spite of the fact that its statutes do not permit it to invest. Among other public companies, the United Company for Construction and Housing bought £E105,000 worth of shares, and the Mamourah Company £E245,000 worth. They too were not legally empowered to invest, but as they came under the direct authority of the Governor of Alexandria they found it advisable to do so.

One of Dr Abu Talib's sons became a director of the Maritime Bank, owning a hundred shares, and the father attended the general meeting of the company holding proxies on behalf of his son. But later Dr Abu Talib emerged as chairman of the bank, with a salary of £E40,000, which was better that the modest £E5,000 he received (simultaneously) as Governor of Alexandria. The bank which was supposed to be going to become active in 'maritime activities', took over the Sursuk Palace in Alexandria as its headquarters at a cost of £E2,500,000. The chairman's office was done up at a cost of £E200,000 and he acquired a large car with a telephone in it ('I could have had a Mercedes, but chose not to' said the chairman in a public statement defending himself, published in the newspapers, giving an example of his restraint). It is not known that the Maritime Bank has ever engaged in any banking activities, and at the time of writing, it and its directors are under investigation.

These five cases are not isolated. True, there is nobody in Egypt who has erected a financial empire on the same scale as Osman Ahmed Osman's Arab Contractors Company, but there have been at least six or seven Rashad Osmans, another dozen Tewfiq Abul Hais, and thousands of Dr Abu Talibs. One of Egypt's leading intellectuals described them as 'the paratrooper class'. Paratroopers, he said, descend on a position either to capture it or to destroy it, and this new class is determined to control Egypt or to destroy it in the process. 'Their idea of the state,' he said, 'is that it is simply a mechanism for protecting the slumber of the rich from the insomnia of the poor.' With what must be assumed to be unconscious irony the paratroopers began to use the word *abur* (crossing) which had been on everyone's lips in its military sense at the time of the October War,[1] to describe their own successes – crossing into the world of millions. I recall talking to one of the President's relatives who was describing the achievements of one of his sisters: 'By God,' he said, 'she's had a wonderful crossing!'

[1] After the October War Sadat had been proud of the title 'hero of the crossing (*abur*)'.

3

NO CHECKS, NO BALANCES

ALTHOUGH as has been said, in a Third World country one man is usually in supreme command, controlling the essential elements – the bureaucracy, the army, the police – and although there will be no true political parties because of the lack of a class structure to bring them into being, this does not mean that life in the country is static. There is always movement of some sort, on the periphery or underground, with new forces trying to consolidate and gain a foothold, old interests regrouping and forming new alliances.

So it was in Sadat's Egypt. Supreme power was his; any loopholes in it had been stopped up, either by legislation or by adminstrative action. Yet there remained some potential checks on the exercise of his power, some balances to his seemingly absolute authority. It is time to consider these and to see what became of them.

In the first place there were the political parties. Either because he was anxious to emphasize the democratic façade for the benefit of foreign opinion, or because he realized that the multiplicity of forces in the country needed some outlet if there was not to be an explosion, Sadat opted for the creation of political parties. This was a different approach from that of Nasser, who had hoped that, by replacing a variety of parties representing special interests with the Socialist Union, this would act as a reconciler of sectional and class interests. The Socialist Union was described as, and intended to be, 'an alliance of social forces'.

Certainly, after May 1971 people were looking eagerly for more democratic liberties and freedom of expression. What they got was a disappointment, but then came the October War and new expectations. These in turn were unfulfilled and this renewed disappointment helped to fuel the flames which burnt out in the rioting of January 1977. This was followed by Sadat's crackdown on all opposition. But the iron fist of repression needed a velvet glove, and this took the form of a measure of freedom for political parties to operate.

The first to take advantage of this opportunity was the Wafd, in the person of its veteran former secretary-general, Fuad Serageddin. He belonged to the landlord class which had dominated Egyptian political life for many generations, but was a decent man and well liked. There was no place for such as him in politics in Nasser's day, but now that Egypt was moving rapidly into a free market economy things were different. Though the Wafd was still legally banned, as it had been from the earliest days of the revolution, Fuad Serageddin felt that the time had come to revive it. So he approached the Prime Minister, Mamduh Salem, asking him to inform the President that there were plans for starting up a New Wafd Party. He would like to emphasize to the President that this party should not be seen as being in opposition to him – on the contrary, his enemies, Communists and Nasserists and the like, were its enemies too. The recent rioting (this was shortly after January 1977) had shown that the government forces, apart from the army and police, had no supporters they could put on the streets to face the oppositon. Serageddin suggested that the Wafd could do better.

This argument appealed to the President. The order which prohibited Fuad Serageddin from engaging in any political activity was lifted, and he was made a member of the Central Committee of the Socialist Union. (The Socialist Union itself was in the process of being dissolved, but the Central Committee was kept in existence pending new elections for a body which was to be called the *Mejlis el-Shaura*, a consultative assembly to represent 'the Egyptian family'.)

Once the New Wafd had begun to function it attracted a lot of support. There were members of the old pre-revolutionary bourgeoisie who had always regarded the Wafd as being their party, as well as new elements for whom the name Wafd still had a certain magic. After the party had been granted a formal licence allowing it to exist it was decided to test its strength at an election in the *Gumruk* (Customs) constituency in Alexandria. Serageddin was billed to speak, and a crowd of forty thousand people turned up to hear him. The reception he got was so enthusiastic that his car was almost lifted off the ground.

Serageddin is a good orator. He said that he accepted the main achievements of the 1952 revolution, including land reform in spite of the fact that personally he had suffered by it. He was careful not to attack Nasser. Then he began to talk about current problems – about the food riots, about corruption, high prices and so on. It was a clever speech, and recordings of it were widely sold on cassettes. As a mark of his new popularity Serageddin two weeks later was invited to address the Lawyers Syndicate, an extremely influential body. Sadat took fright. He introduced new legislation putting restrictions on those who had 'corrupted the life of the nation before or after the revolution'.

This was obviously aimed at Serageddin, so he called a meeting of the founding committee of the New Wafd Party and told them they had a choice – either risk a confrontation with Sadat or decide to dissolve the party. A majority were in favour of dissolution, on the grounds that existing conditions were clearly not those in which a really independent political party could function. They were probably right. Quite a lot of the New Wafd's supporters had benefited from the *infitah* and had no wish to jeopardize their profits for hypothetical political benefits. Serageddin himself, though over seventy, was in the minority which was prepared to continue the struggle in spite of the risks involved.

So the New Wafd was wound up. But this did not stop Sadat from continuing to attack Serageddin, comparing him to the Bourbons who tried to behave after 1815 as though the French Revolution had changed nothing. However, Serageddin had in his possession two documents which he thought ought to protect him from any actively hostile action by Sadat, even if he could make no public use of them – one was a report by the Minister of Interior on the attempted assassination of Nahas Pasha, and the other a copy of a telegram from the Egyptian Ambassador in London referring to a meeting with Ernest Bevin at which the Foreign Secretary had sent a warning to King Farouk that he was playing with fire by allowing his subordinates to use assassination as a weapon.

So one potential check on Sadat's absolutism had been liquidated. But the New Wafd was not the only party to take advantage of the greater theoretical freedom Sadat was now offering. The National Progressive Union (NPU) under the leadership of Khaled Mohieddin had attracted a considerable following. He was one of the few surviving original Free Officers, of considerable ability and wide experience. He was a Marxist, and though undoubtedly some of those who joined his party were Communists, others represented various liberal and progressive elements, intellectuals, and even some Nasserists who felt that the National Progressive Union offered the most hopeful outlet for their activities.

The NPU started to produce a weekly newspaper called *Al-Ahali* which proved extremely effective. The party was shrewd enough to appreciate the damage that might be done to it in the current climate of opinion if it was labelled as in any way atheistical or anti-religious, so it adopted the line of the Italian Communist Party, claiming that progress and religion were in no way incompatible, and even creating a secretariat for religious affairs in the party, headed by a progressive sheikh called Mustafa Assi. He too landed up in prison in September 1981, though Khaled Mohieddin himself escaped, thanks to his status as a former member of the Revolutionary Command Council.

Al-Ahali was a good newspaper and widely read. It was quite prepared to discuss contentious issues and to take up a critical position. It attacked the President's Jerusalem journey, and 'No to a separate peace with Israel' became one of its slogans. It denounced corruption in general and exposed specific abuses. It ran a series called 'The Ottoman Empire' on the activities of Osman Ahmed Osman and the Arab Contractors Company. But in spite of its successes, *Al-Ahali* suffered from one great weakness – it was printed on the presses of one of the government newspapers. This proved its undoing. There was a special court in South Cairo designed to produce quick judgements, presided over by a judge called Anwar Abu Sihly. He belonged to one of the feudal families of Upper Egypt and after Nasser's land reform, in which his family had lost most of their estates, he had been dismissed from his post as judge and gone to work as legal adviser to the Arab Contractors Company. Sadat reinstated him and appointed him to the new court for instant justice. Every week the Public Prosecutor would bring a case against *Al-Ahali* in this court, and every week Judge Sihly would order its confiscation. Very soon publication became impossible. The paper's licence was then withdrawn on the grounds that it failed to appear regularly. The party was obliged to fall back on producing leaflets, some of which had quite an impact, but it was no longer an effective instrument of criticism or opposition.

Like all the other political parties, Misr el Fatat (Young Egypt), which had before the war been fascist in ideology and organization, had been dissolved by the law of January 1953. But some of its ideas had lingered on, as had its founder, Ahmed Hussein. Now Misr el Fatat reappeared as the Amal (Action) Party under the leadership of one of Ahmed Hussein's closest associates, Ibrahim Shukri, a man who, in spite of his landowning background, had been an early advocate of land reform and had a reputation for honesty and progressive thinking. Sadat wanted Amal to become what he called 'my loyal opposition'. But one of the obstacles confronting Amal, or indeed any other party, was the clause in the law regulating political parties which said that no party could be licensed unless it could muster twenty deputies in Parliament. As the deputies had all been elected before the law regulating parties was enacted this meant that somehow twenty converts had to be found among the deputies. This proved no difficulty for the New Wafd, but it did for Amal. What was to be done? Sadat provided the answer. He surprised the founding fathers of the party by turning up at their inaugural meeting and informing them that he himself was to be their patron. In spite of the fact that he was at the time chairman of the National Party, he was prepared to sign the manifesto of Amal. More than that, he was going to lend them twenty deputies from his own party, including his brother-in-law, Mohamed Abu Wafia, so that they could get legally started.

Unfortunately the President's action had the effect of dividing the party. The quorum lent by Sadat continued to act as a loyal opposition under Mohamed Abu Wafia, but the remainder adopted an increasingly independent line. They published a weekly tabloid newspaper, *Al-Shaab* (The People), which gained wide popularity. To begin with the party accepted Camp David, though with reservations; but then it became much more critical. Leading members of the party were very conscious of the accusation that they were stooges, created by the authorities and doing just as much or as little as the authorities allowed them to do. *Al-Shaab* started to discuss some of the real issues of the day, which brought to a head differences between the loyal faction and the rest. Eventually the two factions broke apart, and after shedding the loyalist deputies the remainder became more cohesive, attracting fresh support, particularly from the New Wafd after that had dissolved itself. One of Egypt's leading intellectuals, Dr Hilmy Murad, a brother-in-law of Ahmed Hussein, who had been with the New Wafd, joined Amal and became Deputy Chairman of the party.

Al-Shaab went from strength to strengh. Three oustanding figures in Egyptian public life began to contribute regular columns – Fathi Radwan and Dr Mohamed Asfur, as well as Dr Hilmy Murad himself.

Dr Hilmy Murad was an economist who had been Rector of 'Ain Shams University, and after the student troubles of 1968 had been made Minister of Education by Nasser. The articles which he wrote on the state of the economy were particularly effective, but those which gave most offence to Sadat were ones he wrote attacking the title of 'First Lady of Egypt' bestowed on Jihan, and another which argued that it was the government rather than the people which was using terror as a weapon.

Fathi Radwan was one of the original leaders of Misr el-Fatat, but had differed with Ahmed Hussein and left the party. He had been the first Minister of National Guidance after the 1952 revolution and by now was a widely respected elder statesman, known to be a man of absolute integrity, still with the fires of revolution burning inside him and still extremely effective as a speaker or a writer. One article which he wrote, called *El-'Utaqa* (The Emancipated) particularly infuriated Sadat. In this he rejected the claims Sadat was continually making that he had 'given' the Egyptians freedom and democracy. 'We are not slaves,' wrote Fathi Radwan, 'to be told we have been given our emancipation. If we are free, this is not because of a gift from anyone.'

Dr Mohamed Asfur was an eminent jurist, specializing in constitutional and adminstrative law. In his weekly column he drew attention to infringements by the régime of the law and Constitution. The reports of the weekly meetings of Amal, chaired by Ibrahim Shukri, which appeared regularly in *Al-Shaab,* were another source of offence to the President, especially after the party had come out in opposition to Camp David.

Sadat allowed his irritation with Amal to show, publicly accusing its leaders of ingratitude. They rejected the charge, maintaining that the unsolicited support they had received had been more of an embarrassment to them than anything else.

Their independent stance did not make life any easier for Amal or for *Al-Shaab.* They found it hard to raise money and often the newspaper failed to appear. Their position became even more difficult when they changed their line on Camp David after the Israeli annexation of Jerusalem. *Al-Shaab* declared that, though Amal deputies had voted in favour of the Camp David agreements in Parliament, they could no longer do so: 'No for Camp David; No for normalization' was the headline. This brought Sadat's wrath down on them, and he began attacking them in every speech he made. Naturally most of the leading Amal deputies and the *Al-Shaab* columnists found themselves behind bars in September 1981.

Besides representatives of government parties and of Amal and two or three belonging to the NPU, Parliament included a small but significant number of independents. These were men like Dr Mahmud el-Kadi and Judge Mumtaz Nassar, distinguished parliamentarians who enjoyed strong local support in their constituencies. It was largely thanks to them that Parliament never became a rubber stamp but was forced to debate such controversial matters as the Iranian buses, Boeing, the cement scandal and so on. Never more than twenty or twenty-two in number, they had no newspaper of their own and reports of many of their interpolations were stopped by the censor, though from time to time some newspapers, including the right-wing *Al-Ahrar,* would pick them up.

When the Camp David agreements came to be debated by Parliament only fifteen deputies voted against them though no fewer than fifty-five deputies, including some from Sadat's own National Party, found it convenient to stay away from Parliament on the day the vote was being taken. This was not good enough for Sadat. He wanted to put the agreements in an unassailable position, so he decided to dissolve Parliament and order new elections. This was unconstitutional, since the President is only authorized by the Constitution to dissolve Parliament if there has been a dispute between him and Parliament and a subsequent plebiscite has supported the President's point of view. On this occasion, so far from becoming involved in a dispute with the President, Parliament had voted overwhelmingly in favour of his policies. But the real purpose of the dissolution was to silence the independents once and for all, and this was effected by the usual methods at the subsequent elections, though one of them, Mumtaz Nassar, by what amounted almost to a military operation, managed against all the odds to be re-elected.[1] He became the lone voice of protest in the new Parliament.

★ ★ ★

---

[1] See p. 104.

So much for Parliament. What about the state institutions? When the obliging Judge Anwar Abu Sihly, who had put the left-wing weekly *Al-Ahali* out of action, reached the age of sixty, he became due for retirement and a pension, but instead was appointed Minister of Justice, which took care of that department. But there were also two departments which were meant to act as watchdogs on behalf of the public and which enjoyed a large degree of independence. One of these was the Administrative Surveyance *(el-reqaba el-idariya),* charged with surveillance of official acts and so the appropriate body to draw attention to spurious transactions and crooked deals. Suddenly one day this department was dissolved by presidential decree on the grounds that it had become a bureaucratic nuisance. All the department's records were ordered to be destroyed and its staff were transferred to other departments.[1]

The second watchdog body was the Office of the Public Accountant. This was supposed to send to Parliament reports on nationalized industries and the public sector. Its reports did in fact provide the group of independents with useful material, so these were suppressed and ceased to be circulated. Finally, there was the *mukhabarat,* the General Intelligence Department, but though this later maintained that it had information about everything that was going on it found it did not know what use to make of its information.

So there was only one potential check left on the exercise of absolute power – the press. When I was editor of *Al Ahram* I had tried to persuade Nasser to agree to the idea which had been adopted by *Le Monde,* whereby the paper would be largely owned by the journalists working for it. He agreed to try the idea out on an experimental basis, but after I ceased to be editor in 1974 Sadat cancelled the arrangement, and transferred ownership first to the Socialist Union and then to the Misr Party. Later, after he had created the Assembly of the Family *(Mejlis el-Shura)* he instituted something called the Supreme Press Council, headed by the Chairman of the Assembly. This naturally ensured that all the press was effectively under the control of the government, which appointed all the editors.[2]

---

[1] Since Husni Mubarak became President the department has been reconstituted, but is obviously handicapped by having to start again from scratch, with no records.

[2] The Egyptian press became effectively emasculated, but its total lack of indepen-

The Egyptian press today is in a confused and demoralized state. It has been subjected to too many changes of organization and personnel. In 1973 Sadat ordered eighty journalists, including several of the most outstanding figures in the press, to be dismissed from writing jobs and transferred to administrative posts in the Ministry of Information. This had a chastening effect on those who were left, as was intended. So today on the staff of almost any newspaper it is possible to find appointees from the Sadat period working alongside survivors from the Nasser period, and even from the days of the monarchy. This does not make for harmonious relationships inside the office. Uncertainty is as bad a foundation for a newspaper as for any other institution. To give one example of what this means: *Al Ahram* was founded in 1875, and during the first hundred years of its existence it had six editors, of whom I myself was the sixth, holding that position for seventeen and a half years. In the eight years since I left the paper it has had eight new editors. No newspaper can be run like that.

Shortly before he died, Sadat went in person to a meeting of the Journalists Syndicate in an attempt to silence the murmurs of protest at home, and the increasingly vocal protests in organizations of the press abroad, which the arrest of myself and other journalists had provoked. 'There are some people in this country,' he said 'who think they can copy the American press. They think they can have their Watergates and get rid of the President that way, but they forget where they are living.' His admiration for America and the Americans stopped short of its freedom to criticize the highest in the land.

But there was one way in which America was allowed in the Sadat era to influence the Egyptian press. Most newspapers were in need of new machinery but lacked the resources to invest in it. AID came to the rescue. Eventually almost all the 'national newspapers', as Sadat called the government press, installed new machines, thanks to AID. Loans to these newspapers from AID totalled $120 million, but naturally only after AID officials had obtained satisfactory guarantees for fiscal control.

---

dence could of course cut both ways. The same newspapers which had adulated Sadat day after day as 'the hero of war and peace' were quite ready to change their tune as soon as he was dead. The first question fired at President Husni Mubarak at his first press conference came from an editor who had been closely associated with Sadat: 'Everybody knew that during the past year President Sadat had been psychologically unbalanced. What is your explanation of that?'

4

DETERIORATION AND CHAOS

For Egypt 1980 was a year of increasing frustration and restlessness. It was clear to all that 'the initiative' was going to bring none of the benefits expected from it, neither a true peace nor economic betterment. Indeed, as has since been officially demonstrated, the country's economy was by now in a state of chaos.

Soon after he became President, Husni Mubarak set up a special committee of experts with the formidable task of trying to discover the true state of the economy. Its members included thirty of Egypt's leading economists, who could call on the services of some sixty or seventy specialists. Their work resulted in the production of some highly important reports and some startling findings.

They showed that by 1979 53 per cent of Egypt's Gross National Product went on financing imports. Egypt, normally an exporter of foodstuffs, had now become dependent on imports from abroad for more than half its food supplies. Thus, before 1970 Egypt used to export 40 per cent of its large sugar production, but by 1980 not only was Egypt no longer an exporter of sugar, but as much as 35 per cent of its sugar consumption came from abroad. In fact, the net income from the Suez Canal, one of the country's main sources of revenue, was now, owing to greatly increased consumption, insufficient to cover the cost of imported sugar.

Sugar may be regarded as an essential part of the nation's diet, though the increased demand could have been met by increased home production. But the really alarming increase was in the import of inessential goods. Thus, between 1974 and 1980 the import of textiles doubled (again, increased demand could here, if properly managed, have been met by increased home production), the import of cosmetics was up three times; of cigarettes, watches, furniture and similar goods, ten times; of electrical goods (radios, televisions, refrigerators, etc.), twelve times; of cars, fourteen times; of luxury foods, eighteen times. Between 1974 and 1978 the number of supermarkets and boutiques had been increasing at the rate of 22 per cent a year, part of the reason for this being that many of those Egyptians working abroad, who had previously sent home cash remittances, now preferred to buy goods in the country where they were working, open a supermarket with the help of family or friends in Egypt, and sell these goods at a handsome profit. This is shown in the statistics as 'imports which are not financed by the transfer of money abroad', and whereas in 1974 this item stood at £E45 million, by 1978 it had risen to £E526 million – a twelvefold increase. One example of the effect this had on the way people lived is that in 1980 the consumption of canned food and drinks was three times what it had been in 1974.

By 1980 Egypt's non-military debt had risen to £E21,000 million and three-quarters of the new debt was going towards financing increased consumption. Even the increased revenue from oil, growing at a rate of 40 per cent yearly, was being used to finance consumer imports and not for investment. Similarly, although between 1974 and 1978 the figures for building construction showed a rise of 107 per cent, 90 per cent of this went towards the building of luxury apartments and offices. Of £E2,600 million shown statistically as being devoted to investment much more was squandered on such wasteful projects as the Salhiya reclamation scheme,[1] and the Ahmed Hamdi Tunnel under the Suez Canal. (Nobody could see what the point of the tunnel was supposed to be. Sadat said that it was to avoid the need for another military crossing of the Canal, but if there were to be no more wars with Israel there would never be need for another crossing. Surely the only purpose for the tunnel must be to facilitate communications between Egypt and Israel.) Not surprisingly the value of the Egyptian pound fell until by September 1981 the black market value of the dollar was 110 piastres compared with the official rate of 48 piastres.[2]

By 1980 even the World Bank felt obliged to draw attention to the growing gap which was being created in Egypt between rich and poor and the dangerous political and social implications of this inequality. According to the Bank's own figures, 21.5 per cent of the national income went to only 5 per cent of the population, while at the other

---

[1] See page 189.

[2] There was also what was known as the 'parallel' rate of exchange set up to meet the requirements of 'imports not financed by the transfer of money abroad'. This stood at 82 piastres to the dollar.

end of the scale the lowest 20 per cent of the population had to make do with 5 per cent of the national income. According to the Central Office of Statistics, 80 per cent of government officials had an income of £E600 or less, while 44 per cent of those living in the country and 33 per cent of those in the towns had incomes which put them below the poverty line. When in 1980 Cairo's luxury hotels took advertising space in the newspapers to announce their plans for Christmas celebrations, with tickets at around £E200 a head, some of the editors warned the censorship of what they feared would be the provocative effect of such notices. After reference to higher authority the censor intervened to stop the advertisements.[1]

If the dangers of the situation were apparent to officials of the World Bank it can well be imagined that they were even more apparent to Egyptians themselves. But what could they do about it? The feeling of discontent was almost universal; the channels through which it could express itself were almost nil. Parliament, parties, press and government agencies were, as has been seen, virtually impotent. Only in some of the professional syndicates was there, by 1980, to be found some residual expression of protest.

The Israelis had hoped that one of the advantages they might expect from 'normalization' would be reciprocal exchanges between professional bodies in the two countries. But this all the Egyptian syndicates refused to countenance as long as Israel's part of the Camp David agreements, particularly that relating to the Palestinians, had not been carried out.[2]

Naturally the President tried to bring the professional syndicates into line too. Osman Ahmed Osman was put forward as head of the Engineers' Syndicate, and after discreet canvassing he was duly elected. A change was also organized in the Press Syndicate, though

---

[1] It was said at the time that there were three sorts of goods on the market – capital goods, consumer goods and provocative goods.

[2] The only 'concession' made by Israel under the Camp David agreements related to Sinai, territory over which Israel had never had any historical or theological claims, and which was held onto only as a defensive screen against Egypt. But a separate peace with Egypt, ensuring its permanent non-belligerence, created a far more effective *cordon sanitaire* than ever could have been provided by the continuing occupation of an Egyptian province, which must inevitably have kept Egypt a potentially hostile power.

there the new government-backed chairman had the courage to state that there could be no exchanges at official level with Israeli journalists until the problem of Palestine had been solved. This immediately put him out of favour.

Different tactics were used for the Doctors' Syndicate. The chairman, Dr Hamdi el-Said, much respected in his profession, was surprised to find himself required by the President to accompany him on a visit to Israel to inspect some new piece of medical equipment he had seen there on a previous visit. Dr Hamdi el-Said explained to the President that, though he was obliged to comply, it could make no difference to his own, or to the Syndicate's, attitude towards relations with Israeli doctors. But when, in defiance of the Syndicate's ruling, the President's personal urologist went to Jerusalem to inspect a new piece of equipment, he was, on his return, disciplined by the Syndicate. This so annoyed Sadat, who had sent him there, that he gave the doctor a decoration – a deliberately provocative gesture.

The most effective of the syndicates had always been that of the lawyers. Makram Ebeid, the eloquent deputy leader of the Wafd, had at one time been its secretary-general, and it had always been regarded as the bastion of the nation's liberties. Its fate was to be subjected to what amounted to a *coup d'état*. On one occasion, when a distinguished constitutional lawyer, Mustafa Marei, who had been a Minister several times before the revolution, was addressing a meeting of the Syndicate about the Law of Shame and democracy, thugs from the National Party broke in and attacked members of the audience with chairs and other weapons. The lawyers were not deterred, so on the occasion of the next full meeting of the Syndicate a group of pro-government lawyers held a caucus meeting of their own, at which they declared the existing governing body of the Syndicate dismissed and elected a new one from among themselves. This was going a bit too far, even for the authorities. They accepted the dismissal of the old governing body but did not give recognition to the rebel one, and instead a temporary chairman was nominated to look after the affairs of the Syndicate.

None of this succeeded in silencing the resentment felt inside and outside the syndicates at the way things were going. The feeling against Israel was especially strong. The Israelis had gained so much from Camp David, particularly that separate peace with one Arab country – and the most important Arab country – which had always been one of their main objectives. In addition, by the terms of Camp David, Egypt was bound to supply Israel with two million tons of oil every year. In return what had the Israelis conceded? Virtually nothing.

There was increasing talk about the corrupt deals in which those close to the President were known to be involved, to the extent that he felt bound to defend himself in public. 'I know that there are people who want to attack me, but are frightened to do so,' he said. 'Instead they bypass me and think they can get at me through attacks on Osman Ahmed Osman.' Counter-attacking, the President tried to mobilize the country through the cause of Afghanistan and the threat of world Communism. Committees for aid to Afghanistan were set up throughout the country, but they never achieved anything. If Afghanistan was to be helped in the name of Islamic solidarity, that was playing into the hands of the unofficial Moslem groups which were in a much better position to exploit it.

In this atmosphere of mistrust and suppression it was not surprising that people listened to every rumour and were ready to attach sinister explanations to every event. Thus when on 2 March 1981 a helicopter carrying General Ahmed Bedawi, the Commander-in-Chief of the Egyptian army, and many leading generals, struck a broken lighting standard shortly after taking off from the oasis of Siwa and crashed, burning to death all its occupants, it was widely believed that this was the result of a conspiracy, involving the CIA or Mossad or some other outside agency. The inquiry showed the crash to be the result of poor maintenance not of conspiracy, but none the less reprehensible for that.

On 21 March 1980 there was a plebiscite to approve changes in the Constitution Sadat was proposing. Article 1 of the revised Constitution was now to read: 'The Arab Republic of Egypt is a social, democratic [a new word] country whose structure is based on an alliance of the social forces belonging to it. The Egyptian people form a part of the Arab nation which is working for the achievement of complete unity.' Article 2 stated that Islam was the religion of the state, Arabic the official language, and *sharia* law the basis for legislation. Article 4 stated that the democratic social system in Egypt was based on justice and work, the ending of exploitation, the breaking down of barriers between classes, and the safeguarding of all legal rights and the guaranteeing of a just distribution of responsibilities and duties. Article 5 stated that the political life of the Arab Republic of Egypt was based on the multi-party system within the framework of the basic principles governing Egyptian life.

Article 77 of the revised Constitution was particularly interesting since it had the effect of making Sadat President for life. When he first became President in 1970 Sadat had said, 'My advice to my fellow-countrymen is that one term of six years is enough for the President.' But after the October War he decided that there was nothing wrong with the existing constitutional provision, which allowed the President two terms. Now Article 77 laid down that the presidency would be for a term of six years starting from the date of the plebiscite and that it would be legal for the President to be re-elected for an unlimited number of new terms – that is, for life. The result of the plebiscite was a 98.96 per cent vote in favour of this and all other constitutional changes.

❧ 5 ☙

ANGER EVERYWHERE

THERE WAS ONE ASPECT of the life of the nation which eluded the President's control, and that was religion, and this in spite of the fact that he was doing his best to make himself and his government appear as the champions of religion and guardians of morality; almost daily Sadat could be seen at prayer on television, eyes closed and lips moving. The Speaker of Parliament, Dr Sufi Abu Talib, recommended that all legislation should be looked at to ensure that it was in line with the *sharia*, and the head of the Court of Appeal was instructed to set up a committee to carry this out. All such legislation would apply to Moslems and non-Moslems alike, to foreign citizens as well as Egyptians.

One new law laid down that anyone who apostatized from Islam would be given one chance to repent and return, but if he persisted in his apostasy he would be hanged, and only two witnesses would be needed to convict him. There was talk of putting into practice the strict code which ordained that a thief should be punished by having his hand chopped off, while some judges were so enthusiastic that they began to pass judgement according to *sharia* rather than civil law. At the beginning of 1982 one judge went so far as to punish as well as judge according to *sharia*, condemning a man who appeared before him on a charge of drunkenness to eighty lashes; he could not wait for Parliament to act, he said. Later he published a lengthy explanation of his action, insisting that as a judge his duty towards God was above his duty to human law.

However, one of the reasons why it was hard for the government to make its new religious drive convincing was that the leading Moslem authority in Egypt, the Sheikh of Al-Azhar, had too often been used for purely political ends. While the most distinguished of Azhar sheikhs in recent years, Sheikh Shaltout, had decreed that a vital element in the conflict between Israel and the Arabs was religious, because of Jerusalem, his sucessor was obliged to issue a *fetwa* stating that the Camp David agreements and peace with Israel were wholly in accordance with the teachings of Islam.

* * *

In fact the pattern of religious life in Egypt, and relations between religious and secular, were currently undergoing a profound transformation. As well as Al-Azhar, the recognized religious institutions in Egypt had always included the mosque sheikhs throughout the country and such tolerated organizations as the Moslem Brotherhood and certain Sufi sects. Separate from the religious establishment, but not normally in conflict with it, was the secular establishment, including the bureaucracy, the army, the media, the six universities, the political parties and the professional syndicates.

But now new religious forces were taking over from the old established ones, presenting themselves as more credible defenders of Islam and so finding grassroots support which the others could no longer lay claim to. More than this, the new religious forces had managed to penetrate much of the secular establishment in a way that had not been seen before. They were to be found inside the bureaucracy, the political parties and the universities, and even in the armed forces. As religion had become the only channel open to dissent, this was hardly surprising, but it meant that the delicate balance between religious and secular which had been maintained in Egypt for so long, not always without difficulty, was now tipped towards religion, and tipped in favour of elements which were at work underground, largely unseen and wholly unacknowledged.

As was to be expected, all the talk about the necessity for non-Moslems as well as Moslems to conform to *sharia* had profound repercussions in the Coptic community, and the Copts were now flexing their muscles and extending their activities.

Pope Shenoudah had set up forty-seven new churches in America under the supervision of a bishop, and he had been no less active in Africa. Encouraged by the World Council of Churches, the Coptic Church was seeking converts in Africa, and this was a role it was particularly well suited to perform, since it was unhampered by any imperialist or missionary heritage. In Zambia and Malawi the Church had secured about ten thousand converts, and a bishopric was established with its seat in Kenya.

Back in January 1977 there had been a Coptic conference which had ended by producing a communiqué which, however, was never published. This communiqué read:

> Circumstances have made necessary the calling of a conference of the Coptic people in Alexandria, which was attended by the Pope and priests, the shepherds of their flocks. His Holiness Pope Shenoudah III attended the opening meeting on 17 December 1976, in the great cathedral of Alexandria. The conference proceeded with a discussion of the problems on the agenda, and took into consideration the work of the preparatory committee which met on 5 and 6 July. [This was the first intimation that such a committee had existed.] All members of the conference, priests and laity alike, agreed on two propositions which in their opinion could not be separated from each other. The first is an unassailable belief in the eternal Egyptian Coptic Church, founded by Mark the Evangelist and sanctified by the sacrifices of martyrs through the ages. The second is the sense of responsibility towards the fatherland, for which we are ready to sacrifice our lives, and in which the Copts represent the most ancient, pure and authentic element. No people are more attached to the soil of Egypt, or more proud of their country and of their nationality than the Copts.

The conference suggested that 31 January to 2 February should be a period of fasting, and that the conference should remain in session until its resolutions had been implemented – but it was not revealed what these resolutions were. It was, however, made known that the conference had received messages of support from abroad, and that these messages (but not its resolutions) had been transmitted to the Egyptian Parliament. Most of these messages took the form of protests – 'Why are our brethren in Egypt suffering these hardships?' 'What is this talk about the triumph of Moslems over Christians, and about the Copts being treated as *dhimmi*?' 'What has the government said about *sharia* law?' and so on.

As a counterblast to the Coptic conference in January the Rector of Al-Azhar, Sheikh Abdel Halim Mahmud, convened a conference of Islamic organizations in July. This conference issued a series of resolutions: any law or regulation which runs counter to the teachings of Islam should be treated as null and void and should be rejected by Moslems. The application of Islamic law is mandatory and not the consequence of parliamentary legislation. There can be no questioning God's law. The delay in enacting true Islamic legislation is due to appeasement of non-Moslems, and Parliament should without any further delay pass the legislation which has been already tabled. The conference declared its appreciation of the recent speech by the President in which he spoke of his intention to purge the state machinery of atheists and begged him to act swiftly in this sense. The conference appealed to the President to carry out a purge of the information media to secure the elimination of all atheistical material. The conference also appealed to the President to ensure that religion should be made the basis of all education. Finally, the conference elected an executive committee of its members to supervise the implementation of its resolutions.

Tension between the communities continued to grow throughout 1978 and 1979. Then, on 26 March 1980, Shenoudah delivered a speech in which he angrily attacked the idea that the *sharia* law should be the basis for legislation and claimed that Islam was being made the new form of nationalism. There may have been some substance in this charge, but it was also true that elements among the Copts, with their new international links, were finding a new focus of loyalty beyond Egyptian nationalism. Sadat too, by his alliance with America and his crusade against world Communism, had left the simple concepts of Egyptian and Arab nationalism far behind.

In this same address on 26 March Shenoudah stated that there would be no special services for Good Friday that year. Instead he and his bishops would be going into the desert to pray for deliverance from oppression. He instructed all churchmen not to accept the congratulations of visiting representatives of the state which would, according to custom, be made on the occasion of the Easter Feast.

Instead of negotiating, Sadat decided on a head-on confrontation. Using the occasion of the anniversary of the so-called 'Revolution of 14 May' he gave an address to Parliament in which he said he had knowledge of a plot by Shenoudah to become the political as well as the religious leader of the Copts and set up a separatist Coptic state with Assiut as its capital. 'But the Pope must understand,' he said, 'that I am the Moslem President of a Moslem country.' He harked back to some of the illegal church-building incidents of 1972 and accused Shenoudah of ingratitude: 'He asked for twenty-five churches a year, and I gave him fifty.' He said he had evidence that the Palestinians in Lebanon had arrested three Coptic volunteers fighting in the ranks of the Christian Maronite militias. He declared that his slogan was 'no politics in religion, and no religion in politics', though of course mixing up the two was precisely what he himself was doing.

Sadat ended his attack on a note of pathos. He said that he had been quite determined to take very serious action when, at the last moment, he was shown a letter which had been written to him by an unknown little Coptic girl. In this letter she said: 'My father, I feel you are angry. I wish I could give up my life for you, or add what years are left of my own life to yours.' 'When I read that letter from my Christian daughter,' said Sadat, 'I changed my mind. I decided not to do what I had planned to do.'

After finishing his speech Sadat went to the presidential suite in the Parliament building to rest. One of his aides, who had been listening to the speech, asked him what exactly the action was he had been planning to take before the little girl's letter had dissuaded him. 'I was going to sack him [the Pope],' said Sadat. 'But, Sir,' murmured the aide, 'surely it is not possible to do that.' 'No,' said Sadat, 'I was going to do it by means of a plebiscite.' It is, to say the least, alarming to think what the repercussions would have been if a plebiscite had been held in a predominantly Moslem country to determine the fate of the head of the Christian Church there.

The Pope had been spared for the moment, but he continued to be a cause of extreme annoyance to the President, though the real reason for this was not to be found in any of the charges that had been brought against him in Sadat's speech to Parliament. It was something quite different. By then one consequence of 'normalization' was that Egypt was swarming with Israeli tourists, while only a handful of tourists were going the other way, since few Egyptians wanted to break the Arab embargo. Sadat felt that something must be done to stimulate the flow of tourists into Israel, and he recalled that before the 1967 war between thirty-five thousand and fifty thousand Coptic pilgrims used to go to Jerusalem every year, their journey being organized by the Church authorities and travelling on a collective passport. Since the occupation of east Jerusalem by Israel this pilgrim traffic had ceased, but Sadat was determined that, now there was peace with Israel, it should be started up again, and sent a message to Shenoudah to this effect.

Shenoudah's answer was that, although he was in favour of peace, he had no intention of complying. 'The problems which now separate Egypt from the rest of the Arab world will one day be resolved,' he told the President's messenger, 'and when that day comes I do not intend that the Copts should be branded as the traitors of the Arabs. I will not permit any pilgrimage to Jerusalem.' Privately he told many of the Copts who were prominent in public life that they should cease to be identified with the rapprochement with Israel because of the harm it was doing to the Copts as a community. Sadat was furious. The Israelis were pressing him to do something to stimulate reciprocal exchanges, and he was being shown powerless to do so.

It was not only the Copts who were proving defiant. The new Moslem groups outside the old religious establishment were growing in numbers and confidence. Collectively known as *gama'at el-islamiya*, the Islamic society, this was like a large river in full flow in which separate islands could from time to time be seen raising their heads above the surface. Some of these groups, some of these islands, wanted to organize a camp in the university on the occasion of the 1980 Eid el-Adha, but were prevented by the authorities from doing so. Driven out of the university, they simply crossed the bridge and occupied the Salaheddin mosque on the other side of the Nile. Here they installed loud speakers, and for twenty-four hours broadcast a succession of speeches and sermons denouncing corruption and a separate peace with Israel, and attacking all those who, while claiming to be Moslems, failed to rule in accordance with Islamic law – 'the new Tartars'.

The attitude of these young militants was quite simple. If, as they were continually being told, religion was the basis of the state, they understood better than anyone else what this meant and how to implement it. But if, as seemed in fact to be the case, the basis of the government's policy was not Islam but an alliance with the Americans, peace with the Jews, and fraternization on equal terms with other religions, then they knew who was the real enemy.

Their attitude towards the Copts did nothing to foster religious peace. In their eyes they should be treated in the same way that certain privileged categories of non-Moslems used to be treated in the early days of the Arab empire – as *dhimmi*. These – Christians and Jews – were allowed a large measure of toleration and even of self-government, provided they paid special taxes, but remained essentially second-class citizens. To hear the word *dhimmi* being used again had an ominously retrogressive sound in the ears of Copts and of many Moslem secular elements in the country.

* * *

There was violence in the atmosphere. As early as the occasion of the Shah's first arrival in Egypt as a refugee from the Islamic Revolution in his own country (January 1979) there had been an outbreak of communal disorder. Some of the Islamic groups, though they felt little sympathy with Khomeini as a Shi'a, demonstrated in Assiut. Some Christian shops were looted, but the police moved in, and several of the demonstrators were killed. Later an obscure sheikh in the *gama'at el-islamiya* was to issue a *fetwa* to the effect that if any of the Moslem groups found themselves short of the necessary resources, and could expect no help from the government, it was permissible for them to take what they needed from the shops of Christian jewellers. Increasingly vocal demands for all foreign missionary activities to be closed down began to be heard.

June 1981 saw the most serious communal clash for many years. In the Zawya el-Hamra quarter of Cairo what started as an ordinary quarrel between neighbours turned into an armed battle. Once again, the origin of the dispute was to be found in the illegal setting up of a church, with members of the President's National Party trying to prove their religious zeal by using force to stop its construction. On 21 June the Minister of Interior told Parliament that ten people had been killed in the fracas (the number of dead later rose to seventeen), and fifty-four injured; thirty-four pieces of arms had been discovered and there had been 113 arrests.

This incident was symptomatic of a dangerous polarization which was taking place. Hitherto political life in Egypt had successfully avoided becoming involved in religious extremism. In the Wafd before the revolution, and in the Socialist Union after it, there had been room for Moslems and Copts on equal terms. This was greatly helped by their partnership first in the Egyptian national struggle and later in the wider context of Arab nationalism.[1] A sense of common aims made constructive dialogue possible. But now there were no common aims, and dialogue had broken down. Mistaken policies made it appear as though Egypt was turning its back not only on history and geography but on its own traditions, since these had been formed by history and geography.

---

[1] To begin with Copts were suspicious of the Arab nationalist movement because of its Islamic connotations, but appreciation of the common cultural and historical heritage which they shared with Moslem Egyptians overcame their reservations.

Also a significant shift was taking place in the religious structure of the country. For generations the pattern of life of the village had been the same. Most of the land would belong to some big landowner who, if he did not himself live nearby, would have his representative in the village. The government would be represented by the *omdah* and religion by the sheikh of the mosque. But now the big landowners and their agents had vanished with land reform, the authority of the government had been weakened by the spread of corruption and violence, there had been a general drift of population to the towns, and many of the brighter young men had gone off to seek their fortunes in other Arab countries. The one constant figure in the village was the sheikh of the mosque, and he was now growing in importance. These sheikhs had always been appointed by the Ministry of Waqf (Religious Endowments) and had formed part of the traditional religious establishment – at the top the Sheikh of Al-Azhar in Cairo; at the grass-roots the village sheikh. But now the Sheikh of Al-Azhar, like the Minister of Waqf, belonged to the governmental establishment, and the influence these two had previously exerted was being taken over by the unofficial and underground Islamic groups. This left the village sheikh far more independent than he had hitherto been.

He used this new independence in a manner that was to have wide repercussions. The normal practice had been for the Ministry of Waqf to send out instructions for the weekly Friday sermon in the mosque, telling the sheikh the subject for the sermon and the general lines it should take. But now the bolder sheikhs were choosing their own subjects and treating them in their own way, and often their theme was some aspect of current affairs. Thus the village sheikh became the only spokesman for local or national grievances, and this brought him such prestige that, if there had been genuinely free elections in Egypt in 1981, and the sheikh had chosen to stand as a candidate, more often than not he would have been elected – and the same is true today.

It was not only at village level that this independence found expression. The sheikhs of some of the most important mosques in the country became in effect, through their sermons, leaders of the unofficial opposition – men like Sheikh Mahalawi in the Ibrahim mosque in Alexandria, or Sheikh Eid in the Hidaya mosque there, or Sheikh Kishk in the Kubba mosque in Cairo. Such men were prepared to preach on forbidden subjects, such as the Shah, or corruption, or the true role of religion. In many cases their sermons were recorded on cassettes, and sold like hot cakes just as the sermons of the exiled Ayatollah Khomeini had been sold on cassettes in the bazaars of Iran.

Nor were these sheikhs the only preachers of dangerous doctrines. In the summer of 1981 Sheikh Eid had begun the practice of inviting prominent intellectuals, such as Fethi Radwan and Helmy Murad, to speak to the congregation in his mosque, which they did with great effect. In fact, the mosques had not only usurped the authority of the old religious establishment, but were performing the critical function which, in the days of greater freedom, had belonged to the newspapers. There was nothing comparable to this seething religious opposition among the Christians, but the Copts did have an angry Pope.

Part VI
THUNDERSTRUCK

Who can run the race with Death?

Samuel Johnson

I

3 SEPTEMBER

As the year 1981 developed tension inside Egypt mounted – a tension which Sadat himself both reflected and fostered. Just because he insisted on being always and in all things the centre of the picture, he could not escape becoming more and more identified as the target on which the people's resentment focused. Corruption was the word on everybody's lips, but the President's own entourage was a centre of corruption. The rapprochement with Israel was bitterly disliked, not because it meant peace but because it meant a separate peace which isolated Egypt from the rest of the Arab world; yet the President remained its unceasing and enthusiastic advocate. There was almost universal resentment at Sadat's willingness to let Egypt be used as the springboard for the abortive American raid in the summer of 1980 to rescue the hostages in Tehran. Whatever might be thought of Khomeini, this was not the sort of role which Egyptians, who for a generation had been hosts to liberation movements of every sort, were proud to play. Sadat increasingly talked the language of religion, but most of his critics felt themselves more sincere Moslems than he posed as being. He had declared open war against the head of the Coptic Church. He seemed bent on widening rather than healing the breach between Egypt and the rest of the Arab world. Each press conference he gave, each television appearance, each interview, both by its tone and content served only to deepen the gulf which separated the President from his people.

As had now become the usual pattern, the last months of Sadat's life show him almost continually on the move.

On 20 January he addressed a meeting of the National Party in Aswan and told his audience that on the 29th he was going to make a declaration which would transform the lives of future generations. But when the 29th came it found the President in the new settlement he had founded in Sinai, called Mit Abu el-Kom after his native village, and no declaration was forthcoming.

In February he went to Luxembourg to address the European

Parliament, and on his return gave his opinion that the Arabs ought to have their own Parliament on the lines of the European one – apparently forgetting that he was responsible for driving out of Egypt the only effective forum of cooperation between Arab states, the Arab League.

On his way back from Luxembourg he had stopped off in Paris, where he had a meeting with Alain Rothschild, described in the Egyptian government newspapers as 'the important French millionaire'. While in Paris he also talked to a group of French rabbis and had a meeting with Karl Kahan, the Austrian entrepreneur involved in the controversial telephone deal. At a press conference he announced that he had received reassuring messages from the new American President, Ronald Reagan.

Also in February he laid the foundation stone for the offices of a new magazine he had sponsored, to be called *Mayo*, which was to be the vehicle for yet another version of his memoirs. He spent much time with the staff of the magazine and attended meetings of the editorial board to supervise its layout.

On 21 March he was guest for dinner at the British Embassy in Cairo. This unusual gesture may have been not unconnected with the fact that Jihan was then in London and was known to be hoping to be received by Queen Elizabeth.

On 30 March came the attempted assassination of President Reagan, which greatly shocked Sadat. He issued a statement which said that 'the President felt profound anger when he heard the news.'

On 5 April Sadat had his first meeting with the new American Secretary of State, Alexander Haig. He had wanted to go to Washington as soon as the new administration had been formed, but was told that it was too early to receive him, though Secretary Haig would be shortly visiting a number of countries and Egypt would be his first stop. This visit produced no noticeable results.

On 25 April he received a delegation of American trade union leaders in Mit Abu el-Kom, and on 12 May a delegation of American businessmen.

On 17 May Sadat launched his campaign against the Lawyers Syndicate by attending a meeting in Alexandria of a local branch which had broken away from the main syndicate.

On 24 May, worried by reports of the situation in the Sudan, he paid a one-day visit to Khartoum.

On 28 May he met Sharon and had a long telephone conversation with Begin.

On 4 June he met Begin. Two days later Israeli planes bombed the Iraqi nuclear power station outside Baghdad. Much to Sadat's annoyance, the American Ambassador in Cairo telephoned the presidential office to inquire whether Sadat had been given prior notice of the attack. He issued a statement that he had not been consulted and resented the suggestion that he might have been.

On 29 June Sadat attended naval manoeuvres.

On 1 July he went to Tanta, his helicopter landing in the sports stadium, from where he proceeded to the Sayyed Bedawi mosque where he attended prayers. He went on to Sharm el-Sheikh, where he announced that the cultivation of Sinai was going to make Egypt self-sufficient in food.

The first week of July saw the government-organized coup in the Lawyers Syndicate.

On 11 July Sadat announced that he was concentrating on two things – he was going to see President Reagan, and their meeting would give a big impetus to the peace process, and he was going to ask Parliament to begin an investigation into the crimes committed by the Lawyers Syndicate against the people. He then retired to Mit Abu el-Kom.

On 27 July Sadat attended the dinner customarily given by the staff of Alexandria University to commemorate the fact that theirs was the first university to declare its support for the revolution in 1952. He told his audience that he was going to Washington to discuss common problems, including the conflict between Israelis and Palestinians and Soviet intrigues in the Middle East. He said Egypt and the Sudan were ready to provide America with bases because of the difficult situation in Iran, and added: 'When I come back from the United States I am going to report to the nation about the religious strife.'

On 29 July Sadat let it be known that, because many important decisions had to be made before he left for the States, he was going to spend some time in prayer in Sinai. He spent two days in seclusion at Mount Sinai, accompanied only by Osman Ahmed Osman. He reappeared at Suez on 30 July, and three days later left for Washington.

* * *

What exactly was going on in Sadat's mind in this period? Why was he talking so much about religious strife? The Zawya el-Hamra incident had been in June, and the inquiry by the Minister of Interior had reported that it was the outcome of a quarrel between neighbours, and nothing more, so the incident was officially closed. But Sadat must have realized that there was much more behind it; he must have been aware of the growth of fundamentalist Islamic groups and of the clandestine hoarding of arms, particularly in Upper Egypt. A police raid in one village there had revealed three thousand weapons of one sort or another, including an anti-aircraft gun. He probably felt that he would have to act swiftly and decisively to prevent things getting out of control. It was now or never.

In preparation for Sadat's Washington visit ABC had prepared a special programme, to be shown while he was there, in which he was compared to the Shah of Iran. A video tape of this programme was stolen by the police at Cairo airport and shown to Sadat. It irritated him greatly, for though the Shah had been his good friend he did not relish being bracketed with him. A few days later he burst out in public about 'those crazy people who compare me to the Shah of Iran. There's a campaign against me in the States trying to pretend I'm going to suffer the same fate that he did.' He told newspapermen on the plane taking them all to Washington that when he got back he was going to have a purge. He said that if the editors had any people on their staff they wanted to get rid of, they should give the names to the Minister of Interior.

In the States Sadat was in a bad mood. He sensed that the media's attitude towards him had changed. Nobody seemed impressed when he talked about Egypt's readiness to combat the spread of Communism. They questioned Egypt's ability to act as 'policeman of the area' (another echo of the Shah), and seemed more interested in his country's internal difficulties, including the religious question. To make matters worse, the Coptic community took half-page advertisements in the *Washington Post* and the *New York Times* listing their grievances, and staged two demonstrations while Sadat was in Washington, one in front of the White House and one in front of the Metropolitan Museum, where he was billed to attend a dinner and open a new wing devoted to Egyptian antiquities. These took place in spite of the fact that Shenoudah had sent Bishop Samweel to the States in advance of the President's visit asking the community to lie low and not provoke him. Sadat ended his visit uncomfortably aware that, though he had tried hard to speak the new administration's language, the Middle Eastern country by which it set most store was still Israel, with Saudi Arabia next, and Egypt only in third place.

Sadat returned to Egypt an angry and frustrated man. Only two people now had any influence with him – Osman Ahmed Osman and his wife, Jihan. She realized that he would get no good advice from the sycophants around him and was anxious to widen his contacts. There was a Professor of Political Science at the American University in Cairo she had heard well spoken of, and she managed to arrange a meeting between him and Sadat. They were together for four hours, from 11.00 a.m. to 3.00 p.m. on 29 August. The professor suggested that one way of breaking down Egypt's isolation from the rest of the Arab world might be to call a conference of intellectuals from various Arab countries to discuss the problem. Sadat listened non-committally. Then he went out for a walk and came back for his siesta, leaving the professor talking to Jihan until five. The professor went away rather pleased, feeling he had achieved something, but in fact he had made no impression.

There is nothing in the records to show exactly whom Sadat was seeing in these days immediately preceding the mass arrests of 3 September. Certainly he saw the Minister of Interior and the Director of Intelligence, but there must have been others. The Minister of State for Presidential Affairs, Mansur Hassan, sensed that something was being prepared, but he did not know what. Sadat had let out that he was going to make an earth-shaking pronouncement which would put an end to sedition, but refused to be more specific. Mansur Hassan tried to see the President, but failed to do so.

The crackdown came before dawn on 3 September, one week after Sadat returned from America and five days after he had listened to Jihan's professor. It was a massive operation, involving over three thousand arrests, and names were being added to the list of those to be pulled in up to the very last minute. Some of the arrests – of students and rank-and-file fundamentalists – were comparatively easy, but the arrest of leading politicians and religious dignitaries required more elaborate planning. I only realized the full scale of the operation when I got to the prison and found there people like Fuad Seraggedin, the

Wafd leader, Helmi Murad, secretary-general of the Action Party, Fathi Radwan, a Minister from the early days of the revolution, half the members of the central committee of the left-wing NPU, all except one of the independent deputies, and many others. All the leading members of the Lawyers Syndicate and of the Newspaper Syndicate were there, as well as many priests and prominent sheikhs, such as Sheikh Mahalawi, Sheikh Kiskhk and Sheikh Eid. About two hundred and fifty of the most prominent figures in Egyptian public life were now behind bars, including all those who had spoken or written any criticism of Camp David, of corruption, or of Egypt's isolation from the Arab world. These arrests had nothing whatever to do with the religious strife which was advanced as the reason for the crack-down.

While I was in Paris in August I had read reports in the press that Sadat might be planning some spectacular move against his critics, and I knew that if this did materialize I was unlikely to escape. I foresaw the possibility of my being expelled from the Newspaper Syndicate, which would prevent me from carrying on as a journalist, but never in my wildest dreams did I imagine my being arrested in the course of an action purporting to be directed against religious extremists. In fact Sadat used a more general term to describe those whom he had now locked up – *'arzal,* the vicious. Almost the entire population of Egypt, it now seemed, was potentially vicious.

I think it is worth describing my own arrest in some detail because what happened to me was happening simultaneously to hundreds of others in every walk of life throughout the length and breadth of Egypt.

At 2.15 in the morning of 3 September there was a knock on the door of my flat in Alexandria where I and two of my sons were staying. My second son heard the knocking, went to the door, and found that there were two officers from the state security police demanding to be let in. He asked them to wait until later in the morning, but they said that if the door was not opened immediately they would have to break it down. My son woke me up. I opened the door and spoke to the police officers, who told me I was to accompany them to security headquarters. Looking at my watch, and seeing what the time was, I reminded them that it was I who had coined the phrase 'the visitors of the dawn' to describe such intrusions, and that I had often in print condemned these as tyrannical. They said they were sorry, but they were simply obeying orders.

I was told I had ten minutes in which to get ready. 'Should I take a bag with me?' I asked. 'Oh yes,' they said, 'that is what the ten minutes are for – for you to pack in.' I asked how big a bag I ought to pack, and they said enough for one or two days. 'Shall we be going to Cairo?' I asked, and was told no, we should be remaining in Alexandria. I suggested that if, after all, we did go to Cairo we might make the journey in my car rather than a police van. 'No,' they answered. 'There are other arrangements. Please hurry.' So I packed, said goodbye to my son, but did not embrace him, nor did I wake my younger son who was still asleep. 'I am at your disposal,' I told the policemen.

When I came out of my flat I was horrified by what I saw. On the small landing (there are only two flats to each floor) were at least ten soldiers, all armed with automatic rifles. The glass in the door leading to the service stairs had been broken and soldiers were stationed there too. Every floor in the block of flats was occupied by troops, and I could hear them speaking to each other over their walkie-talkies: 'Mission number nine completed . . .' 'Am I mission number nine?' I asked. It appeared that I was.

The lift doors had been left open, and the two police officers and two of the armed soldiers indicated that I was to get into the lift with them. I pointed out that the maximum load for the lift was four persons and we were five. 'Never mind,' they said.

When we reached the ground floor I found that the entrance was filled with troops. Our apartment building is in a narrow street leading to the sea and both ends of this had been blocked by trucks loaded with security police. 'It looks like a scene from Z,' I said to the officer, but he did not understand the reference.

As we walked towards the officer's car I asked him what this was all about, but he said he was not permitted to tell me anything. I would have to wait until we reached headquarters; I would find out there. The officer tried to be friendly. He told me how much he used to enjoy the articles I wrote in *Al Ahram* in the old days. He asked if this was the first time I had been arrested. I said it was. 'Ah well,' he said, 'times change.'

An amazing scene greeted us when we arrived at the headquarters of

Alexandria State Security Police. Hundreds of police were milling around, marshalling their prisoners into the specially built Peugeot station-wagons, which then disappeared in convoys along the Cairo road, sirens blaring and lights flashing. I saw young and old, sheikhs and priests, all suffering the same fate. Among familiar faces I recognized that of Dr Kadi, just about to leave in one of the convoys. I hailed him. 'We'll meet later,' he shouted. 'Now you know what is going on,' said the officer who had brought me in. 'Will you please telephone to my son and tell him we are going to Cairo?' I asked. 'With pleasure,' he said. 'What is your telephone number?' 'Surely the Security Police know that,' I said. But he never did telephone.

Among those in the same convoy as myself were Ibrahim Talaat, a former Wafd deputy, now aged sixty-six, Adel Eid, a former judge and one of the group of independent deputies, Kamel Ahmed, a Nasserite deputy who had been got rid of at the last election, Abu el-Ez el-Hariri, a prominent labour leader who had been a deputy several times and was a highly respected parliamentarian, and Ahmed Farghal, a deputy from the Action Party. We headed off down the agricultural road towards Cairo, no doubt terrifying out of their wits the villagers who were awoken by these fearsome cavalcades. For me the most alarming aspect of the journey was that the soldier driver was obviously half asleep, the truck lurching from side to side as he tried to keep up with the motorcycle escort. I begged for him to be given a cup of tea to wake him up, but we sped on.

We were crowded together in our police truck, since more were crammed into it than it was supposed to hold, so we chatted together, trying to come to some conclusion as to what was happening, though discreetly because the guards were listening. I said I thought the operation betrayed a bad case of nerves. Then we speculated about where we were being taken, and listened to the radio, but as this was only tuned to the Koran station we got no enlightenment from it. The only light relief on the journey was provided by Ibrahim Talaat who insisted on stopping the convoy so that he could piss. 'I suffer from prostate trouble,' he explained. 'If you don't stop you will have my death on your hands.' So the convoy was stopped.

We reached Cairo at seven o'clock and asked to be allowed to buy newspapers but permission was not granted. We drove past the turning that would have taken us to the office of the State Prosecutor, which was where we thought we were probably heading. We also passed the turning off to the Citadel prison, and from this we concluded that our destination was to be Maadi and the Tora prison. This was Egypt's newest gaol, a triumph of American penal technology transplanted onto Egyptian soil and tastefully named *sijn el-salam*, 'the prison of peace'.

I had imagined that I would be treated as I knew politicians or intellectuals or journalists were usually treated in gaol and so had brought some books with me. But I was quickly undeceived. At reception everything we had was taken from us – not only books, but paper and pens, medicines, wallets, money and even our clothes. All we were allowed to keep was the underclothes we had on, a towel and a toothbrush – but no toothpaste; we might have concealed poison in the toothpaste. We were told that next day a medical team would come round and issue us with toothpaste and any medicaments we needed. At reception I found many of the distinguished figures in Egyptian public life – politicians, economists, writers, intellectuals, but the priests I had seen under arrest in Alexandria were not with us in Tora.

I was taken to cell 14, where for the time being I was by myself. It was a small cell, the floor covered by ten rubber mattresses strongly impregnated with DDT. There was a hole in the floor to serve as a toilet and in one corner a pile of battered tin bowls. As there was nobody else in the cell I piled the mattresses on top of each other and tried to get some sleep.

But after only an hour the door of the cell was opened and a sergeant came in. 'Where's your bowl?' he asked brusquely. 'I haven't got a bowl,' I said. 'There they are,' he said, pointing to the pile in the corner. 'Take one for your food.' I saw that behind him was a soldier carrying a bucket full of horrible-looking molass and another soldier carrying a basket of bread covered in flies. 'I'm not going to eat that,' I said. The sergeant insisted, but I continued to refuse. 'I'll tell the officer you're refusing to eat,' he said. 'Tell anybody you like,' I said. He went out. After a short while an officer came in. 'Why won't you take your food?' he asked. 'I know this is your first time in prison, but you'll have to get used to prison ways.'

I asked the officer if I was to be alone in this cell. He said, 'No, you aren't. But because we respect you we want to make sure you have people you like sharing with you.' I asked him where the people were who had been in the same convoy with me from Alexandria, and he said that they were in cell 13, 'but it's full.' 'Why don't you ask if some of them would care to come in here with me?' I suggested. So he went out, and when he came back reported that Ibrahim Talaat and Kamel Ahmed had volunteered, as well as some of the young fundamentalists, led by a young man called Akmal, who wanted to have discussions with me. I said they would all be welcome, so in a short time cell 14 was full to capacity.

At 3.00 p.m. another officer came in and told me I was to accompany him. 'You're lucky,' said Ibrahim Talaat. 'Obviously there has been pressure from outside and you are going to be released. It's a miracle.' 'Don't be silly, Ibrahim,' I told him. 'Once they decided to lock me up, nothing is going to make them change their minds.' 'Bring your things,' said the officer; so, still uncertain what it was all about, I collected my toothbrush and towel and went out.

I found a general and three brigadiers waiting for me. They said they wanted to search my flat, my office and my house in the country. I pointed out that the road to the country house was very bad; 'Can't it wait till tomorrow?' 'No,' they said. 'We have our orders.' So we all got into a car and set off. I learned that this part of the exercise was known as Operation 5.

We drove to my flat, and I saw that the whole apartment block was surrounded by Security Police. 'What's the point of all this?' I asked. 'Even if I had been in Paris, and you had told me by telephone that there was a warrant for my arrest, I would have come. And if you wanted to search my flat, one soldier would have been enough.'

However, I found that my flat was already occupied. My escort undertook a thorough search, opening all the drawers and cupboards. 'What exactly is it you are looking for?' I asked the general, who belonged to the State Security Police. He made no answer but began to inspect my books. When he found some dealing with Islam (my last book had been about the Iranian revolution) he seemed pleased. 'Aha!' he said. 'Are you going to accuse me of being an Islamic fundamentalist?' I asked. 'These are some of the books I needed for my own book on Iran.' Again he made no answer, but handed the books that had aroused his attention to one of his assistants. He also confiscated some of my files.

Then we moved into the bedrooms. Again I asked him what it was he was looking for. This time he answered: 'Papers.' 'What papers?' I asked. 'Political papers.' I told him all my important papers were in

London. 'If you give me back my passport,' I said (it had been taken from my desk during the search) 'we could go together to London to look at them.' He did not seem to think much of the idea.

Another document which cheered up the general was a copy of a statement by the New Wafd Party of their attitude towards the Camp David agreements. This had a card attached to it on which was written 'with best regards, Fuad Seraggedin.' (I had met Seraggedin at a funeral and he had asked me if I had seen their statement. I said I had not, and he had promised to send me a copy.) 'You might leave the card,' I said as he put the statement away with the other confiscated documents. 'No, no,' said the general. 'It's important.'

Search of the flat completed, we all got into the car again and set off for the country house at Birgash. The unmetalled road to it is extremely uneven, and by now I was very tired. When we arrived I found that the farm too was under occupation, in this case by the police belonging to Giza province. Some of their trucks were being driven over the flower-beds, and I protested, but when one of their officers tried to stop his men from picking and eating my mangoes I told him to let them go ahead. For my own part, though by now I was extremely hungry, having had nothing to eat all day, mangoes on an empty stomach were not what I wanted. The wife of the watchman offered to produce some eggs, but unfortunately she fried them in butter, and because I suffer from stones in the kidney and gall-bladder I could not eat them. But just before we all left – the searchers having found nothing more suspicious than a book about Karl Marx, which presumably meant that in addition to being a Moslem fundamentalist I was a Marxist – the watchman pressed into my hands five loaves of flat bread and five hard-boiled eggs.

We got back to the prison at about 10.30. I was determined not to complain about any of the events of the day, because I knew that the intention was to wear down our resistance and make us lose our self-respect. I asked the officer on duty if I could keep the food I had brought with me, and he agreed. My cell-mates were rather disappointed to see me return and to find that I had not been released, but they were happy to share the food, and we spent the night talking together.

I found that my experience as a reporter enabled me to take quite a detached view of everything that was happening. I could see myself as a spectator at an historical drama rather than as a victim of injustice, watching myself as dispassionately as I watched all the others in prison. I found that the prison was constructed on four floors and had three thousand inmates, all of them arrested on 3 September.

For the first eleven days we were locked up in our cells with no newspapers or information of any sort of what was going on in the outside world, and no periods of exercise. I tried to compensate by doing physical jerks in the limited space available. We had no tea or coffee, but only tap water to drink. The young Moslem fundamentalists, who had some prison experience, tried to teach me how to wash all over using only the contents of a small bowl of water, and when after three days I was finally obliged to use the hole in the floor they formed a screen round me.

We slept packed close together on the floor, our mattresses all touching each other. We suffered from the attacks of flies by day and of mosquitoes by night – bombers by day and fighters by night, as I used to say. After four days a medical team at last appeared and handed out some of the medicines we needed.

The third of September found Pope Shenoudah in a monastery at Wadi Natrun. Ever since Sadat's attack on him in Parliament on 14 May 1980 Shenoudah had expected some action to be taken against him. He knew that the President enjoyed some support in the Coptic community, both from those who had profited from the *infitah* and from those of his fellow-religionists who were opposed to him. He was also well aware that some leading churchmen, including Matta el-Miskeen, were in close touch with the President.

On 3 September, 170 bishops and priests were arrested, though no move was made against the Pope himself. But two days later troops began to take up positions round the monastery, and as it was known that the President was going to make a speech that day explaining the arrests, it was clear that action was now imminent. The Pope's secretary, Anba Ibshwy, asked his master if he was going to watch the President's speech on television. He said he did not propose to, and went into his room to read. Anba Ibshwy, however, listened to the President's speech, and so heard the announcement that the Pope had been suspended and his functions transferred to a patriarchial committee of five, in which Bishop Samweel was the most prominent figure. With some embarrassment Anba Ibshwy gave the news to his master, who commented that this was not as serious as he had expected.

Shortly after, the commander of the troops now in position round the monastery knocked at its door. The monk who opened it asked what he wanted, and was told that the man they wanted was not the Pope but Anba Ibshwy. This was reported to Ibshwy who in turn told the Pope and asked for instructions. The Pope told him, 'Go.' The troops took him away and the door of the monastery was sealed.

A month later Bishop Samweel was to be killed by the side of the President. For many Copts his fate was divine judgement for his having usurped the position which rightly belonged to another, and popular credulity was further encouraged when a journalist who had written an article in *Al Ahram* attacking Shenoudah suffered a heart attack three days later.

Only once in the succeeding months was Shenoudah permitted to leave his monastery, and this was to attend the requiem mass in Cairo Cathedral for Bishop Samweel. Leading Copts from government and business were in the congregation, but few ordinary people. Although the service was conducted in the name of Shenoudah, as Patriarch and head of the Church, he was not allowed to officiate in any way, and after the conclusion of the service he returned to his monastery, where, at the time of writing, he remains.

Though we did not know it at the time, Sadat said that it had been necessary to take action against 'certain elements which threatened the unity and security of the country', and that he would give an explanation of the action he had taken to Parliament on 5 September. Also unknown to us – and of course not reported in the newspapers – was the fact that the Minister for Presidential Affairs, Mansur Hassan, had tried in vain to see the President immediately before the arrests, and now they were accomplished felt strongly that this was the wrong way to do things. He believed it was a serious mistake to lump Moslem fundamentalists and politicians together and to treat them all in the same say; they were different categories of people and should be treated differently. Sadat's attitude was that Mansur Hassan didn't understand, and that in any case it was none of his business. So he relieved him of his post and made him Deputy Speaker of the Parliament instead.

In his speech to Parliament Sadat said that the arrests had been made under article 74 of the Constitution. This was copied from article 16 of the Constitution of the Fifth Republic in France, which gives the President in a time of emergency the power to abolish constitutional guarantees and take whatever action he thinks necessary. But though this was De Gaulle's own Constitution, he only invoked article 16 once, and then only for twenty-four hours, during the riots of the summer of 1968 when he went to meet the generals in Germany. There was no remotely comparable emergency in Egypt in September 1981. Yet Sadat not only ordered the arrest of three thousand people, but also carried out a purge of universities and the press and confined the head of the Coptic Church to a monastery, transferring his authority to a committee.

Probably realizing that in spite of the applause which greeted his statement to Parliament not everyone was convinced by his explanation, Sadat decided to give a press conference. This was held on 7 September in Mit Abu el-Kom, and was attended by a number of foreign correspondents. The first question he was asked was about me, which was annoying enough, but the next one was even worse. The correspondent of the American television network, ABC, said, 'You were in the States little more than a week ago. Did you clear your action with President Reagan?' At this Sadat completely lost his temper. 'If this was not a free country,' he said, 'I would have you shot.' It was all extremely embarrassing, particularly for members of his family who were present. Sadat's daughter left the press conference in tears.

What particularly infuriated Sadat was the fact that it was his own medium, television, which had let him down. He realized that instead of appearing in his normal role as a benevolent father figure he had been a flop. He felt betrayed. His only solution was to try again, in the same medium but without questioners. He would treat the nation to a televized fireside chat in the manner of President Roosevelt. So on 15 September he went before the nation and at first seemed reasonably relaxed. But he rambled on from one subject to another, and spent an hour attacking Fuad Serageddin – 'This pasha, this child of feudalism, living in luxury,' comparing him to Louis XVIII and the Bourbons of the Restoration who had learned nothing and forgotten nothing. Then he devoted another hour to attacks on me, making five principal accusations. The first was that I was an atheist and had confessed as much to him, and that in my book on Iran I had said that the Moslem fundamentalists represented the wave of the future (which was simply not true and in any case hardly squared with the charge of atheism). Secondly, I had so many friends among kings and presidents and leading politicians in the Arab world and elsewhere that I had become a rival 'centre of power'. Thirdly, I made money by writing scurrilous things about Egypt – but he failed to give a single concrete example to back up the charge. Fourthly, I presented the outside world with a distorted and defamatory picture of Egypt; and finally that I was plotting with Fuad Seraggedin to produce a newspaper for the Wafd. The card signed by Fuad Seraggedin which had been removed from my flat by the searchers was produced as evidence that he and I had been in frequent contact over the past years, whereas in fact we had only a few casual meetings on occasions such as funerals of common friends.

Then Sadat turned his attention to some of the religious leaders, but this was probably his greatest mistake. He was particularly bitter about Sheikh Mahalawi, who had openly criticized the President's luxurious life-style and even attacked Jihan. 'Now this lousy sheikh finds himself thrown into a prison cell, like a dog,' he said. This created an extremely bad impression. People were unhappy too at his sneering references to the fundamentalists. He mocked the girls wearing *chadors* – 'going about like black tents' – and the young men with beards. But, after all, the Prophet Mohamed had a beard. So the final result of this marathon four and a half hour discourse explaining what Sadat now called 'The Revolution of 5 September' was that it left people more confused than ever as to what he was really up to. More and more people now tuned in to foreign broadcasts in an attempt to find out.

2

6 OCTOBER

ONE OF THE MANY listening to outside broadcasts was a first lieutenant in the army called Khaled Ahmed Shawki el-Islambouli. He was aged twenty-four when he first made his appearance in the pages of history, on Wednesday, 23 September 1981, a day that was to be fateful for him and for Egypt.

At 10.15 in the morning of that day Lieutenant Islambouli was summoned by his commanding officer, Major Makram Abdel A'al of 333 Artillery Brigade, to inform him that he had been chosen to take part in the parade on 6 October to commemorate the beginning of the 1973 war. He was to lead a detachment of twelve guns with their trailers. Lieutenant Islambouli asked to be excused. He said he had already made arrangements to spend the feast (8 October was the start of the Eid el-Adha) with his family in Mallawi, their village in Upper Egypt. The major refused to accept his excuses, and after a bit of an argument Islambouli said: 'Very well, I accept. Let God's will be done.'

The significance of this remark was, not surprisingly, lost on Major Abdel A'al. All he could see was one of his junior officers, who was known to be religiously inclined but to whom no suspicion attached, accepting, albeit reluctantly, a routine order which had been given him. But we now know that it was in the split second before Islambouli's 'I accept' that the idea of assassination came to him, together with the resolve to carry it out.

How had this young man become prepared for so momentous a decision? All he knew was that he belonged to a small group of like-minded fundamentalists in the main stream of Islamic thought, the *gama'at el-islamiyeh*. Though now largely driven underground, this stream had flowed continuously for a long time, nourished by publicists like Rashad Ridha and semi-legal or clandestine organizations like the Moslem Brotherhood and *takfir wa hijra*. The new groups, such as that to which Khaled belonged, were known as *'anquds*, the Arabic for a bunch of grapes, each *'anqud* being separate and self-contained, so that if plucked from the main bunch none of the other *'anquds* would suffer, nor would the removal of one grape on a bunch affect the other grapes. This was not exactly an organization on the traditional cell basis of conspirators, but something at the same time very compact and very loose. The mainstream of Islamic fundamentalism was shared belief and common experience for all its adherents, but the islands which broke the surface of the mainstream were out of sight of each other. There seems to have been some organized contact, probably in mosques, between the heads (*umara*) of different *'anquds*, amounting to a consultative assembly (*majlis el-shura*), but whether there was ever an effective overall direction of all *jihad* groups is still not clear.

Islambouli was aware that since the beginning of the year the word had been circulating in the *gama'at el-islamiyeh* that President Sadat had been condemned to death. A theoretical question had been put to the Mufti Dr Omar Abdel-Rahman Ali Abdel-Rahman: 'Is it lawful to shed the blood of a ruler who does not rule according to God's ordinances?' His answer – though neither answer nor question mentioned any specific name – was that the shedding of such blood was lawful. Later, when he was asked to give a specific opinion about Sadat, but without being told of the action proposed against the President, he hesitated: 'I cannot say that he has definitely crossed the line into infidelity.' After this the conspirators had no further use for him.[1]

Members of the *gama'at el-islamiyeh* divided mosques into three categories. The first category was called *el-mesajid el-derar*, that is to say mosques built for some mundane reason – by a monarch to enhance his fame or by a wealthy man to perpetuate his memory. In their eyes such mosques did not owe their existence to any genuinely Islamic inspiration, but to some person's playing at being a Moslem, as the Tartars had done in the Middle Ages. Such mosques they would not attend, even though they included some of the oldest and most famous in Cairo. The second category was known as *el-mesajid el-majhoula*, 'unknown mosques', meaning that it was not known how or why

[1] Dr Omar Abdel-Rahman was to be tried with Islambouli and the others at the first trial, which was concerned solely with the actual assassinations, but was acquitted. He is due to appear with almost four hundred others at the second trial, which is concerned with the conspiracy. He had for some time taught in Saudi Arabia, where he seemed to have done well since $20,000 were found in his flat after his arrest.

they had been built. These mosques were not given the benefit of the doubt and were also boycotted. The only mosques they accepted belonged to the third category, *mesajid el-taqwa*, 'pious mosques', mostly new ones in the poorer quarters of the cities or in the countryside with names like 'The Light', 'The Islamic Path', 'Glory of Islam', 'Lights of Mohamed'. These were frequented by the new fundamentalists, and it was in them that they met each other, and in them that the word went round that Sadat must die.

Lieutenant Islambouli knew this. He knew too that the *fetwa* denouncing Sadat placed a particular responsibility on members of *'anquds* in the armed forces because they had a better chance of obtaining access to the President than had civilians. He knew too that in his own *'anqud* there was a senior officer, but he did not know his name or rank or branch of service.

Khaled el-Islambouli was born on 14 November, 1957, at Mallawi in Upper Egypt. His father was Ahmed Shawki, a lawyer, in 1981 aged sixty and head of the legal department of the sugar company in Nag Hamadi. He had married in 1952 a girl five years younger than himself, called Kadria, and they had four children, two boys and two girls. The elder son, Mohamed, now aged twenty-six, was in his last year in the Faculty of Commerce in the University of Assiut. The elder daughter, Anisa, was aged twenty-eight, a graduate from the Commercial Institute in Assiut, and married to an official in the Ministry of Social Affairs living in Heliopolis. The younger daughter, Somaya, had taken her BA in education at the University of Assiut and was married to an accountant working for the Arab Contractors Company. The atmosphere in the house was conservative and nationalist. (It is significant that the parents had married in the year of the revolution and that their younger son had been given the name Khaled, which was the name of Nasser's son and so, like Nasser's own name, extremely popular for children born immediately after the Suez crisis.)

Khaled's primary education was in the Notre Dame missionary school in Mallawi, after which he had three years in a school run by the sugar company in Nag Hamadi, followed by another three years at a secondary school called the Aruba (Arabism) School. (It had originally been an American missionary school, but had been taken over and its name changed when all such institutions were Egyptianized.) Khaled had always wanted to go into the air force, but when his aim of becoming a pilot was thwarted by his failure to pass the examination for the Air Academy he settled for the School of Artillery, and graduated with honours in 1978.

Khaled's unit was stationed at Huckstep Camp near Cairo, which still retained the name of the American general after whom it had been called when it was built for American forces during the war. This made it possible for him to spend most of his weekends – Thursday and Friday nights – at his sister's house in Heliopolis, not far away. He would take his laundry there, wash it himself, and take it back with him clean to camp on Saturday morning. This Heliopolis link was to prove useful.

It is now possible to trace the origins of the conspiracy through the report compiled by the Deputy Minister of the Interior, General Hassan Abu Basha (since appointed Minister of the Interior). Interrogation of the prisoners after the assassination revealed that a meeting of some members of Khaled's *'anqud* took place at the end of January or the beginning of February 1981. Those present at this meeting included Mohamed Abdel-Salam Farag Attiya, the religious head of the group, and Lieutenant-Colonel Abboud Abdel-Latif Hassan el-Zumr, the military head, the senior officer whose existence, but not whose name, had by September become known to Khaled.

The subject for discussion at the meeting was nothing less than taking over power in Egypt, and this naturally also involved the problem of disposing of Sadat. Colonel Zumr came from a village just across the Nile from the presidential Barrage rest house, and it was suggested that this might provide a suitable opportunity. But the consensus of opinion was that the whole area of the rest house was too well guarded for a direct attack on the President to offer any real chance of success. An alternative – to shoot down the President's helicopter as it landed at the rest house – was put forward only to be rejected because it was never known in which of the three machines the President was travelling. Also rejected was a proposal to demolish the rest house with shells from an anti-aircraft gun, because there was no guarantee that Sadat would die in the ruins. So the conclusion was reached that a more detailed and precise plan was necessary.

It was then that the 6 October parade was first mentioned. The President and most of the leading members of his government were certain to be there, very conspicuous, and it was suggested that they could be attacked by one of the planes in the display. Khaled was not present at this meeting, but through his *'anqud* heard of the idea to use the opportunity of the parade for the assassination. It was when ordered to take part in the parade that he realized the possibilities of a ground attack. In the course of his interrogation he said: 'I was reluctant to take part in the parade, but then I agreed to do so because it suddenly flashed into my mind that it was the will of God that I should take part, not for the sake of the parade but for the sake of the sacred mission.'

But had he already received an order as to what he should try to do? Or was he simply aware of the general aims of the *'anqud*? In other words, was the formative decision which led to the assassination his alone, or was it from the outset shared with others? Unfortunately this is something which was not properly investigated, the reason being that some military authorities wished to keep the trial of army officers and NCOs, who had, it was felt, disgraced the service, as far as possible in their own hands. The more the inquiry went into the ramifications of the conspiracy, the more it would become a matter not for the army alone but for the state security courts, and this they wanted to avoid. So the military inquiry concentrated on the single point of how exactly the actual act of assassination had been carried out.

A clear picture of how Khaled's resolution was formed is therefore lacking. But during his interrogation he did give three explanations in answer to the question: 'Why did you do it?' The first was that the existing laws in the country were not consistent with Islamic law and in consequence Moslems were suffering. The second was the peace which had been made with the Jews, and the third the recent arrest of Moslem leaders, their persecution and humiliation. Decoded, his grievances can be summed up as the social and economic conditions in the country, the Camp David agreements and government oppression. A fourth and more personal explanation might have been added – Khaled's elder brother, Mohamed, was among those members of Moslem groups who were rounded up on 3 September.

On that day Khaled was due in Mallawi, his father having written to him about a piece of land in the village where he wanted to extend his house with the help of both his sons. When Khaled arrived he found his mother and one of his sisters in tears. They told him that Mohamed had been arrested in the middle of the night and taken away without anything to eat or drink and without even a chance to dress. They did not know where he had gone. When Khaled heard of his brother's arrest he too wept. He knew that his brother was at risk because he had been in trouble with the police some months earlier for tearing down a poster of Sadat, hundreds of which had been stuck up on walls everywhere. Also Mohamed had happened to be in Mecca in December 1979 at the time of the attack by a group of fundamentalists led by Juhaiman el-Oteibi on the Great Mosque (the Haram). It may be that it was he who gave Khaled a copy of Oteibi's book *Seven Letters*, which was later found in his possession. Mohamed had always been very religious, and had in fact dropped out of college for a year for religious reasons.

Later Khaled's mother reported that he tried to comfort her by saying: 'There is an end to every tyrant.' He took her back to Cairo with him, in an attempt to distract her and so that she could stay with her daughter in Heliopolis. They also hoped to be able to visit Mohamed in Tora prison, but, like all other prisoners' relatives, in this they were unsuccessful. While Khaled's mother was in Heliopolis her son seemed to be always busy, and she assumed it was because he was preparing for the examination for promotion to captain. She did not know that on the day of his brother's arrest Khaled had written in his memorandum book a quotation from one of the books lent to him by Mohamed Abdel-Salam Farag Attiya: 'The greatest prize for a believer is salvation, and to kill or to be killed in the cause of God.'

Nothing is known of how Khaled spent the rest of the day after receiving and accepting the order to take part in the parade, but the very next morning, on Thursday, 24 September, he and his unit took part in a rehearsal for the parade, passing the empty stand in which the President and his party would be seated two weeks later. Khaled stated at his interrogation that at this rehearsal he studied the layout, and decided that his plan was feasible, but that great daring would be called for and he would need assistance. After the rehearsal he went back, as usual at weekends, to his sister's house in Heliopolis and spent the night there.

At seven o'clock in the evening of Friday, 25 September, Khaled went to see Abdel-Salam Farag, the spiritual leader of his *'anqud*, to tell him what had happened. This meeting took place in a friend's house where Farag was staying, his leg being in plaster after he had broken it, perhaps in his hurry to escape arrest on 3 September. Khaled reported the conclusions he had come to during the rehearsal – that the job could be done, but that he would need three people to help him. What did Farag think of the idea? Could he provide the three assistants?

It is time to take a closer look at Abdel-Salam Farag, the spiritual leader of Khaled's *'anqud* and so one of the key personages in the conspiracy. As has been pointed out,[1] the Pakistani fundamentalist, Abu el-A'ala Mawdudi, had drawn a distinction between the two stages which contemporary Islamic communities would have to pass through – the stage of weakness (*istidhaf*), and the stage of action (*jihad*). Those belonging to the *takfir wa hijra* group, who had achieved notoriety by the 1974 assault on the Military Technical College and the 1976 kidnapping of the ex-Minister of Waqf, believed that they represented a minority of true believers in a basically infidel society, and that during this stage of weakness their real duty was to withdraw themselves from society and prepare for the next stage, that of action. (These two acts of violence were uncharacteristic exceptions to their rule, to be justified only by special circumstances.) Others rejected this attitude. There was, they argued, nothing basically wrong with society, only with the rulers and the laws. Get rid of the rulers, change the laws, and it would be shown that the people are capable of responding. In other words, this was not the moment for weakness, but the moment for action.

Among these others was Abdel-Salam Farag. In 1980 Farag, who was by profession an electrical engineer, then aged twenty-seven, wrote a small, badly printed book of less than a hundred pages, called *The Absent Prayer*. In this he included a number of quotations from Moslem theologians (*fuqaha*) of the past, particularly Ibn Taimiya, the purport of which was that, just as the head is the most important part of the human body, so the ruler and the laws by which he rules are the most important part of the social and political body. If the rulers are hypocritical Moslems as the Tartars had been in Ibn Taimiya's day, they should be eliminated. The mass of the people would then be

---

[1] See p. 126.

revealed as basically sound. So Farag's 'absent prayer' was *jihad*, action. He did not believe that the time for action should be postponed, or that Egypt should be regarded as in the stage of *istidhaf*. Postponement could mean waiting for generations. But if the righteous seized power straight away, then they could ensure that the country was ruled justly according to *sharia* law.

The printing of *The Absent Prayer* created a problem inside Farag's own *'anqud*. Farag wanted his ideas to be given as wide a circulation as possible, but Colonel Zumr disagreed. He told Farag that the book would simply have the effect of drawing the attention of the authorities to their movement, and so he thought it ought to be suppressed. We should go on with our plans for seizing power without giving them dangerous publicity, he said. So all the five hundred copies of the book which had been printed, except for fifty or sixty which had already been distributed, were burned.[1] Khaled el-Islambouli was one of those who had read *The Absent Prayer*, and he had been convinced by it. So it was that on that Friday evening he went to see Farag.

Khaled and Farag had first met in the summer of 1980 when Khaled had been looking for a flat. He wanted to get married – not that, as far as is known, he had any particular girl in mind, but he felt that the time had come for this step to be taken. Flats in the Heliopolis area were hard to come by, and someone suggested that there might be a better chance in some of the new housing projects in the Boulak el-Dakrur area. So Khaled went to Boulak el-Dakrur, and going into a mosque to pray found there Farag discussing religious matters with some of his disciples. He got the impression that Farag must be a man of influence in the district and so approached him and asked for his help in finding a flat. Learning that Khaled was an army officer, Farag realized his potential usefulness, and used the flat-hunting pretext to see more of him. He gave him a copy of *The Absent Prayer* and some of the works of Ibn Taimiya and of the historian Ibn Kathir, another of the authors who had a considerable influence on fundamentalist thinking.

The very next day, Saturday, 26 September, Farag was able to

---

[1] The military court investigating the plot could not decide what to make of *The Absent Prayer*, so sent it to the Grand Mufti of Egypt for his opinion. He wrote a refutation of its arguments, which was published, but, as nobody had seen the book he was arguing against, his refutation was puzzling rather than enlightening.

produce the assistants Khaled had asked him for. They all met at the house of a common friend and fellow member of their *'anqud*, Abdel-Hamid Abdel-Salam Abdel A'al. He was a former army officer, very religious, who, having decided that the army was not the best way in which to serve God, had resigned his commission and opened a bookshop. He appears to have acted as contact man for the *'anqud*.

The two volunteers Farag had brought with him to the meeting were Ata Tayel Hemeida Reheil, aged twenty-seven, a reserve officer now working, like Farag, as an engineer, and Hussein Abbas Mohamed, a sergeant instructor in the Civil Defence School and for seven years champion marksman of the army. It was he who was to fire the first fatal shot at Sadat from the stationary truck. For Farag to be able to produce within twenty-four hours two such well-qualified assistants for such a desperate enterprise shows what a wide pool of like-minded men he must have been able to call upon.

Farag told the others present at this meeting – Khaled, Abdel-Salam, Abbas Mohamed, and Reheil – that what was proposed involved certain martyrdom; were they ready for that? They all said they were. Khaled then explained his plan to them. It was very simple. He would lead the column of twelve 131mm guns with their trailers taking part in the parade. He would arrange for a letter to be written purporting to come from his unit which would give them access to the assembly area; but they would have to shave off their beards. He would arrange for them to travel with him in the leading gun-trailer. He told them that he had measured the distance which would separate them from the reviewing stand and thought it was about thirty paces. Further particulars would be given later. All five swore to maintain absolute secrecy, and agreed to meet again in a week's time. After spending an hour or more in reading the Koran together they dispersed.

Farag told Khaled that the weapons he had asked for would be provided. Khaled had said he needed four hand grenades, a pistol and some ammunition, because, although those taking part in the parade would be armed, security had been considerably tightened over the past two years and not only would they not be allowed to carry any ammunition for their weapons but the firing-pins would be removed.

So on Sunday, 27 September, Farag sent a messenger to a group of fundamentalists then engaged in the communal cultivation of some of the newly reclaimed land in Tahrir province (the large land reclamation scheme on the edge of the Delta inaugurated by Nasser). These men were all former members of *takfir wa hijra* who had been implicated in the kidnapping of Sheikh Mohamed el-Dhahabi, the ex-Minister of Waqf. They had received prison sentences, but later been released and had decided, in accordance with their *istidhaf* principles, to remove themselves from ordinary society to a remote area. Although these men were conscious of being under continual police scrutiny they were able to supply Farag's messenger with the four grenades and the pistol he had asked for as well as 120 rounds of ammunition for a Kolashnikov rifle.

It was now time for Farag to consult the military head of the *'anqud*, Colonel Zumr. Colonel Zumr had been employed in military intelligence – ironically, any clandestine meetings he arranged had been held in the mosque which was located inside the Intelligence headquarters. But some months earlier he had begun to feel that he was under suspicion, so without waiting to be arrested he had simply disappeared and gone underground. The police were in fact even now searching for him, and the Minister of Interior had told Sadat that Zumr had escaped the police net. Sadat sent Zumr a direct challenge, though without naming him, in the television speech he made on 25 September, the day when Khaled and Farag had their first meeting. 'I know,' he said, 'that there is one officer left at large, and he must be watching me now. We picked up all the others in five minutes, but one escaped. He will be listening to me, and I warn him that we shall catch him too.'

Farag's messenger, another engineer named Saleh Ahmad Saleh Jaheen, told Zumr, code-named Mansur (Khaled's code-name was Zafer, which like Mansur means 'victorious') what was proposed, but Zumr immediately vetoed it. He said it would be much too difficult to carry out, and in any case assassinating the President would not be enough. The aim they had in view was to take over power, and much more time would be needed to prepare for this.

When Farag heard of Zumr's veto he rejected it. He said he was confident that Khaled could carry out his plan and that it would be successful. The act of assassination would create an entirely new situation which they would be able to exploit, and other pillars of the state might be expected to fall at the same time as Sadat. This would not only decimate the top ranks of the government but would disperse the terror which at present held the masses in subjection. They would rise as the Iranian masses had risen. He accused Zumr of faint-heartedness. 'You must play your part,' he said, 'and not try to prevent others from playing theirs. And whatever you say, we are going to go ahead.' Zumr appreciated that Farag as a *faqih* had greater authority than he, so he withdrew his veto. Khaled was given final permission to go ahead, though with or without the sanction of his superiors he was now determined to act.

At their second meeting, on Friday, 2 October, Khaled told his fellow-conspirators that there was a problem over the driver of the truck. This man was, of course, not aware of what was being planned, and would somehow have to be got out of the way or made innocuous. Khaled suggested that before the parade he should be given a sleeping pill which would make him feel drowsy. Khaled could then explain to the rest of the column that, owing to his driver having been taken suddenly ill, he would have to drive the truck himself. So a pill was obtained from a chemist and given to Abbas Mohamed to see what effect it would have on him. It had none, so they had to think again. Khaled told them not to worry. He would threaten the driver with his pistol (as leader of the column he would naturally be sitting next to the driver) and terrify him into inactivity. Khaled decided to keep only eighty-one rounds of ammunition, among them four with green markings. These were pencil burners, and he gave them to Abdel-Salam to hide in the roof of his house.

By the evening of Friday, 2 October preparations were virtually complete, but it was agreed to have another meeting on Sunday, again in Abdel-Salam's house. So far it had not been decided whether Abdel-Salam himself should take part in the action as well as the other three – four, he felt, might be too many. But on Sunday it was seen that he had shaved off his beard, so it was clear that he meant to be included.

Khaled had prepared the ground well. He had got rid of three of the regular members of his gun crew; one had opportunely gone sick, another had been given leave and a third given a special duty elsewhere. The rest of his unit had been told that three other private soldiers had been posted to the unit to replace the absentees. It was hinted that these might in fact be from some branch of the intelligence, sent to check up on security in the parade in view of the somewhat tense atmosphere in the country.

So when the conspirators met on Sunday, Khaled told the other three that he was going to see his sister and would meet them later in front of the Maryland Casino in Heliopolis. He would drive them in Abdel-Salam's Fiat to the parade concentration area, drop them off and follow them to the camp shortly afterwards. He had provided them with passes authorizing them to go in.

While Khaled was at his sister's house, for the last time, he wrote a note which he put in an envelope and left for her, but which was not discovered until after he had been arrested. In this he wrote: 'Please give me your understanding. I have not committed any crime. What I have done, I have done for the sake of God, the Merciful, the Powerful. I do not want anything for myself. I am not seeking promotion or reward. If any of you suffer injury because of me, please forgive me.' Later, when Khaled's aunt visited him in prison, she asked him if he had not considered the effect his act would have on his father and mother. 'No,' was his answer, 'I thought only of God.'

Ata Tayel and Abbas Mohamed spent Friday and Saturday nights in Abdel-Salam's house, not talking about the enterprise before them, but spending most of their time reading the Koran. On Sunday everything went as Khaled had arranged. The three, now beardless and in uniform, got out of Abdel-Salam's car two hundred yards from the camp gate and went in (without, as it happened, being asked to show their passes). They went to Khaled's tent and asked for him. They were told he was not there, but that they themselves were expected. So they waited for him outside the tent. About a quarter of an hour later Khaled arrived, carrying the ammunition in a Samsonite briefcase. He greeted the newcomers brusquely and sent them off on fatigues.

The next morning, Monday, 5 October, the day before the parade, Khaled's batman was surprised to find that his officer had not eaten his breakfast himself but had handed it over to the three newcomers. He thought that perhaps Khaled was trying to ingratiate himself with the intelligence people.

Soon a brigadier drove through the camp giving orders through a loud-speaker that all arms were to be concentrated in special storage tents. He was followed by an officer from the Presidential Guard with orders that all strikers and firing-pins should be removed from weapons and handed over to each unit commander, who would be personally responsible for them. Khaled detailed two of the new arrivals 'from intelligence' to be in charge of security, one to guard the tent where the arms were stored and the other to collect all the strikers and firing-pins.

Tuesday, 6 October was the day of the parade. Khaled roused his unit at three o'clock because they had to be ready to move off at six. He took four machine-guns from those in the storage tent and loaded them, and instructed Abbas Mohamed to mark them so that they could be identified and put them back with the others. Abbas Mohamed put a piece of cloth in the four barrels. Khaled found that the strikers he had been supplied with by Farag were of an obsolete pattern and did not fit the guns, but as he now had a whole tent-full of strikers to choose from this presented no problem.

Before six they were all ready to move off. Khaled wanted to conceal the grenades under his seat in the cab, so he sent his driver off to buy him a sandwich from the mobile canteen in the camp, and while he was gone the grenades were put in position.

The order for the parade to move off was given. Khaled's vehicle was on the right of the column, nearest the reviewing stand, at a distance of about forty yards. As they came abreast of the stand Khaled suddenly drew his pistol and turned it on his driver, ordering him to stop. The driver did as he was told, putting on his brakes so violently that the truck slewed out of line. (Later, during his interrogation, Khaled was asked why the driver had stopped; was he an accomplice? Khaled said no, he was just scared. Why was he scared? 'Probably because he was a coward.')

As soon as the truck had come to a halt Khaled leaped out and hurled a grenade to create confusion. Meanwhile Abbas Mohamed stood up in the truck and began firing in the direction of the President. His first shot hit Sadat in the neck, and was almost certainly fatal. As soon as the firing started the driver and the rest of the crew jumped out on the side away from the stand and took shelter as best they could. Reheil threw a grenade which exploded half way between the truck and the stand. Later a fourth grenade was found unexploded in the chair where the Minister of Defence had been sitting.

The surprise was so complete that for at least thirty seconds there was no effective retaliation. Khaled reached the front row of chairs on the stand, followed by Abbas Mohamed, the other two racing to the sides of the stand and giving covering fire from the flanks. Khaled's defending counsel was later to claim that he shouted to Vice-President Mubarak and the Minister of Defence, 'Get out of my way. I only want this son of a dog!' Whether in fact he uttered these words will never be known for certain. If he did, they were inconsistent with the conspirators' plan to dispose of as many top-level members of the government as possible. On the other hand, it is conceivable that when Khaled came face to face with Sadat he forgot everything else in his hatred for the man he regarded as the arch-tyrant. Whatever the explanation, he continued to fire round after round into the body of the President, probably thinking that he was wearing a bullet-proof waistcoat and not wanting to leave anything to chance. By the time the firing had ceased and three of the four conspirators had been seized, Sadat and seven others were dead and there were twenty-eight wounded. For the first time the people of Egypt had killed their Pharaoh.

3

AFTER THE PARADE

LET US RETURN to Wednesday, 23 September, the day which was to prove fatal to Sadat, and see how he spent it.

In the morning he had a meeting with members of the newly instituted Supreme Council of the Press and told them what he proposed to do about the journalists who had been arrested on 3 September, with particular reference to those of them who thought they could copy their American colleagues and get a President turned out of office. Later, at the Barrage rest house, he met an envoy sent by President Mitterand to patch up a row which had blown up between them. After the 3 September arrests Mitterand had issued a statement deploring this 'undemocratic action', and this had greatly annoyed Sadat. The envoy explained that Mitterand had been speaking as a member of the French Socialist Party and not in the name of the French government.

On the same day Sadat gave another interview, this time for the NBC 'Today' programme, in which he referred to Egypt's sending arms to the guerrillas in Afghanistan 'because they are our Moslem brothers and in trouble'. The interviewer brought up the question of the Moslem fundamentalists; had they engaged in any terrorist activities? he asked. 'No', said Sadat, 'it's all a matter of meetings, not arms.'

Interviewer: 'If it is true that everybody in Egypt backs your policies, why have you arrested your political opponents as well as the Moslem fundamentalists?'

Sadat: 'I did not have any clampdown on my political opponents at all. The whole thing was because of the religious strife. These politicians I have arrested joined the religious elements, and would have exploited my arrest of the fundamentalists.'

Interviewer: 'What do you think of the comparison being made between you and the Shah?'

Sadat: 'I am really puzzled. This comparison is quite out of place, and those who make it are people filled with hatred. As you have seen from the plebiscite I have a 100 per cent support from my people, so this comparison must have been made by people filled with hatred. Unfortunately they mix opposition with their hatred. They are trying to tarnish my image and the image of Egypt. As for my own image in the world, I don't care, but I will not allow the image of Egypt to be tarnished.'

The newspapers of 23 September reported the possibility that the date of the parade might be brought forward from 6 October to 5 October, because 6 October was the day before the eve of the Eid, and so a holiday. The newspapers also said that in this parade for the first time the proportion of arms from the West would equal that of arms from Communist countries. Hitherto the latter had always predominated. It was pointed out that the President and other spectators would see many new American arms, including Phantoms and M131 armoured cars as well as French Mirage 2000s. New helicopters would also be on view, including the gigantic American Chinook, the British Sea King and the French Gazelle. The papers carried a report by the Institute of Strategic Studies in London which said that the Egyptian army was the most powerful in the Middle East.

The newspapers also quoted a statement by the Minister of Interior to the effect that all the underground organization of the Moslem Brotherhood was known to the security services. The leaders of the Brotherhood were making the biggest mistake of their lives if they thought that the security services were only concerned with the Brotherhood's old members and were unaware of the new recruits to the movement. 'We know them all,' said the Minister, 'the new as well as the old, and we are watching them all, including those who have been brought in since 1970.'

On 23 September the Patriarchal Committee, appointed to manage the affairs of the Church following the detention of Pope Shenoudah, made known some important resolutions, including one declaring that the Coptic Church was 'in complete obedience to the regulations of the Egyptian state'. *Time* magazine of the same date reported Bishop Matta el-Miskeen as declaring that the measures taken by President Sadat had saved Egypt.

September 23rd also saw the annual film festival at which prizes were awarded for the best films and actors. The film which won the first prize was called *The Devil Preaches*, and winner of the second prize was *The Fugitive*.

The papers of that day devoted a good deal of space to a human interest story concerning the President. Sadat always liked to remember people who had helped him before he became famous, and he talked about them in his numerous broadcasts. There was, for example, the man who had given him a cup of tea in Tel el-Kebir, and the man who had given him a lift when he was in a hurry – both at the time when, after coming out of prison, he was working as a contractor. In his last birthday broadcast Sadat had referred to the second of these simply as 'the man from Demru' (the village he came from). One of the President's listeners identified himself as 'the man from Demru', and was rewarded for his act of kindness, which was said to 'represent traditional village values', with the gift of a house. Now it was reported that the President had given 'the man from Demru' and his wife two tickets so that they could go on the *haj*.

Twelve days later, on Monday, 5 October, the eve of the parade, President Sadat was at his residence in Giza. The following morning, Tuesday, he awoke as usual at about 8.30, did some physical exercises, followed by massage and a shower. He then ate a light breakfast and began to prepare for the parade. He was determined that the occasion should be as big a success as possible, because he still had an uneasy feeling that he had not entirely succeeded in silencing criticism. A new uniform had arrived a few days before from his London tailor, and Jihan noticed that he was not putting his bullet-proof waistcoat on under the tunic. Sadat explained that it would spoil the set of the uniform. He remembered seeing a film of his Jerusalem journey, when he had worn the waistcoat, and this had made him look much fatter than he really was.

Sadat announced that he would travel to the parade in an open car. He had been in Mansura in an open car a few days before, where there were crowds in the streets, whereas today he would be surrounded by his army. So why hide himself? Adjusting the Sash of Justice completed his dressing, and he went out, failing to pick up his Field-Marshal's baton which had been put out on a table near the door but overlooked. Later Jihan was to interpret this omission as a bad omen.

Sadat arrived at the parade in an excellent humour. He indicated to the Sheikh of Al-Azhar and Bishop Samweel that he wanted them to sit close to him – the object being, of course, that the pictures should show him not only adorned with the emblem of justice but surrounded by the representatives of religion. Most of Sadat's conversation with his neighbours was about the new weapons on display, and everyone was listening to a broadcast commentary on the parade which was being relayed inside the stand as well as over the national radio and television services.

Units of the Egyptian air force performed spectacular aerobatics, their Phantoms emitting different coloured smoke, which was much applauded. 'Now comes the artillery,' said the commentator, though this was inevitably something of an anti-climax. Then suddenly one of the trucks swung out of line and halted. Those on the stand assumed that it had broken down and was being moved slightly nearer to the stand to avoid blocking the rest of the parade.

The first thing that made the spectators in the stand aware of anything unusual happening was when they saw two grenades in the air, followed by the sound of a shot. All those with any military training automatically ducked. The nearest member of the Presidential Guard to Sadat was a young brigadier, Ahmed Sarhan. In the testimony he later gave to the court of inquiry he stated: 'I ran to where the President was, and shouted repeatedly to him "Duck your head, Mr President." But it was already too late. He was covered in blood. I tried to clear the space around him. I drew my revolver and fired five rounds in the direction of someone I saw aiming his fire against the President.'

There was in fact almost forty seconds of total confusion and the first retaliatory shots were not heard until after about the first twenty seconds. Some of these were effective, because both Khaled and Abdel-Salem Abdel-Al received bullet wounds in the stomach, though this did not prevent them from continuing to fire into the stand. Hussein Abbas Mohamed, the marksman, went unscathed and was even able to get clean away from the parade area without being stopped. He went to the house of some of his relatives and was not arrested until two days later. Probably the others could have escaped too, such was the confusion, if they had given their minds to it.

On the stand everybody was now either dead, wounded, taking cover or starting up into frenzied activity. Mamduh Salem, the former Prime Minister and an ex-policeman, threw chairs in the direction of the President in an attempt to give him some protection. A former deputy Prime Minister was seen by all television viewers sneaking out of the stand to make his getaway. The Vice-President, Husni Mubarak, was unhurt, as was the Sheikh of Al-Azhar, but the President's principal aide-de-camp, General Hassan Allam, his personal photographer, and Bishop Samweel were among those who died.

Later there was inevitably to be an argument about where the blame lay for the security failure which had made assassination possible. The Americans had, at Sadat's request, taken over responsibility for protecting him, and had installed the most sophisticated precautions of every description at a cost of about $20 million. These included a special military unit trained to deal with international terrorism, but as it was not thought desirable to make them too conspicuous they had, during the parade, been stationed behind the stand, which meant that a distance of sixty yards separated them from the President. By the time they reached the scene it was too late.

There was in fact some confusion between overall responsibility for security of the parade and security inside the stand. The Presidential Guard was charged with protection of the President at all times, but Brigadier Ahmed Sarhan explained that his duties had been primarily to identify all those on the stand, to see that no unauthorized persons were admitted, and then to check on everything the President had to eat and drink. The fact is that nobody expected any trouble from the armed forces in the parade, knowing that they were all supposed to be effectively disarmed.

In the motorcade which, on this as on all occasions when the President travelled by road, had taken him from his residence to the parade, the presidential car had been followed by a first-aid truck. But it was quickly obvious that the President was in need of much more than first aid. It was essential for him to be taken as quickly as possible to the military hospital at Maadi, and this meant moving him by helicopter.

While all this was happening Jihan had been in a glass-fronted balcony attached to the stand. Now she rushed into the main stand, crying out: 'Where is the President? Where is the President?' She was able to get into the helicopter with him. This took off at 12.40 p.m.

According to the official hospital report the presidential helicopter arrived at Maadi at 1.20 p.m. – that is, forty minutes later – but the journey would normally take only five minutes. How is the delay to be explained? There is no clear answer to this question, but the helicopter was seen to land shortly before one o'clock at the helicopter pad adjoining the President's Giza residence. Jihan is known to have rushed into the house and put through two telephone calls to the United States. One was to her elder son Gamal, who was then in Florida. She learnt that Gamal had gone with some friends to an island off the coast of Florida, so she told the person who answered the telephone to get hold of him immediately at any cost and tell him to call his mother on a matter of the greatest urgency. Who the other call was to Jihan has never revealed, but it is certain that it must have been someone of the highest importance, and that her purpose was to obtain from the most authoritative source possible some outside indication of what was happening in Egypt. After these two telephone calls had been made Jihan rejoined the helicopter which continued its course up the Nile to the Maadi hospital.

The official report from the hospital stated that when the President arrived he was in a state of complete coma, with no recordable blood pressure or pulse, 'the eyes wide open, with no response to light', and no reflexes anywhere. The report went on to list his injuries, which included two bullet entrances under the left nipple, one entering below the knee and exiting at the top of the left thigh, as well as several wounds in the right arm, chest, neck and round the left eye. There was 'a foreign substance which can be felt by touch under the skin of the neck', which was presumably the first and fatal bullet fired by Abbas Mohamed. The doctors detailed the attempts made at resuscitation, but by 2.40 it was concluded that there was no activity in either heart or brain and that the President must be declared dead. The cause of death was given as shock, internal haemorrhage in the chest cage, lesions in the left lung and all main arteries. The report was signed by twenty-one doctors.

From the outset Jihan had realized that there was no hope of her husband's survival. As she waited outside the room where the doctors were operating the call came through from Gamal in Florida. 'Gamal,' she said, 'I am going to tell you something important, but you must not let anything show in your expression or behaviour. This must be kept secret for the time being. Your father has been shot. You must come back immediately.'

Gamal rang the Egyptian Embassy in Washington, and then the Embassy in London to see whether arrangements could be made to fly a surgeon to Cairo, if that could be of any use. But hearing on the news that his father was dead, he flew to Washington where a special plane belonging to a friend was put at his disposal and he was flown back to Cairo.

Other members of the family, who had heard the news, were by now hurrying to the hospital. Among these was his elder brother, Talaat, who was shown into the room where Sadat was lying, his whole body encased in bandages, with only part of the face visible. Sadat had once sent his brother, who refused to have anything to do with the get-rich-quick activities of other members of the family, to prison on a trumped-up charge, as proof of his worthiness to be called 'the just'. This, Talaat said, broke his heart. But, as he looked at the body of Anwar, he spoke these words to it: 'Now, go. I have forgiven you.'

To begin with nobody could be certain whether the assassination was an isolated incident or part of a wider conspiracy. Most of the senior members of the government had been on the reviewing stand since ten o'clock; now, as they hurriedly dispersed, they desperately sought for information – how widespread was the trouble? Who else had been killed? Even the Minister of Interior could do no more than telephone to his own office to ask what was happening. It was in fact from Monte Carlo radio that most Egyptians first heard the news that their President had been assassinated.

The only place where there was any trouble was Assiut. Colonel Zumr was there and he had contacts with member of another *'anqud*. Their belief was that news of the death of the tyrant would release the masses from the fear which had so long inhibited them, and they would start a spontaneous uprising. The University of Assiut was a stronghold of the *gama'at el-islamiya,* so it was hoped that Assiut could be taken over as the nucleus of the new order until Cairo and the rest of the country had swung into line. Zumr and his accomplices made their way to the governerate. There was considerable bloodshed, and over a hundred policemen were killed. But the uprising attracted little or no popular support and was soon overwhelmed, Zumr himself being taken prisoner two days later in Giza.

In fact life in most parts of Cairo and other cities continued to be more or less normal after the initial shock of the news of the assassination had been digested. In some of the poorer quarters of Cairo the authorities even took the precaution of switching off the electricity for fear that there might be demonstrations of popular jubilation. For three days radio and television broadcast nothing but Koran recitals. The conspirators had managed to recruit an official of the state broadcasting service, and a proclamation had been written and recorded by Farag which was to be read over the air, appealing to the people to rise in the name of religion and asking the armed forces to remain at least neutral, if they did not feel able immediately to support the Islamic revolution. But this part of the conspiracy was very imperfectly prepared and never came to anything.

Khaled's mother was one of those listening to the broadcast account of the parade. She was now back at their house in Mallawi, Khaled having persuaded her that she was not going to be allowed to see Mohamed in prison, and that she had better go home for the Eid. He gave her £E70 to buy a sheep for the Eid and told her he would join her a little later and they would slaughter and eat it together. She heard the sound of firing on the radio and the announcer say that the President and Vice-President 'had left the parade'. She said later that this somehow made her feel uneasy, and she tried tuning in to foreign stations to see if she could pick up any more news. But of course she had not then the slightest suspicion that her son was in any way involved.

The next day her husband bought copies of the newspapers which carried photographs of the assassination. He recognized Khaled, and with trembling hands thrust the paper in front of his wife. 'Look at that!' he cried. She asked him what he meant. 'Look at who is firing,' he said. 'Who do you think he is?' She now realized that this was indeed their son, but refused to admit it. 'No, no,' she cried, 'it's not him.' In later editions there was a picture of the assassin, but taken after he had been beaten up by his captors so that much of his face was covered in bandages. 'They've killed him,' screamed his mother when she saw this photograph. 'They have taken him out of the morgue just so that they can take a picture of him!'

4

WHO AND WHY?

AFTER THE ARREST of those involved in the conspiracy their houses were searched by Group 75 of the Intelligence. In every house a compass was found, for they all wanted to be absolutely certain that they were facing towards Mecca whenever and wherever they prayed. Almost all possessed cassettes of sermons by Sheikh Kishk, Sheikh Mahalawi and others. The house of Abdel Salem el-A'al, the contact man, was to some extent typical, containing sixty-four cassettes, two military uniforms, one pair of khaki trousers, an air defence beret, a first lieutenant's badge, several army buttons, religious books, leaflets put out by the Students' Union, and a photograph of Menachem Begin which had been torn into pieces.

The arrested men were savagely beaten up, as official medical reports testify. They were kept chained to their cots, and beaten with whips and hosepipes, sustaining fractures of the skull, knees and other parts of the body. Khaled's interrogation started ironically enough in the same military hospital at Maadi where the body of Sadat was lying. His interrogators tried to break him down by telling him that the President had only been wounded, but though he was in agony he was not deceived. 'You can't fool me,' he said. 'I put thirty-four bullets into his body. Try another trick.'

The police who were sent to Farag's house questioned his wife Aisha. They told her: 'Here you've only got two rooms – a living room and a bedroom. But lots of people were coming to the house all the time. How could you, a good Moslem, deal with them? Did you wear your *chador* inside the house?' She said: 'No. People used to knock at the door. I would release the latch but not open the door. Then I would tell whoever was knocking to wait while I went into the other room. So I never knew who came to the house and they never saw me.' The authorities gave strict instructions that any questioning of women suspects should never be carried out by men.

* * *

When the trial of the conspirators opened Khaled was asked whether he pleaded guilty or not guilty. He answered: 'I killed him but I am not guilty. I did what I did for the sake of religion and of my country.' All the other accused answered in similar words. When questioned about the services of defending lawyers their answer was 'God defends those who believe in Him.'

When Farag was asked what they had hoped to achieve by killing the President, his answer was: 'To warn all who come after him and to teach them a lesson. My aim at this stage of the struggle is to deter all those rulers who may follow.' Abbas Mohamed, the champion army marksman, said in evidence: 'Before I was asked to join the conspiracy I had come to the conclusion that the man ought to be killed, and I was praying to God that I would be given the honour of making the tyrant pay for his sins.' He was asked whether he had felt hatred against the President. His answer was: 'No. I have no hatred against him. I am a Moslem, and I pray. I care only for Islam.'

All the accused stated that their sole target was the President (though they never referred to him during their interrogation by his title). According to Khaled: 'I said to Abu Ghazala [Minister of Defence] and Mubarak "Out of the way; I only want this dog!"' Describing his part in the operation Ata Tayel Reheil said: 'I went to the stand. I was the last to arrive. I could not see my target [i.e., Sadat] but I saw the front row of chairs with nobody on them. I began to fire at the empty chairs, and then I was hit by someone firing at me, I think from about the fifth row. But I did not return his fire, although he was in easy range. We wanted to kill him [Sadat] alone, to make him an example for those who came after him.' Abbas Mohamed was asked whether he had not realized that innocent people might be killed in the shooting. He said, yes, he had been aware of the possibility, but he was prepared to fire on anyone who obstructed his path to the tyrant. He regarded it as valid in religious terms to do this. When Reheil was asked the same question his answer was that at the Day of Judgement everybody would be judged according to his intentions, and if an innocent man had been killed, God would ensure his resurrection.

Farag was questioned about *The Absent Prayer*. He said: 'I collected it myself from the works of the *salafyin* (the old theologians), from those learned Moslems who were following the path of the Prophet, may the blessings of God be upon him. I made this collection in the latter part of 1980. I had it printed at a press in the Embaba district near the mosque of Khalid ibn Walid. I gave the manuscript to a man called Abu Sariya who is part-owner of the press. He printed five hundred copies and I paid him £E90 for this. We had only distributed fifty or sixty copies when Abboud Zumr objected, being afraid of the harm it might do to our organization, so I burnt the remaining copies.'

Farag was asked whether he thought it was right to attack a man who was trying to introduce democracy into Egypt. 'What sort of democracy is this with jaws and claws?' said Farag. (Sadat once said that people made the mistake of thinking that democracy was defenceless, 'but in fact it has jaws and claws'.) 'Besides,' he went on, 'what is this democracy you are talking about? Is it like the democracy in England where the House of Lords passes a law making homosexuality legal? Is that democracy?'

How could he go ahead with the plan after Zumr had vetoed it, he was asked. He said: 'I am the *faqih*. Zumr knew that we were going to do it.' He said he gave Zumr permission to attack Christian jewellers, and they did in fact raid several shops in the Shubra area and at the first attempt got half a kilo of gold and jewels. Farag pointed out an additional advantage was that this prevented the jewels from going to the Church, as would otherwise have been the case.

Farag still had a leg in plaster when he was arrested. After the first full day of his interrogation, 15 October, he denied all the charges, but the next day he signed a written confession. It is not difficult to imagine how he was persuaded to change his mind.

The official investigation shed a good deal of light on the thinking of the whole *jihad* movement, of which this one particular *'anqud* was in many ways representative. The alternative courses of action, as they saw it, were either individual or collective, assassination or a popular uprising, though of course preferably the two should be combined, the first leading on to the second. As Reheil put it: 'You see, we had no army, no power, so no other way was open to us except assassination.' He added that he did not belong to *takfir wa hijra* 'because they make infidels of everybody, but we don't do that.'

Farag was asked why he had not been prepared to wait. If one of his grounds of complaint against the President was his arrests of 3 September, could he not at least have waited until those arrested had been brought to trial? His answer was that the *jihad* could brook no delay. The aggression Sadat had committed was not against individuals but against God. Why, he was asked, was he not prepared to wait until he was older and perhaps a little wiser. 'The fact that we are young,' was his answer, 'does not mean that we are not equipped to carry out the task required of us by God.' When he was reminded that the Prophet Mohamed had known how to bide his time, Farag said that the Islamic movement had been persecuted in Egypt ever since the 1952 revolution. Its members had been prepared to wait, but there was a limit to their patience.

Abboud Zumr was the main advocate of the alternative course of action. He had wanted a period of two or three years preparation, during which time he would have recruited a sufficient nucleus of army officers to ensure the success of the uprising. But he knew that, because of its size and because most of its officers were professionals, who would therefore be likely to warn the authorities about any hints of disaffection, the army would be a difficult recruiting ground. Zumr said that, as a military man, he had explained to the civilian members of the *'anqud* the necessity for proper planning. They would have to be prepared, he told them, to take over key points in the country, such as the Ministry of Defence, the Ministry of Interior, the broadcasting station, the headquarters of the State Security Police, and so on. (Plans of the layout of a number of these buildings were found in his possession after his arrest.) Above all, he said, it was essential that they should organize revolutionary committees in every district of Cairo. When the time came they would have to be able to put sufficient numbers in the street to make it impossible for the security forces to control them. The example of Iran had shown that no army and police are able to overcome the mass of the people, provided they are sufficiently numerous and determined. Their own committees must be in a position to seize and maintain control of the street, because if they failed to do so the Communists would exploit the situation. Zumr's arguments were overruled, but he still hoped that the casualties on 6 October would be sufficiently heavy for a state of chaos to develop which would give the *jihad* movement its chance. It was, after all, known that all the *jihad* groups, not just one or two *'anquds*, had agreed that Sadat was an infidel and a tyrant who should be eliminated, so that the basis for a popular uprising, sparked off by the news of his assassination, might be expected to exist.

* * *

It is hardly to be wondered at that there were many people who remained dissatisfied with the official explanation of how the assassination of the President had been carried out. As happened after the assassinations of President Kennedy and Martin Luther King, several 'conspiracy theories' gained ground. One of the most widely held of these, naturally enough, put the blame on the Americans and the CIA. According to this theory, the American government had been growing increasingly worried by the situation in Egypt. It was aware of the mounting internal opposition, both political and religious, to Sadat's policies, the unrest caused by corruption, the rapprochement with Israel, Egypt's isolation from the rest of the Arab world and so on. The arrests of 3 September had finally convinced America that Sadat was no longer in control of the situation. He had served his purpose, particularly by his recognition of Israel, which had for years been the main objective of American policy. He was now a liability rather than an asset, and so had become expendable, like Diem and other earlier American protégés. It was time for him to be replaced by someone more liberal and so more acceptable.

Though in many ways plausible, this theory does not stand up. In spite of its admitted weaknesses, Sadat's régime was still able to serve American interests in the Middle East and still strong enough to deal with its internal opponents. Sadat's Egypt was the chief bulwark in the Middle East of Reagan's anti-Communist crusade, and able to intervene effectively in African trouble spots such as Libya, Chad and Zaire. It was most unlikely that the Americans would have relished the idea of losing a second Shah within the space of two years, nor was it easy to imagine fruitful collaboration between the CIA and the *gama'at el-islamiya*.

The second 'conspiracy theory' is that the assassination was the work of the Egyptian army. Certainly, some aspects of the official version required a good deal of explanation. The assassination took place, after all, in the middle of an army parade, the assassin's truck stopping immediately beside the main reviewing stand which, for the first time, was completely open to the front (though this was to be explained by the fact that Sadat did not want too many guards to be visible on the television screens). The timing of the killing, when everyone was looking upwards at the air display, seemed almost too exact to be a coincidence. And why was the Presidential Guard so slow to react?

Many people found Khaled's role in the killing full of suspicious circumstances. There was the fact that he had not originally been detailed to take part in the parade, but that his commanding officer had insisted that he should. Why choose him? The investigators asked Khaled if the officer in his unit responsible for security had not known about the report on his file from Military Intelligence that he was a Moslem fanatic. Khaled's answer was: 'All the brigade knew, and so did the commander of my battalion.' It was also widely known that his brother had recently been arrested with other fundamentalists, and that he had frequently urged his fellow-officers to spend more time in prayer and less in the pursuit of worldly pleasures. Yet everyone kept silent about what they knew and seemed to do all they could to facilitate his taking part.

Then there was the matter of the ease with which he got his accomplices into the parade. He was asked at his investigation: 'Didn't anyone notice that you had given three members in your company leave for the day of the parade, or sent them away on special duty?' His answer was: 'Yes, this was to be seen in the company diary, and that was sent to battalion office in the normal way on the Friday before the parade.'

Khaled was asked who had inspected his detachment to ensure that its arms had no live ammunition and no strikers. His answer was: 'Nobody inspected the ammunition. There was an order to remove the strikers, but there was no inspection to see that the order had been carried out. Each officer was responsible for his own unit.' He said his commanding officer had asked him if the order had been carried out, and he told him that it had.

There is a lot in all this to encourage the idea that there must have been a master plan behind the assassination, but there is no real supporting evidence. All the admitted mistakes can reasonably be put down to familiar bureaucratic bungling. There was also an almost universal belief that the one place where nothing of this sort could happen was a well-organized military parade.

Finally, there is the theory that the assassination involved a much wider conspiracy than the single *'anqud* which actually executed it. This in fact is the line which the official inquiry has taken, and which has led it to investigate the whole *gama'at el-islamiya* and the *jihad* groups.

The basic concept in the *jihad* groups is that the *hakimiya*, the authority by which men are governed, depends on the *ba'ya*, the consent or approval of the people, and this can only be given to someone who rules in accordance with the *sharia,* the *ba'ya* being given not to the ruler himself but to the *sharia.* So if the ruler ceases to obey the *sharia* it is legitimate to oppose him. In this case he represents the *hakimiya* of man instead of the *hakimiya* of God. This gave the *jihad* groups justification, as they saw it, to move from the realm of ideas to the realm of action.

At his trial Khaled was asked whether it was right that someone like Farag or himself should have given and accepted a *fetwa* that the ruler of their country was a renegade and an infidel. Khaled agreed that probably the *fetwa* should have come from higher up. He was asked who there was in a position to give such a ruling and he answered with the Arabic expression '*ahl el-hal wa el-aql*' (those who can speak with authority). 'Are you one of them?' asked the judge. 'No,' said Khaled. 'Did any of them speak to you in this sense?' asked the judge. 'No,' said Khaled, 'and even if I had wanted to consult them, they were all in prison.'

The result of the investigation into the *jihad* groups will presumably come out when the second and larger trial takes place. But already over a hundred officers in the armed forces have been dismissed.

5

WHERE TO?

THE SADDEST THING about Sadat's death is that none of his dreams came to anything. As I heard someone say of him soon after I had been released from prison: 'He died when he died'. Even in the days immediately after the assassination this verdict was justified. Egyptians experienced a sense of relief not of grief; there were no regrets for the departed President or for anything he stood for. The trial of the assassins was converted in effect into the trial of their victim. The legacy bequeathed to Sadat's successor became plain for all to see; it was simply to begin undoing what he could of his predecessor's work.

In retrospect it can be seen that Sadat's chief mistake was to sacrifice long-term strategic assets for short-term tactical manoeuvres. It is true to say that after the October War he had a greater opportunity than had fallen to any ruler of Egypt in modern times – greater than was open even to Mohamed Ali or to Nasser. But he threw it all away. Perhaps, in view of the sort of life he had led and his lack of education, it is unfair to blame him, but he never showed any knowledge or understanding of Egypt's place in history and geography, and so misjudged the social and economic – and even the cultural – conditions in his own country. His approach to problems was based on fantasy, not on reality. Lack of knowledge and understanding could be concealed for a time by the make-believe contemporary world of cameras and microphones, but as soon as the actor was removed, the stage he had occupied was seen to be deserted, the scenery and props dismantled, and the audience vanished.

Had Sadat been asked what he had given Egypt he would in answer have pointed to five things – firmer state institutions, more democracy, more prosperity, a new international status and peace.

When he addressed the nation after the food riots of January 1977 Sadat stressed several times that 'ours is a state of institutions'. He maintained that as early as 1971 he had given Egypt a new and definitive Constitution ('my Constitution') and a broad measure of democracy. It is true that a written Constitution now existed, but, as has been seen, when its provisions proved inconvenient Sadat was prepared to ignore them. It is true that for a time Parliament and press enjoyed a certain freedom of expression, but when genuinely independent deputies began to ask awkward questions rigged elections were arranged to silence them, and journalists who had departed from the official line lost their jobs – many from both categories of course eventually ending up in prison. Sadat's main contributions to the institutional life of the country were the Law of Shame and the Socialist Prosecutor, two of the most absolutist weapons ever devised or implemented in any country in any age.

When talking of his achievements Sadat could never resist the temptation to compare what he had done with what he alleged his predecessor had failed to do. Nasser had lost a war, he had won a war; Nasser had put people in prison, he had released them; Nasser had been a dictator, he was a democrat; Nasser had ruled by emergency laws, he by statutory law. This vendetta – in fact it amounted almost to a *jihad* – against his predecessor started quite early. I protested to him that, while undoubtedly Nasser had made mistakes, to denigrate him in this way was, apart from anything else, extremely short-sighted. It was bound to erode his own legitimacy, because he was where he was primarily as the legitimate successor to Nasser – as the person who, on first assuming the presidency, had pledged himself to follow the path laid down by Nasser. 'If you want to be a Khrushchev to Nasser's Stalin,' I told him, 'at least I suggest you don't do it so openly. Khrushchev's address to the Twentieth Congress of the Communist Party of the Soviet Union was leaked through foreigners, not broadcast to the Russian people. And in many ways it backfired on Khrushchev. The question inevitably asked of him was "And where were you while all this was going on?" People are bound to ask the same question of you. After all, for ten years you were Speaker of the Parliament, and if all these mistakes were being committed you were in a better position than anyone to draw attention to them.'

I suggested to Sadat that a better plan would be to order a comprehensive and public evaluation to be made of all the achievements of the Nasser era, out of which could come a report criticizing some aspects of it but giving due recognition to other positive aspects. I felt obliged to ask him where he thought the credit lay for the revolution, or for land reform, or for Suez, or for the socialist laws and the social transformation of the country, for the High Dam and industrialization, for Egypt's position as leader of the Arab world and architect of Arab unity. Did he claim the credit for these for himself? And if not, would it not be wiser, while rejecting what he felt to be his predecessor's failures, to acknowledge the successes and build on them in his turn?

Regarding the question of Egypt's prosperity, enough has been said to demonstrate how limited and unevenly distributed were the benefits accruing during Sadat's years of power, and at what a cost to his own and future generations they were bought. '*Infitah*' (opening) was Sadat's own word to describe his economic policies, and here again he could not resist the temptation to attack his predecessor. His argument was that Egypt had been living in what he called a closed (*inghilak*) society and that it was time to open it to modern technology. This was a strange reflection on a régime which had been responsible, in the High Dam, for one of the greatest technological achievements of the age, and which had welcomed the participation of foreign capital and expertise, including Swiss and American, in fields where it was really needed, such as oil and pharmaceuticals. The truest commentary on *infitah* were the food riots of January 1977. Even the State Security High Court which tried the rioters was bound to admit that 'the government made the mistake of surprising the people with something for which they had not been prepared. They had in fact been expecting the exact opposite – some measure of relief rather than fresh burdens. Their anger was justified.' This verdict did not save those who were released from being re-arrested, the President using for this purpose his prerogative as martial law administrator.

But of course Sadat's greatest claim to fame, in foreign eyes at any rate, is that he was the man who planned and executed for Egypt a successful war and then planned and executed a successful peace. This is a sweeping claim. How far can it be justified?

Sadat was not the first Egyptian leader to want peace in the Middle East or to work for it. Too often it is forgotten that when Nasser, together with other Arab delegates, objected to an invitation being sent to Israel to attend the first non-aligned conference at Bandung in 1955, he was asked by several of his friends to explain his reasoning and to suggest what he thought a solution to the Arab-Israel conflict might be. In his speech to the comprehensive gathering, which included such influential figures as Nehru, Chou En-lai and U Nu, he committed

Egypt to acceptance of the 1947 UN partition plan – if Israel would agree too. The same position was elaborated in his correspondence with President Kennedy in 1961. But Nasser feared then – with good reason, as is now plain to everyone – that what Israel really wanted was not peace but territory.

The October War was a strategic victory for the Arabs. It was almost a tactical victory for the Arab armies, Egyptian and Syrian, which fought the war, but this in the end eluded them owing to miscalculations in the field and America's determination to rescue Israel, whatever the cost. Yet it is a fact that, as 1973 ended, the world was waiting with bated breath to see what this new political and economic giant, the Arab world, would make of its opportunity. Now, as I write, nine years later, with the war in Lebanon recently ended, the contrast between original hopes and present reality is almost too bitter to contemplate. If it can be said that in 1967 Arab policies were betrayed by Arab arms, it is no less true that in 1973 Arab arms were betrayed by Arab policies. Israel's invasion of Lebanon revealed to all the Arabs' total impotence – political, military, economic. It was the moment of their greatest humiliation and shame.

How Sadat would have reacted to the Israeli invasion of Lebanon is impossible to say. But what is certain is that, by stating categorically in Jerusalem that there would never be another war between Egypt and Israel, he had given a one-sided pledge of non-belligerence of which Israel was to take full advantage. If there had been no such pledge, if Egypt had still been an active element in the Middle East military equation, the Israelis would never have dreamed of committing a hundred thousand troops to the invasion of their northern neighbour. The fact that Sadat's policies had ensured the total and inevitable isolation of Egypt from the rest of the Arab world did more than anything else to give a clear passage for Sharon's tanks on the road to Beirut.

Looked at dispassionately, it can be seen that the siege of Beirut was the logical outcome of the Camp David agreements. From the outset it was perfectly clear that Begin knew exactly what he intended these agreements to mean – no Palestinian state, no independent Palestinian entity, and if the Palestinians in the West Bank and Gaza insisted on claiming to be represented by the PLO, then the PLO would have to be destroyed. The first stage of destruction involved the arrest and expulsion of all prominent PLO supporters living under Israeli occupation, seizing land, cutting off water and various other forms of harassment. The second stage took the form of outright war.

The Arabs could do nothing to stop Israel because by making a separate peace the state which was the Arab world's natural leader had effectively disarmed all the others as well as itself. The free hand which Sadat gratuitously presented to the Israelis was not exploited by them at the expense of the Palestinians alone; all Arabs east of the Suez Canal thereby became immediately exposed. Lebanon is the most obvious victim, but Syria too has felt the full weight of Israeli weaponry, and even Iraq became the target for the Israeli air force.

Egypt's opting out had a centrifugal effect on all other Arab countries, diverting their attention from what had for long been the dream of unity – however imperfectly understood or pursued, yet a noble and stimulating dream – into barren territorial rivalries, religious conflicts and social strife. The Arab world had become well and truly balkanized.

No contrast could be greater than the increased practical support by all Arab governments for the Palestinians in general, and for the PLO in particular, during the 1960s and 1970s, and the reluctant agreement by these same governments in the summer of 1982, under American pressure, to receive some of these same Palestinians, after they had fought the Israeli army for nearly three months without support, as permanent and unwanted exiles. On foreign insistence the Arabs were dismantling all they had tried for the past generation to achieve. Nor is the Palestinian cause the only one to suffer by Egypt's defection. The Arab League, removed from Cairo to the periphery of the Arab world in Tunis, has lost most of its former authority; the Organization of African States and the non-aligned movement are shadows of what they once were. Under Nasser the three circles of which he saw Egypt as the centre – Arab, Islamic and African – had a reality; Sadat made Egypt the centre of nowhere.

Worse than that, he divided Egypt against itself. A sense of common nationality had been the cement which bound Egyptians of different religions and classes together, but now religious distinctions were exaggerated. The President became Mohamed Anwar el-Sadat, the pious, the leader of the faithful. He told the nation that sometimes, when confronted with a particularly difficult problem, he would go to sleep and wake up to discover that by some mysterious transcendental aid the solution to the problem had been given to him as he slept. But at the same time that he presented himself as the most devout of Moslem rulers he was talking of harmonizing the worship and worshippers of the three religions of the book – Islam, Christianity and Judaism. It is not surprising that the freedom with which he used the term 'atheist' to abuse his political opponents should have encouraged others to apply the same term to himself.

It is possible to see the recent history of the Arab world as falling into a series of fairly well-defined eras. There was the imperial era, when Britain and France were busily taking over as much as they could from the slackened grip of the Ottomans. There was the nationalist era of opposition to imperialism led by men like Zaghlul. Then came the Arab era, linked inevitably with the name of Nasser. This was succeeded by what must be called the Saudi era, when it seemed to many that Saudi oil riches and the leverage this produced would enable them to exert an influence that would benefit all the Arabs, particularly by persuading America to modify its total commitment to an expansionist Israel.

This hope was disappointed. So far from the position of Israel being in any way weakened, we can now see the Saudi era giving place with hardly a struggle to the era of imperial Israel. This is a prospect which can only be regarded with the greatest foreboding, particularly for the West which probably stands to lose more by it than even the Arabs. Sharon has defined what, in his view, Israel's imperial boundaries should be with as much clarity as if he was writing the political testament of a new Augustus Caesar. There are to be the immediate border areas, Lebanon, Syria and Jordan (including the Palestinians) held under close control; beyond them the glacis of Saudi Arabia, Iraq and the Gulf States; and beyond that a third sphere of influence, extending all the way from the Mediterranean to the Indian Ocean and including Turkey and Pakistan, in which Israel, the fourth strongest military power in the world (as Sharon specifically claims), would be the sole dominating authority.[1]

---

[1] Already the world has been presented with the paradox of an acknowledged nuclear power, and the would-be fourth-ranking military power in the world, demanding from the head of a neighbouring state, Lebanon, the expulsion of two thousand of its own citizens (the *Murabitun*) on the grounds that they represent a threat to Israel's security.

In the end, of course, dreams such as these for the future role of a state with fewer than four million inhabitants, wholly dependent for everything on the United States, will be shown to be madness, and if seriously pursued can only end with the physical destruction of Israel. But meanwhile, as one of Zionism's most notable representatives, Nahum Goldmann, pointed out shortly before he died, they are destroying the moral and spiritual elements of the Zionist heritage of which Israel was supposed to be the custodian.

The empire of Israel would be unlike any of those that came before it because it must be built on nothing and would have nothing to offer those it rules. The empires of Turkey or Britain or France had at least the backing of centuries of self-realization of political and economic evolution, with skills and culture to be imparted which many of those who came into contact with them found desirable for their own sake. There was also often a sense of obligation to those placed in subordination to them. Israel, on the other hand, has none of the prerequisites of empire. Its new, insecure, unproductive, neurotic base has only two ways of extending its power – blackmail and terror. The state which came into being on the back of terror has started to create an empire based on terror, and the only thing which is absolutely certain is that this will be met by counter-terror.

Sadat bequeathed to his successor an almost impossible legacy. Some errors could be rectified quickly. Prisoners could be released, laws enforced, corruption exposed to the light of day. The mood of the country could be changed, tensions slackened, hopes revived. But the fundamental political, social and economic problems remained, just as daunting in their magnitude as ever.

Consolation is to be found in the evidence that the tragedy of Sadat's murder showed the eternal Egypt to be capable, as so often in the past, of taking over in an emergency. Egypt is still basically an agricultural land, its people dependent, as they always have been and always will be, on a just distribution of the water which gives life to all of them. Deep in the consciousness of every Egyptian is the knowledge that the greatest misfortune which can befall the state is the breakdown of order. It is most significant that several of those who had been imprisoned by President Sadat and released by President Mubarak should have brought a case before the Council of State claiming that their arrest had been illegal since it had been ordered under article 74 of the Constitution, which covers a state of emergency, while there had been no such emergency.[1]

Still more significant is the fact that on 11 February 1982 the Council of State should have upheld the justice of their case, ruling that the arrests carried out on 3 September 1981 were indeed unconstitutional.

Egypt is beginning to feel her way back onto the road which history and geography have dictated for her and from which she temporarily strayed. It is, admittedly, a road beset with difficulties and dangers. By the end of the century the country is expected to have a population of eighty million. To feed, clothe, employ and educate all these men, women and children represents a challenge which will tax to the utmost the wisdom and cohesion of the nation. The problems ahead are not such as can be solved, or even masked, by the television lights or the smooth subterfuges of advertising, but solved they can be. History and geography may be hard taskmasters, but they are also good guides.

---

[1] Pope Shenoudah declined to take any comparable legal action, even though several lawyers volunteered to appeal on his behalf. He preferred to remain shut up in his monastery, a martyr to the temporal power. But when Husni Mubarak was about to pay his first visit to Washington as President, Shenoudah was persuaded by leading Copts who feared he might be greeted with hostile demonstrations by their fellow-religionists, as Sadat had been, to send them a letter pointing out the great importance the visit had 'for the internal peace of Egypt and for a just solution to the Middle East problem'. He said he was confident the President would be given a welcome 'befitting the head of our state, obedience to whom is ordered by our Holy Book.' The Pope's letter was taken to Washington by Bishop Gregorious.

INDEX